AF600337

# THE JURIDIC EFFECTS OF MORAL CERTITUDE ON PRE-NUPTIAL GUARANTEES

THE CATHOLIC UNIVERSITY OF AMERICA
CANON LAW STUDIES
No. 150

# The Juridic Effects of Moral Certitude on Pre-Nuptial Guarantees

A HISTORICAL SYNOPSIS
AND COMMENTARY

A DISSERTATION

*Submitted to the Faculty of the School of Canon Law of the Catholic University of America in Partial Fulfillment of the Requirements for the Degree of Doctor of Canon Law*

BY

THE REV. DAVID J. BOYLE, M.A., J.C.L.
*Priest of the Diocese of Fargo*

THE CATHOLIC UNIVERSITY OF AMERICA PRESS
WASHINGTON, D. C.
1942

NIHIL OBSTAT:
CLEMENT V. BASTNAGEL, J.U.D.
Censor Deputatus
May 28, 1942

IMPRIMATUR:
✠ALOISIUS J. MUENCH
Episcopus Fargensis
June 13, 1942



MURRAY & HEISTER
WASHINGTON, D. C.

PRINTED BY

TIMES AND NEWS PUBLISHING CO.
GETTYSBURG, PA., U. S. A.

To

His Excellency

The Most Reverend Aloisius J. Muench, D.D., LL.D.

Bishop of Fargo

## TABLE OF CONTENTS

## PART TWO—CANONICAL COMMENTARY

# INTRODUCTION

The Church has always justified herself in opposing the marriages of the faithful with pagans, heretics, and schismatics, because such marriages often constitute an occasion of sin and place the faith of the Catholic spouse and the offspring in jeopardy. Experienced pastors can recount the evils of mixed marriages in their parishes, offering as evidence five mixed marriages which have done spiritual harm for every one which may have been a success.

In the sixteenth century with the opening of new missionary fields to the Church and a rapid spread of heresy through the erstwhile Catholic countries of Europe, the Church granted dispensations for the first time from the impediments of mixed religion and disparity of worship. It was a necessary compromise with her strict discipline in this matter, chosen as the better course for the welfare of souls. There could be no compromise, however, with error, and consequently permission to enter a mixed marriage was conditioned upon the serious promise of the parties concerned to safeguard the practice of the Catholic's religion and to assure the Catholic baptism and education of all the children. These promises constituted the first *cautiones* to mixed marriages. At first, lengthy and detailed, *cautiones* finally came to embrace the two points just mentioned. Substantially consisting of them, they are received into the present law of the Church.

The *cautiones* or "guarantees" in mixed marriages are not incidental adjuncts, but form a true condition in ecclesiastical legislation required for the valid granting of the dispensation. A dispensation for disparity of worship without the *cautiones* would, therefore, be invalid and would correspondingly render invalid the subsequent marriage. Since mixed religion is merely a prohibitive inpediment, there does not follow this last-mentioned juridic effect as in the case of disparity of worship. Although they are of ecclesiastical origin, *cautiones* have an evident foundation in the natural divine law, for they constitute the normal means whereby the Church certifies the Catholic party's freedom to practice his religion and to attend to the Catholic baptism and education of the offspring. *Cautiones* alone, however, are not sufficient. The Church, cognizant of human weakness and fickleness, demands a *moral certitude* on the part of the one granting the dispensation that the *cautiones* are sincere in the present and will be fulfilled in the future. Such moral certitude is also required for the validity of the dispensation. The interplay of *cautiones* and *moral certitude* in the matter of mixed marriages has given rise to various juridic doubts and problems, some of which have been settled by authentic decrees of the Holy See, some of which still remain.

The following pages will attempt to trace the historical background of the problem of mixed marriages with particular emphasis upon the origin and development of the *cautiones*. Against this background the problems arising in present-day canon law regarding the *cautiones* and the attendant *moral certitude* required of the one who dispenses may be better appreciated. An attempt will be made to analyze the basis for the natural law and the ecclesiastical law prohibition of mixed marriages. Consideration will be given to the juridic interrelationship of the *cautiones* given by the parties and to the *moral certitude* concerning their sincerity in the present and their fulfillment in the future, for the agent who dispenses needs to obtain this certitude if his act of dispensation is to be valid. Attention will particularly be turned to the content of the *cautiones*. Finally some practical problems of everyday occurrence will be discussed.

Throughout the study it will be necessary to hold fast to the distinction between the impediment of mixed religion on the one hand, and the impediment of disparity of worship on the other. Unless otherwise explicitly distinguished, however, the term *mixed marriages* will be referable to both impediments.

The writer wishes to take this occasion to express his profound appreciation to the Most Rev. Aloisius J. Muench, Bishop of Fargo, whose kindly interest and encouragement has made possible a three years' graduate course of study in Canon Law. The writer likewise desires to use this present opportunity to manifest his gratitude to the members of the Faculty of the School of Canon Law at The Catholic University of America for their helpful cooperation, and to his classmates and all others who have so materially aided him in the preparation of the present study.

# PART ONE

## Historical Synopsis

## CHAPTER ONE

### Early Traces and Background of Pre-Nuptial *Cautiones*

The canonical institute of pre-nuptial *cautiones,* commonly referred to as the "guarantees," which are demanded by Canon Law today as a condition that must be present before mixed marriages are permitted by the Church, came formally into being only after the Protestant upheaval in the sixteenth century. Arising out of the *stylus Curiae Romanae,*[1] the *cautiones* as a condition for the dispensation were exacted first of the nobility. Dispensations and *cautiones,* crystallized as canonical institutes, eventually obtained among the common people as well toward the end of the eighteenth century.

The Protestant "Reformation" and the spread of heresy on the one hand, the movements of the Church in her ardent extension of missionary work in pagan lands on the other, and the inevitable clash of these two counter-forces, hastened the climax of the mixed-marriage problem in those troublesome times. The result was a compromise. The Church was constrained by the grave danger of loss in her membership to effect a compromise *in her policy* towards heretics and to permit what she had always considered an item replete with jeopardy, namely, the marriage of Catholics with those who were not of the faith. If she relaxed

---

[1] Cicognani, *Canon Law,* authorized English version by J. O'Hara and F. Brennan (2. ed., Philadelphia: Dolphin Press, 1935), p. 105; Schenk, *The Matrimonial Impediments of Mixed Religion and Disparity of Cult,* The Catholic University of America Canon Law Studies, n. 51 (Washington, D. C.: The Catholic University of America, 1929), pp. 63-64 (hereafter cited as *Mixed Religion and Disparity of Cult*); White, *Canonical Ante-Nuptial Promises and the Civil Law,* The Catholic University of America Canon Law Studies, n. 91 (Washington, D. C.: The Catholic University of America, 1934), p. 12.

her discipline on this score through expediency, the Church did not alter her position as guardian and custodian of the faith. She insisted, after this shift of policy as before, on safeguarding the faith and morals of the Catholic spouse and on securing the Catholic baptism and education of all the children of such a marriage. To accomplish this purpose the *cautiones* were required.

There is a background to the history of the *cautiones* which runs from Biblical days through the centuries to the Council of Trent. During this entire period there is no mention in law of the word *cautio* as it is now used by the Church in its peculiar significance regarding mixed marriages; there is no consideration of any dispensation in their regard. If the word *cautio* did not find its way into the language of ecclesiastical legislation as regards mixed marriages until later, it is significant to note, however, that the substance of the idea was not unknown. Again and again with regard to the mixed marriage, the Church insisted on conditions which amounted substantially to *cautiones*. If the early *cautiones* seem strict and uncompromising, that apparent fact becomes all the more intelligible if it be remembered that then mankind still lived in the centuries of faith, and that heresies of all kinds were unequivocally condemned and shunned by the clergy and by the believing laity alike. All of Europe was united in Catholicism before the Protestant "Reformation." Heretics were considered rebels by both Church and State. Consequently they were held liable for punishment by both powers. If the Church permitted the marriage of a Catholic with a heretic, it was only on the condition of a previous abjuration of heresy and of a profession of the true faith, which connoted a return on the part of the heretic to the one true Church. After the time of Luther and of Henry VIII religions other than that of the Catholic faith received the endorsement of civil governments. Thus the situation was changed. No longer could the Church demand the complete conversion of the heretic as a condition for his prospective marriage with a Catholic. She could have forbidden marriages of Catholics with heretics entirely, but the common good of souls dissuaded her from such drastic action. Hence the *cautiones,* in the canonical sense in which they are known today, were devised to protect the Catholic spouse in a mixed marriage and to safeguard the offspring of such a marriage against the danger of perversion from the true faith. When these measures of moral safety could be invoked, the mixed marriage became a factor which the Church could tolerate.

## I THE EARLY FATHERS

Few and infrequent are the words of the Fathers regarding the problem of mixed marriages. This is probably due to the freshness of the Scripture injunctions against them, as well as the fact that the Christian was a social outcast in Roman society, a member of a hated sect, an enemy to the traditional religion of the Roman.[2]

One of the earliest attestations of ecclesiastical jurisdiction in the matter of Christian marriage is found in the writings of St. Ignatius (✠ 107): "But it becomes both men and women who marry, to form their union with the approval of the Bishop, that their marriage may be according to the Lord and not after their own lust. Let all things be done to the honor of God."[3]

Tertullian (✠ ca. 223)[4] the African Father, writing in the second century is perhaps strongest in his expression of the prohibition of Christians' marrying pagans. His interpretation of St. Paul's words which allowed widows to marry "only in the Lord" regards them as a command rather than a counsel. His warning to Christians not to marry pagans was based on the danger of idolatry.[5] Tertullian becomes oratorical in his condemnation of

---

[2] Feije (also Feye), *Dissertatio Canonica de Matrimoniis Mixtis* (Lovanii, 1847), p. 65 (hereafter to be cited as *De Matrimoniis Mixtis*); Esmein, *Le Mariage en Droit Canonique* (2. ed., 2 vols., Paris: Libraire du Recueil Sirey, 1929-1935), I, 5.

[3] *Ante-Nicene Fathers* (14 vols., American Reprint of the Edinburg ed., New York: Scribner & Sons, 1903), I, 95.

[4] "De nubendo vero in Domino, cum dicit tantum in Domino, iam non suadet sed exerte jubet."—*Ad Uxorem*, Lib. II, cap. 1—Migne, *Patrologiae Cursus Completus, Series Latina* (221 vols., Parisiis, 1858-1864), I, 1292-1293 (hereafter cited as *MPL*); cf. also *Adversus Marcion*, Lib. V, cap. 7—*Corpus Scriptorum Ecclesiasticorum Latinorum* (Vindobonae, 1866-), XLVII, 592-596 (hereafter cited as *CSEL*).

[5] *Liber de Corona*, Cap. XIII,—*MPL*, II, 96.

such marriages, particularly in one passage,[6] where he seems to have the doctrine of the mystical body in mind as expressed by St. Paul.

This same doctrine forms the basis and background for the condemnation of such marriages by St. Cyprian, Bishop of Carthage (✠ 258), who refers to them as a "prostitution of the members of Christ."[7]

The writings of St. Ambrose (✠ 397) in Italy introduce for the first time the consideration of baptism as forming the basis for the distinction between Christian marriage and pagan marriage.[8]

Only later, however, was it authoritatively acknowledged that baptism determined the essential and juridic difference between the impediment of mixed religion and disparity of worship.[9]

When Bishop Vigilius on his election asked St. Ambrose for some paternal advice, he was told first of all to put a stop to mixed marriages, for there could scarcely be a more grave threat to faith than marriages with those who were alien to the faith,

---

[6] ". . . fideles gentilium matrimonia subeuntes stupri reos esse constat, et arcendos ab omni communicatione fraternitatis, ex litteris Apostoli dicentis 'cum ejusmodi nec cibum sumendum.'" (I Cor. V: II)—*Ad Uxorem,* Lib. II, cap. 3—*MPL,* I, 1292-1293.

[7] ". . . iungere cum infidelibus vinculum matrimonii, prostituere gentilibus membra Christi." *De Lapsis,* Cap. VI—*CSEL,* III, P. I, 240; cf. also, *Ad Quirinium,* Lib. III, cap. 62—*CSEL,* III, P. I, 166, where Cyprian reminds his readers of the defection of Solomon through such marriages; see also for the same text, *MPL,* IV, 767.

[8] "Cave, inquam, gentilem, aut Iudaeam atque alienigenam, hoc est haereticam, et omnem alienam a fide tua uxorem arcessas tibi . . . si Christiana sit, non est satis nisi ambo initiati sitis sacramento baptismatis . . . non possunt hoc dispares fide credere ut ab eo quem non colit putet sibi conubii inpertitam gratiam. . . . Primum in coniugio religio quaeritur." —*De Abraham,* Lib. I, cap. 9, n. 84—*CSEL,* XXXII, P. I[a], 555-556. The passage does not indicate that Ambrose considered the unions invalid. This is perhaps the only passage from the early Fathers in regard to such marriages which was taken over bodily by Gratian in his *Decretum.* Cf. *infra,* p. 10-11.

[9] C. 7, X, *de divortiis,* IV, 19; Pope Innocent III (1198-1216) first called attention to the fundamental difference in marriage between the baptized and unbaptized. Cf. Schenk, *Mixed Religion and Disparity of Cult,* p. 39, who cites Smisniewicz.

for such unions were seared with the flames of lust and dissension and branded with the crimes of sacrilege.[10]

The note of sacrilege in marriage with a pagan is also struck by St. Zeno, Bishop of Verona (✠ 371),[11] though his reference is more to the body of the Christian, which is the temple of God, as being defiled by the pagan.

These few references to the writings of the early Fathers find their way in whole or in part into later conciliar legislation or decrees of the Pontiffs[12] and thus laid a foundation for the tradition of ecclesiastical legislation in regard to such marriages. There is no mention of dispensations. The promise of conversion to the Faith was the only condition upon which such a marriage could be contemplated.[13]

## II CONCILIAR LEGISLATION

### *A. Ecclesiastical Law*

Since the early councils were concerned chiefly with matters of discipline, the nature of a particular canon often bespoke the presence of an abuse against which the authorities intended to legislate. In Elvira, for instance, the large Jewish population was probably the occasion for several canons directed against Christians intermarrying with infidels.[14]

---

[10] ". . . nihil gravius quam copulari alienigenae, ubi et libidinis et discordiae incentiva, et sacrilegii flagitia conflantur . . . quomodo potest conjugium dici, ubi non est fidei concordia?"—*Epist. XIX* (Ad Vigilium)—*MPL,* XVI, 984-985.

[11] *Tractatus,* Lib. I, Tract. V, nn. 7-9—*MPL,* XI, 307-311.

[12] S.C.C., declar. *Matrimonia,* 4 nov. 1741—*Codicis Iuris Canonici Fontes cura Emi, Petri Card. Gasparri Editi* (9 vols., Romae [postea Civitate Vaticana]: Typis Polyglottis Vaticanis, 1923-1938, Vols. VII, VIII, et IX ed. cura et studio Emi. Iustiniani Card. Serédi), n. 3527 (hereafter cited as *Fontes*); Benedictus XIV, ep. encycl. "*Magnae Nobis,*" 29 iun. 1748, ad 2 —*Fontes,* n. 387; Ter Haar, *Mixed Marriages and Their Remedies* (New York: Pustet, 1933), pp. 20-21.

[13] "Dolorem . . . meum ex aliqua parte consolabatur, quod audivi te illam ducere noluisse, nisi prius catholica fuisset facta,"—St. Augustinus, *Ep. CCXX* (Ad Bonifacium), n. 4—*CSEL,* LVII, 433-434.

[14] Dale, *The Synod of Elvira and Christian Life in the Fourth Century* (London, 1882), pp. 254-262. The word "synod" is used interchangeably with the word "council."

The Council of Elvira (305-306) not only forbade such marriages but severely punished offenders in this regard as well as parents who permitted such marriages.[15] Social intercourse with Jews was forbidden both to clerics and to the faithful, so that they were not so much as to eat with them.[16] This Council marks the beginning of extreme measures against the marriages of Christians with Jews, which were considered more perilous in the eyes of the Church than marriages with pagans.

The Council of Arles (314)[17] also enacted punishments of a temporary deprivation of communion for girls who married pagans.

The Ecumenical Council of Chalcedon (451) forbade chanters and lectors to marry heretics.[18] If such clerics were already so married, their children who were not yet baptized were forbidden to be baptized as heretics, but they were to enter the Church and were forbidden to marry heretics, Jews or pagans "unless such

[15] C. 16: "Heretici si se transferre noluerint ad ecclesiam Catholicam, nec ipsis Catholicas dandas esse puellas; sed neque Judaeis, neque hereticis dare placuit; ea quod nulla possit esse societas fideli cum infideli. Si contra interdictum fecerint parentes, abstineri per quinquennium placet." Mansi, *Sacrorum Conciliorum Nova et Amplissima Collectio* (53 vols. in 59, Paris-Leipzig-Arnhem, 1901-1927), II, 8 (hereafter cited as Mansi); Feije, *De Matrimoniis Mixtis,* pp. 28-29; note the condition expressed in the canon. Marriage was forbidden with heretics if they did not wish to join the Church. It is not certain whether the condition had to be fulfilled prior to the marriage, or after; cf. also c. 17 of the same Council, whereby parents were to suffer denial of communion for all time if they gave their daughters in marriage to priests who served the idols.

[16] C. 50—Mansi, II, 14.

[17] C. 11—Mansi, II, 472.

[18] C. 14: " Quia in quibusdam provinciis conceditur *psalmistis* et *lectoribus* uxores accipere, statuit sancta synodus, prorsus non licere cuiquam ex his alterius sectae accipere uxorem. . . . Qui [filii] vero adhuc baptizati non sunt, omnimodo non posse eos in heretica ecclesia baptizari nec in matrimonio jungi haeretico, Judaeo vel pagano; nisi forte spoponderit se venire ad orthodoxam fidem, dum conjungitur personae orthodoxae. Si quis vero hanc definitionem sanctae Synodi praeterierit, regularum condemnationibus subjaceat."—Mansi, VII, 388. Cf. Reiffenstuel, *Ius Canonicum Universum* (5 vols. in 7, Parisiis: 1864-1882), Lib. IV, tit. 1, n. 363, who renders the condition expressed in the canon as ". . . nisi forte promittat ad Orthodoxam fidem se per personae Orthodoxae copulam transferre." Cf. also, Feije, *De Matrimoniis Mixtis,* p. 211.

shall have promised to join the orthodox faith." An offender against this law was to be excommunicated. The same condition of conversion had been expressed in canon 31 of the Council of Laodicaea (343-381) with the added provision that the heretic was to be received (*"sed magis accipere"*) into the home of the Catholic and not vice versa. Apparently the conciliar Fathers considered it a danger of perversion for the Catholic to live with the family of the heretic in spite of the promise which had been made.[19]

The problem of Christian-Jew marriages must have become acute in France and Spain in the sixth century, for the language of the councils could lead one to consider the marriage between Christian and Jew as invalid. Thus the II Council of Orleans (533)[20] without qualification called such unions *illicitas* and ordered the parties of such a marriage to separate under pain of excommunication to the Christian. This council thus appears to offer the first instance in which mention is implied of the existence of a diriment impediment relative to the prospective marriage of Christians with Jews, though the separation which was demanded may in reality have been the separation *from bed and board.*

The Jewish question was no less a concern of the Church in Spain, where already the Council of Elvira had legislated against Christians' intermarrying with Jews. Solicitous for the faith of the Christian spouse and the offspring, the IV Provincial Council of Toledo (633)[21] obliged bishops to admonish Jews who were married to Christians to become Catholics if they desired their unions to persist. If the warnings were ignored, the spouses were to be separated and the children were to be entrusted to the custody of the mother if she was the Catholic.[22]

---

[19] Cf. Feije, *De Matrimoniis Mixtis,* pp. 211-212.

[20] C. 19—*Monumenta Germaniae Historica, Legum Sectio III, Concilia Aevi Merovingici* (Tom. I, recensuit Fridericus Maassen, Hannoverae, 1893), I, 64 (hereafter cited as *MGH*); cf. also Mansi, VIII, 838.

[21] C. 63—Mansi, X, 634.

[22] Later Councils of Toledo in Spain increased the restrictions of Christian-Jew marriages. These strong measures may well be the basis for the diriment impediment for such marriages as it evolved later. Cf. Schenk, *Mixed Religion and Disparity of Cult,* p. 28.

The uncompromising attitude of the Church towards the marriages of her members with Jews was undoubtedly prompted by the dangers, inherent in such marriages, to the faith and morals of the Christian. This explains the severity of the councils in this matter. They allowed such marriages upon one condition—conversion to the true Faith.[23]

### B. *Civil Law*

Roman Law contained few prohibitions against the marriages of Christians with Jews, but the laws which were made were very extreme. The Theodosian Code went so far as to enact capital punishment for a Jew who married a Christian.[24] This law dates from the reign of Constantius in 339. Such marriages, too, were branded as adulterous[25] and were subject to all the penalties provided therefor. There is some question as to whether these laws were endowed with a binding force in the Church. It is certain, however, that Roman Law alone did not furnish a sufficient basis for an ecclesiastical diriment impediment in this regard. Still, hand in hand with the Church, Roman Law did much to further the growth of the custom of outlawing Christian-Jew marriages.[26]

### C. *Summary of Conciliar Legislation*

The period from the fourth century to the time of Gratian in the twelfth century was a time of abundant conciliar legislation in the Church. It was marked by a number of ecumenical and particular councils in the East and numerous particular councils in the West. The theatre of conciliar legislation centered in the

[23] ". . . nisi perfecte crediderit Christo et baptizatus fuerit. . ."—Council of Rome (743), c. 10—Mansi, XII, 384.

[24] C. Th. (16. 8) 6.

[25] C. Th. (3. 7) 2; C. (1. 9) 6.

[26] Justinian Law adopted the laws of the first four general Councils (Nice, Constantinople, Ephesus, and Chalcedon) and considered them part and parcel of the *Corpus Iuris Civilis.* Cf. N (131) 1; Benedictus XIV, ep. *"Singulari Nobis"* 9 feb. 1749—*Fontes,* n. 394.

East, partly because of the number of heresies that were rampant there and partly because of the Caesaro-Papistic tendencies of the Byzantine Emperors.[27] In the East the councils were not slow to condemn the marriages of Christians with heretics, permitting them, however, on condition that the heretic promised to become a Catholic. Whether the promise had to be fulfilled before the marriage, or only thereafter, is not certain. It is significant that the conciliar Fathers saw this condition as the only effectual safeguard to the faith of the Catholic; no other condition, however, could be countenanced at that time, for the Catholic Church was the only juridically recognized religion in the Eastern Roman Empire as well as in all Europe. All outside the pale of the Church were considered rebels, dissidents.

It was a slightly different picture in the West where the particular councils of France, Spain, Africa, and Italy fashioned legislation to meet the menace to the faith in the person of the Jew. The Council of Elvira as early as the year 306 forbade the intermarriage of Christians with Jews, and subsequent councils in France and Spain added sanctions of anathemas and excommunications against Christians who flouted this prohibition. It was apparently out of these vehement measures against marriages with Jews that the diriment impediment of disparity of worship became crystallized perhaps by the twelfth, but surely by the thirteenth century.[28] It seems warranted to conclude that by the close of this conciliar period particular ecclesiastical legislation had begun to differentiate the diriment impediment from the prohibitive, the former causing the marriage to be invalid and illicit, the latter branding the marriage as illicit but leaving it stand as

---

[27] Arianism and Nestorianism arose in the East and spread westward; a popular treatise of the Caesaro-Papistic problem appeared recently in Don Luigi Sturzo's *Church and State* (New York: Longmans, Green & Co., 1939), pp. 44-69.

[28] Many and divergent are the opinions as to the time when disparity of worship became an established universal impediment arising out of custom. The opinions cover a span of eight centuries, from the sixth to the fourteenth. Most authors accept the twelfth century as the time of its origin, though a few place it as late as the thirteenth century. Cf. Schenk, *Mixed Religion and Disparity of Cult,* pp. 41-44, for complete details of authors and opinions.

valid. It remained for Pope Innocent III and particularly the scholastics of the thirteenth century, however, to develop what St. Ambrose had suggested, namely, the juridic basis for the essential difference between the marriages of the baptized and the marriages of the unbaptized.[29]

Thus far, it is true, one cannot point to a *universal* prohibition against marriage between Christian and infidel, which involved in addition the character of a diriment impediment. The few canons which allege the invalidity of such marriages are found in the Fathers or in Provincial councils, or they refer to the marriages of Christians with Jews. Inclusion of these canons in the canonical collections gave them added prestige, to be sure, but their juridic force and extension remained what they were in their original enactment. Some few canons, as has been seen, prohibited in the same tenor the marriages of Christians with heretics, infidels, and Jews.[30]

## III GRATIAN TO THE COUNCIL OF TRENT

In making his collection, Gratian drew upon the Scriptures, the Fathers of the Church, the canons of the councils, the letters of the Roman Pontiffs, the Penitentials and upon civil law. It is not surprising, therefore, to see included in the *Decretum* much of what has already been examined.[31] The warning of St. Ambrose to Christians not to marry gentiles, Jews, and heretics is sub-

[29] Innocent III (1198-1216) seems to have been the first to have made the juridic distinction. Cf. *infra,* p. 13.

[30] Cf. Sanchez, *De Sancto Matrimonii Sacramento Disputationum Tomi Tres* (Lugduni, 1669), Lib. VII, disp. 71, n. 8 (hereafter to be cited *De Sancto Matrimonii Sacramento*).

[31] Canon 14 of the Council of Chalcedon (451) is incorporated in c. 15, D. XXXII; St. Ambrose's doctrine in his *De Abraham,* Lib. I, c. 9, n. 84, is found in c. 15, C. XXVIII, q. 1; Canon 67 of the Council of Agde (506) in c. 16, C. XXVIII, q. 1; Canon 6 of the Council of Auvergne (535)—Mansi, VIII, 861, is incorporated in c. 17, C. XXVIII, q. 1; Canon 19 of the II Council of Orleans is similar to canon 6 of the Council of Auvergne and is omitted from the *Decretum;* Canon 10 of the IV Provincial Council of Toledo (633) in c. 10, C. XXVIII, q. 1.

stantially repeated in the *Decretum* and is preceded by the following *dictum Gratiani:*

> "Illa itaque auctoritate iubentur separari ab invicem qui contra Dei vel Ecclesiae decretum copulati sunt, utpote infideles cum fidelibus, consanguinei cum consanguineis, vel affines cum affinibus. Hi omnes, si sibi invicem copulati fuerint, separandi sunt."[32]

Thus Gratian's own teaching seems to conform with the import of some of the former councils, particularly those of France and Spain, which sensed the presence of a diriment impediment in the marriages of Catholics with infidels. The inclusion of these conciliar enactments in the *Decretum Gratiani* as well as Gratian's own *dictum* did not, of course, reflect a universal law of the Church, but it had great influence upon the future legislation and doctrine. Since Gratian included the marriages of *fideles* with *infideles* in the same category in which he placed the invalid marriages of the people related by blood or affinity, and further stated that all those who had entered such marriages were to be separated —*"iubentur separari"* and *"separandi sunt"*—it appears fairly evident that he considered these marriages as interdicted by means of a diriment impediment.[33] By his inclusion in the *Decretum* of only such canons as implied the unlawfulness but not the invalidity of marriages between Catholics and heretics and by the omission of any mention of such marriages in the *Dictum* already reported, Gratian seems to have inclined to the view that the marriages between Catholics and heretics were not branded with invalidity.

Huguccio's clear comment on canon 67 of the Council of Agde (506), as it appeared in the *Decretum,* showed definitely what direction he took in deciding the latter issue for himself, for he explicitly stated that "the marriage was to hold."[34]

---

[32] *Dictum* ante c. 14, C. XXVIII, q. 1.

[33] Wernz, *Ius Decretalium* (6 vols., Romae et Prati, 1898-1905; Vol. IV [*Ius Matrimoniale*], 1904), IV, 761, note (20) (hereafter cited as *Ius Matrimoniale*); Leitner, *Lehrbuch des katholischen Eherechts* (3. ed., Paderborn, 1920), p. 184.

[34] "Haereticus non potest contrahere cum Christiana. Dixit Hugutio quod, si contrahit, tenet matrimonium sicut si contraheret cum excom-

On the contrary, some twelfth century canonists and theologians regarded the diriment impediment as extending also to the marriages between Catholics and heretics.[35] It is difficult to determine the basis for their opinion. It appears as a sudden inversion of doctrine on the part of Bernard of Pavia and Peter Lombard, after centuries of canonical legislation, in which for the greater part marriages with heretics were considered valid even though they were forbidden. Perhaps they likened heretics to Jews as a source of danger for the perversion of Christians and thus classified them together on the basis of the strong injunctions against Christian-Jew marriages as seen in the French and Spanish councils. It is sure that they had no basis for their opinion in Gratian. The twelfth century marked the beginning of scientific speculation in Canon Law. Starting with Gratian, theologians attempted not merely to record the legislation of the past, but to interpret it from a scientific and philosophical standpoint. An erroneous interpretation of past legislation may well have been the basis for the opinion held by several twelfth-century theologians that marriages between Catholics and heretics were invalid. Be that as it may, the thirteenth-century theologians, in reverting to the traditional opinion which upheld the validity of such marriages, had the ad-

municato."—Joh. Teutonicus et Barth. Brixiensis, *Glossa Ordinaria* ad c. 16, C. XXVIII, q. 1, v. "haereticus"; cf. Esmein, *Le Mariage en Droit Canonique,* I, 244; for note on Huguccio cf. Van Hove, *Commentarium Lovaniense in Codicem Iuris Canonici* (Vol. I, Tom. I, *Prolegomena,* Mechliniae: H. Dessain, 1928, Tom. IV, *De Rescriptis,* 1936, Tom. V, *De Privilegiis,* 1939), I (*Prolegomena*), pp. 228, 241 (hereafter cited *Commentarium Lovaniense, Prolegomena,* or *De Rescriptis,* or *De Privilegiis*); Kuttner, *Repertorium der Kanonistik, 1140-1234,* Studi e Testi, 71 (Citta del Vaticano: Biblioteca Apostolica Vaticana, 1937), pp. 155-160; Cicognani, *Canon Law,* p. 329. Wernz (*Ius Matrimoniale,* p. 761 nota 20) cites St. Raymond and Guilielmus Durantis as agreeing with Huguccio.

[35] E.g., Bernard of Pavia (✠ 1213), *Summa Decretalium* (ed. E.A.T. Laspeyres, Ratisbonae, 1861), pp. 291-292; Peter Lombard (✠ 1160), *Libri IV Sententiarum* (studio et cura PP. Collegii S. Bonaventurae in lucem editi, 2. ed., 2 vols., Ad Claras Aquas, 1916), Sent. IV, D. XXXIX. Cf. Chelodi, *Ius Matrimoniale iuxta Codicem Iuris Canonici* (4. ed., Tridenti: Libreria Moderna Editrice A. Ardesi, 1937), p. 94 (hereafter cited as *Ius Matrimoniale*); Schenk, *Mixed Religion and Disparity of Cult,* p. 38, note 6.

vantage of the twelfth-century speculations as well as the decretals upon which to base their stand.

Thus in a decretal contained in the collection of Gregory IX (1234), the response of Innocent III (1198-1216) to the Bishop of Ferrara called a marriage between two members of the faithful a *"verum et ratum"* matrimony and based it on the Sacrament of faith, which when once admitted is never lost.[36] The reference to the Sacrament of faith was later to be more fully developed by the scholastics and applied to the Sacrament of baptism to form the theological and juridic basis for the essential distinction between mixed religion and disparity of worship.[37]

While Innocent IV (1243-1254) did not explicitly state that the marriages of Catholics with heretics were valid, yet by enacting a punishment which called for the confiscation of the dowry if a Catholic woman knowingly married a heretic, he implicitly stated that they were valid.[38] The parity of the contracting parties based on sacramental baptism was also recognized by Abbas Panormitanus (1386-1453), even though one party was a heretic.[39]

---

[36] "Si vero alter fidelium coniugum vel labatur in haeresim vel transeat ad gentilitatis errorem, non credimus quod in hoc casu is, qui relinquitur, vivente altero, possit ad secundas nuptias convolare, licet in hoc casu maior appareat contumelia creatoris. . . . Inter fideles autem verum quidem et ratum exsistit, quia Sacramentum fidei quod semel admissum, nunquam amittitur, sed ratum efficit coniugii sacramentum ut ipsum in coniugibus illo durante perduret."—c. 7, X, *de divortiis,* IV, 19.

[37] St. Albertus Magnus, *Commentarii in IV Sententiarum,* Dist. XXXIX, art. 2, ad 4—*Opera Omnia* (38 vols., cura ac labore Steph. Caes. Aug. Borgnet, Parisiis, 1890-1899), XXX, 429; St. Thomas Aquinas, *Summa Theologica,* III[a], Suppl., q. 59, art. 1, ad 5; St. Raymundus de Peñafort, *Summa* (Veronae, 1744), Lib. IV, tit. 10; Guilielmus Durantis, *Speculum Iuris* (3 vols., Venetiis, 1577), Lib. IV, Partic. 4, tit. *de divortiis,* n. 2; Joannes Duns Scotus, *Quaestiones in Quartum Librum Sententiarum—Opera Omnia* (26 vols., Parisiis, 1891-1895), XIX, 510.

[38] "Decrevit felicis recordationis Innocentius Papa IV, quod propter haeresim maritorum uxorum catholicarum dotes non debeant confiscari. Quod intelligendum fore censemus, nisi forte mulieres ipsae cum viris matrimonia contraxissent quos haereticos tunc sciebant."—c. 14, *de haereticis,* V, 2 in VI°; cf. Feije, *De Matrimoniis Mixtis,* p. 8; Esmein, *Le Mariage en Droit Canonique,* I, 245.

[39] C. 7, X, *de conditionibus appositis in dispensatione vel in aliis contractibus,* IV, 5—*Commentaria in Quinque Libros Decretalium* (5 vols. in 7, Venetiis, 1588), ad *cap. cit.;* Esmein, *Le Mariage en Droit Canonique,* I, 245.

### GENERAL SUMMARY

In the early Church there was no question of permission to enter a mixed marriage. Marriages of Catholics with any and all who were not of the faith were simply forbidden without distinction of diriment or prohibitive impediment. The Scriptures and early Fathers beat the path for the conciliar legislators in this regard. If marriages with heretics were permitted in some of the councils, it was only on the condition or at least the promise of conversion. It cannot completely be determined, however, whether that promise had to be fulfilled prior to marriage. Gratian seems to have differentiated the impediment of disparity of worship from the impediment of mixed religion. No theological basis was offered for the distinction, however, until the speculative theologians of the thirteenth century or the late decades of the twelfth century, following the decretals, established the foundation of the *matrimonium ratum* in valid baptism. A strange interlude was seen in the twelfth century wherein a few theologians, apparently departing from the already established traditional view, declared the marriages of Catholics with heretics to be invalid. Since there was no juridic precedent for such a position, it is difficult to assign the reason they held such a view. It may have been that they erred in their speculation. By the thirteenth century the two distinct impediments were established beyond question. The diriment impediment of disparity of worship may have had its origin in the French and Spanish councils legislating on Christian-Jew marriages. None the less, apart from custom, the origin of this impediment is indeed shrouded in the uncertainties of the past.

This was the picture of the mixed marriage problem from the time of the Fathers to the time of the Council of Trent, after which the *cautiones* as a canonical institute were developed to meet the new problems arising out of the Protestant "Reformation."

# CHAPTER TWO

## The Council of Trent and the Origin of the *Cautiones*

### I THE COUNCIL OF TRENT AND SUBSEQUENT COUNCILS

The Council of Trent (1545-1563) did not legislate directly on the question of mixed marriages, but indirectly struck at them through the issuance of the famous *Tametsi* decree, which established that all marriages be celebrated before the proper pastor and two witnesses under sanction of nullity.[1] The decree thus set the canonical form to be required for valid Christian marriage and took the first step to outlaw clandestine marriages.

The result of the *Tametsi* decree was restricted, however, for it did not receive promulgation in England, Scotland, Saxony, Asia, almost all of Africa and parts of America.[2] In fact much confusion as to where or where not this decree of the Council of Trent was in force kept the Holy See preoccupied in determining the validity or invalidity of marriages.[3]

---

[1] "Qui aliter quam praesente parocho, vel alio sacerdote de ipsius parochi seu Ordinarii licentia, et duobus vel tribus testibus matrimonium contrahere attentabunt, eos Sancta Synodus ad sic contrahendum omnino inhabiles reddit: et huiusmodi contractus irritos et nullos esse decernit. . . ."—*Conc. Trident., sess.* XXIV *de ref. matrim.*, c. 1,—Mansi, XXXIII, 152-153.

[2] The decree was to be promulgated in each parish and was to take effect thirty days thereafter—*Conc. Trident. sess.* XXIV *de ref. matrim.*, c. 1, *in fine*,—Mansi, *loc. cit.;* Cicognani, *Canon Law,* p. 363. For complete enumeration of places where the *Tametsi* was promulgated, cf. Perrone, *De Matrimonio Christiano* (3 vols., Romae, 1858), II, 256-274.

[3] Cf. for examples, S.C.C. declar. *Matrimonia,* 4 nov. 1741—*Fontes,* n. 3527; S.C.Prop. Fide (Constantinopolitan.), 21 mart. 1759—*Collectanea S. Congregationis de Propaganda Fide* (2 vols., Romae, 1907), I, n. 415 (hereafter cited as *Coll. S.C.P.F.*); S.C.C. (Rosnavien.), 20 aug. 1780—*Fontes,* n. 3811; S.C.S.Off. (Quebec.), 10 sept. 1820—*Fontes,* n. 859. In the last named response occasion was taken to condemn the practice of giving the nuptial blessing to the parties of a mixed marriage in certain places in America. As to the Tridentine form binding heretics for validity of marriage, cf. Carrière, *Praelectiones Theologicae—De Matrimonio* (2 vols.,

It was in those countries where heresy had gained a foothold as well as in pagan lands where missionary activity was opening new fields to Catholicism, that the Church was finally to take her stand in establishing the conditions for dispensations, the *cautiones*, as well as in indicating which causes were alone sufficient to warrant a dispensation, and was to set a strong barrier to those who urged that contrary custom could derogate from the necessity of a cause if the *cautiones* were obtained.[4]

If the Council of Trent was not explicit and direct in its stand against mixed marriages, one can not say the same for a score or more of provincial councils and diocesan synods held throughout Europe during the following two centuries. From 1570 to 1750 more than thirty such councils included in their decrees an unmistakable prohibition of mixed marriages.[5]

The II Provincial Council of Milan (1569), held under St. Charles Borromeo (✠ 1584), was particularly expressive of the conditions under which bishops could freely transmit favorable testimony of the status of a Catholic subject who intended to contract marriage in a distant place where heresy was strong and flourishing. Assurance that the Catholic party would not contract marriage with a heretic was one of these conditions.[6]

---

Parisiis, 1837), II, 423-428 (hereafter cited as *De Matrimonio*); cf. also Roskovány, *De Matrimoniis Mixtis inter Catholicos et Protestantes* (8 vols., Pestini et Nitriae, 1842-1887), I, 8-9 (hereafter cited as *De Matrimoniis Mixtis*).

[4] S.C.S.Off. (ad Archiep. Corcyren.), 3 ian. 1871: "Quamobrem etsi iamdiu, uti affirmas, opinio isthic inoleverit, licite posse mixtas inire nuptias absque Sanctae Sedis dispensatione, haec tamen opinio, qualibet non obstante consuetudine, tolerari nequit."—*Fontes*, n. 1013; Gregorius XVI, ep. encycl. "*Summo iugiter*," 27 maii 1832—*Fontes*, n. 484; litt. ap. "*Quas vestro*," 30 apr. 1841—*Fontes*, n. 497.

[5] Aich, "Ueber die gemischten Ehen mit besonderer Rücksicht auf die Verhältnisse in Würtemberg"—*Archiv für katholisches Kirchenrecht*, XIV (1865), 322 (hereafter cited as *AKKR*); Roskovány, *De Matrimoniis Mixtis*, I, 9-14.

[6] Tit. I, decr. 25—Mansi, XXXIV A, 113. In this connection cf. Synod of Muenster (1753) in Westphalia, which decreed that dimissorial letters of testimony regarding the religious status of a diocesan be denied if he intends to marry in a pagan land unless the pastor of such place would vouch for a Catholic marriage.—Schannat-Hartzheim, *Concilia Germaniae* (11 vols., Coloniae Augustae Agrippinensium, 1759-1790), X, 586-587 (hereafter cited as Schannat-Hartzheim).

The injunction for pastors to guard against mixed marriages by having no less concern in making the pre-nuptial examination regarding the possible attendant dangers to the faith of the Catholic party than in exploring the contingencies of possible attendant impediments is contained in at least one of these particular councils.[7] Again pastors were urged to point out in their preaching the dangers to the faith arising from mixed marriages and to show how the divine-natural law is often flouted in such unions.[8]

Not a few of these provincial councils were satisfied merely to pronounce a prohibition against mixed marriages,[9] while one or the other, recalling the strict attitude of conciliar legislation in the early Church on marriages with heretics, permitted them only on condition that the non-Catholic was willing to abjure heresy and make a profession of faith.[10]

---

[7] Provincial Council of Cambrai (1586), Tit. XI, c. 7—Mansi, XXXIV B, 1240. The first Synod of Antwerp (1576), Tit. VI, c. 2 repeated the 16th canon of the Council of Elvira (305-306)—Schannat-Hartzheim, VII, 818.

[8] Provincial Council of Bordeaux (1583) Tit. XV—Mansi, XXXIV A, 763; cf. also Synod of Antwerp (1610), Tit. X, cap. 7—Schannat-Hartzheim, VIII, 993; the Synod of Augsburg (1610), P. I, cap. 5, n. 3, which enjoins upon tutors, parents, priests, and all who have the care of youth, to deter them from marriage with heretics and not to condone such a marriage unless the danger of perversion to faith and morals was rendered remote according to the judgment of the vicar general.—Schannat-Hartzheim, IX, 29; compare this last with P. II, cap. 10, n. 30 of the same Synod—*idem,* 55; the Synod of Bois-le-Duc (s' Hertogenbosch) (1612), Tit. X, cap. 24—Schannat-Hartzheim, IX, 221; Synod of Paderborn (1688), P. II, tit. 10, n. 24—Schannat-Hartzheim, X, 166.

[9] Provincial Council of Toulouse (1590), P. II, cap. 8, n. 5—Mansi, XXXIV B, 1290; Synod of Coutances (1609), P. I, tit. 16, n. 17—Schannat-Hartzheim, VIII, 874; the Provincial Council of Narbonne (1609) forbade such marriages because a heretic was unable to receive grace—Mansi, XXXIV B, 1501.

[10] Synod of Lisieux (1580), n. XVIII—Roskovány, *De Matrimoniis Mixtis,* II, 1; Provincial Council of Cambrai (1586), Tit. XI, cap. 7: ". . . eos non Coniungant [parochi] nisi parati sint haeresim abjurare et fidei professionem facere."—Mansi, XXXIV B, 1240; Synod of Cologne (1651), P. IV, n. 25—Schannat-Hartzheim, IX, 775. The Synod of Gap (*Vapincentia*) (1672) demanded of the heretic a certificate of his solemn abjuration of heresy, a public profession of faith and the assurance that he was sufficiently instructed in the mysteries of the faith—cited from Feije, *De Matrimoniis Mixtis,* p. 42; see also Mansi, XXXVI[a], 431 for information about this synod.

The Synod of Liege (1618) is a particularly good example of the latter requirement, for it insisted on the abjuration of heresy in the hands of the vicar general before a marriage was permitted with a Catholic.[11] Another synod, held at Antwerp (1643), insisted that the pastor strive to effect the conversion of the heretic before he proceeded to assist at the marriage.[12] Several of the synods, too, did not hesitate to put sanctions upon their laws, threatening excommunication to those in authority who were neglectful of their duty to safeguard the faith and morals of the Catholics in their charge by permitting them to marry heretics. In this respect the synod held at Evreux (1576) is remarkably like to a canon of the early Church which forbade social intercourse with Jews.[13]

By 1750 the *cautiones* as elaborated by the Church through decrees of the Roman Pontiffs had been fairly well established. It is not surprising, therefore, that subsequent to that time particular synods and councils adapted their statutory language to the examples offered by the Pontifical decrees. One such instance of this adaptation is found in the Synod of Chełmno (Kulm), Poland (1745).[14] Though the word *cautio* in this case was employed in the sense of a safeguard against danger, it was also

---

[11] Tit. IX, cap. 4: "Si parochi alterum contrahentium haeresi infectum aut non temere suspectum inveniant, eos non conjungant, nisi haeresi in manibus Vicarii nostri prius abjurata."—Schannat-Hartzheim, IX, 298.

[12] Tit. X, n. 17—Schannat-Hartzheim, IX, 645.

[13] *De Officio Curatorum et Vicariorum*, n. 10—Roskovány, *De Matrimoniis Mixtis*, II, 1. Cf. the Provincial Council of Bordeaux (1624), cap. VIII, n. 1—Mansi, XXXIV B, 1561-1562, by which priests who admitted Catholics to mixed marriages to their spiritual loss were to suffer suspension *ipso facto* from both orders and benefice; cf. also the Synod of Glandèves (1656) in France, cap. 7, n. 9—cited in Feije, *De Matrimoniis Mixtis*, p. 42; see also Mansi, XXXVI°, 345.

[14] Schannat-Hartzheim, X, 545; cf. also Provincial Council of Prague (1860)—*Acta et Decreta Sacrorum Conciliorum Recentiorum, Collectio Lacensis* (7 vols., Friburgi Brisgoviae: Herder, 1870-1890), V, 522, wherein it was determined that if the *cautiones* were denied and the Catholic party could not be deterred from the marriage, the pastor could assist at the marriage passively by virtue of an apostolic indult; cf. Planchard, "Dispense de Disparité de Cult et de Religion Mixte"—*Nouvelle Revue Théologique*, XV (1883), 514 (hereafter cited as *NRT*).

used to denote, as the Roman law had done, a security for the stipulations attaching to a contract.

Thus during the sixteenth century and seventeenth century a vast number of diocesan synods and provincial councils were concerned about legislation in one form or another against mixed marriages. The authors are silent as to why the Council of Trent did not include direct legislation on this subject; it may be that the Tridentine Fathers considered their indirect attacks against these marriages as sufficient. But because of the uncertainties in the promulgation of the *Tametsi* decree, much of its force in regard to mixed marriages was rendered ineffective. It may be, too, that in the politico-religious difficulties of the times the Church considered it more politic, in her dealings with the new dissidents from the faith, to leave the direct attack and condemnation of such unions to the smaller local units of the Church, the dioceses and provinces. This may have been the better method in the circumstances by force of which not all the territories and kingdoms contained a mixed population of Catholics and heretics, for there were some which were still solidly Catholic, and others which were already totally Protestant. Thus it could have been a question of policy rather than one of principle with the Conciliar Fathers of Trent to leave the question untouched. It must be remembered, however, that the pre-Tridentine laws against mixed marriages were still in force. Furthermore, the problem was met squarely, if not in the Council, then by the letters, instructions, decisions, councils, and diocesan synods which followed the spirit of the papal utterances in their legislation. It was out of the papal dealings with the royalty in connection with the question of mixed marriages that the insistence on formal *cautiones* and the prerequirement of certain conditions came to apply to the common people as well. Hence a brief consideration will be given to several of the more important cases in which the popes and the members of the royalty of Europe entered into lengthy deliberations preparatory to the eventually recognized mutual agreements and concessions that made possible the contract of marriage between Catholic and Protestant royalty with the toleration of the Holy See.

## II ORIGIN OF *cautiones* IN MIXED MARRIAGES

As early as the year 770 Pope Stephen IV in his solicitude for the faith of the Franks addressed a letter to their Kings, the jointly reigning Carloman (✠ 771) and Charlemagne, dissuading them from marriage with the Arian Desiderata, daughter of Desiderius, King of the Longobards. Bertrada, Pepin's widow and the mother of Carloman and Charlemagne, meant to ensure peace between the Franks and Longobards when she proposed to Desiderius this matrimonial union of his daughter to one of her sons.[15] The proposed union was not at all to the liking of Pope Stephen, for the Catholic religion as well as Italy and Rome had suffered much from the hands of the Longobards. Consequently he wrote to both Frankish Kings. The strong, uncompromising language used by the Pope on this occasion lets one think that such marriages were unheard of in those days when Catholics had a holy fear of associating with heretics.[16] Hence, Pope Stephen took a firm stand in the case and pointed to the threat and danger that was involved by such a marriage for the religion of the subjects of the kingdom. Though Charlemagne married Desiderata in 770 he repudiated her in 771.

In the political scheming of nations through the ages, the question of marital alliances has played a very important part. It is understandable that the Holy See, in its regard for the faith of entire nations, would be much interested in the marriages of princes, particularly in the post-Reformation days in which the principle *Cuius regio, illius religio,* held sway. After the Protestant "Reformation" in which whole nations broke away from the unity of the Church, it was inevitable that a clash would

---

[15] *Cambridge Medieval History* (8 vols., New York: Macmillan, 1911-1936), II, 218-219 and especially 595-596.

[16] "Nullus . . . qui mentem sanam habet, hoc suspicari potest, ut tales, nominatissimi reges, tanto detestabili atque abominabili contagio implicentur. 'Quae enim societas luci ad tenebras? aut quae pars fideli cum infidelae?' "—Jaffé, *Bibliotheca Rerum Germanicarum* (6 vols., Berolini: Apud Weidmannos, 1864-1873), IV, 159; the text of Stephen's letter also appears in *MGH, Epistolae,* Tom. III (Berolini: Apud Weidmannos, 1892), 560-563; see also Feije, *De Matrimoniis Mixtis,* p. 8.

result between the Church and the civil rulers on the matter of marriages. In order to satisfy the natural expectations of certain nations the Church sometimes had to choose the toleration of the lesser evil. As long as there was present the required safeguard for the faith of the Catholic prince or princess, and as long as the Catholic religion of the royal offspring was properly guaranteed, the Church could still fulfill the essential demands of the divine law despite her toleration of the intermarriage between Catholic and non-Catholic. And so the Church saw herself constrained to devise such politico-religious agreements which according to the more recent point of view can be regarded as the substantial equivalent of formal *cautiones*. In earlier ages the Church had simply condemned mixed marriages and permitted the prospective marriage between Catholic and heretic only upon the latter's abjuration of heresy and profession of faith, that is, upon the heretic's outright or at least sincerely promised conversion. In later times the Church did not demand that the heretic give up his or her professed belief as a condition for marriage with a Catholic, but permitted such marriage provided that due *cautiones* in protection of the true faith and religion were properly covenanted and signed by the parties who contracted a mixed marriage.

The *cautiones* did not follow a uniform pattern in their outward expression, for each marriage presented its own peculiar problems. In one case it was possible that the heretic was well disposed to the Church or was perhaps in a state of vassalage relative to the royal house of which the Catholic prince or princess was a member; in another the heretic may have been entirely opposed to the Church or politically independent of feudal service to the Catholic royal house. In all cases, however, it was insisted that the Catholic party to the marriage was to be granted freedom to practice his religion and that all the children of both sexes were to be baptized and reared in the Catholic religion alone. These *cautiones* had to be signed always by the non-Catholic party, and usually by the Catholic party also. At times even an oath was demanded to fortify the agreement. The entire procedure was subject to notorization by at least two witnesses.[17]

[17] Feije, *De Matrimoniis Mixtis,* pp. 213-214; Schenk, *Mixed Religion and Disparity of Cult,* pp. 51-52; White, *Ante-Nuptial Promises and the Civil Law,* pp. 10-12.

The marriage case of Henry, Duke of Lorraine (1563-1624) is indicative of the reluctance with which the Holy See adopted the post-Tridentine discipline in the matter of granting dispensations for mixed marriages.

On January 30, 1599, Henry married his third cousin Catherine (1559-1604), the sister of Henry IV of France, without a dispensation and against the express prohibition of Pope Clement VIII. In addition Catherine was a Calvinist. Cardinal D'Ossat labored for years to obtain a dispensation in their favor. Because of the existence of the two impediments in the case, the one of consanguinity and the other of mixed religion, Clement was averse to grant the dispensations. A precedent was discovered in a like dispensation granted some years previous in the reign of Pope Gregory XIII at the intervention of St. Charles Borromeo. Thus, more secure in mind, Clement dispensed from consanguinity. The dispensation for mixed religion was also granted, but its execution was subject to the condition of conversion on the part of Catherine, and hence marks an example of the old Canon Law *cautio*. Catherine died before the dispensation became effective.[18]

Perhaps the best example of these politico-religious agreements is that which was connected with the marriage of Prince Charles of England with Henrietta Maria of France, sister of Louis XIII, in 1625. This marriage took place only after Charles strove for months for the hand of the Infanta Maria of Spain to satisfy his father King James I of England in a political alliance. The deliberations were long and involved between England, Spain and two of the Roman Pontiffs,[19] and involved an agreement on 23 public articles touching the marriage ceremony, the most important of which were:

> II—"That the marriage be once only celebrated in Spain and ratified in England . . . so as no ceremony or other thing intervene which shall be contrary to the Roman Catholic Apostolic Religion.

---

[18] Pastor, *History of the Popes* (32 vols., St. Louis: Herder, 1906-1940), XXIII, 161-162; Schenk, *Mixed Religion and Disparity of Cult*, p. 52; Feije, *De Matrimoniis Mixtis*, pp. 9-10; Roskovány, *De Matrimoniis Mixtis*, I, 19-20; Aich, "Ueber die gemischten Ehen. . ."—*AKKR*, XIV (1865), 326.

[19] Gregory XV (1621-1623) and Urban VIII (1623-1644).

XX—"That the sons and daughters which shall be born of this marriage shall be brought up in the company of the Most Excellent Infanta, at the least until the age of ten years and shall freely enjoy the right of succession to the Kingdoms . . ." (Pope Gregory XV corrected this to read 12 years for girls, 14 for boys).[20]

The 23 articles were sworn to by the King, Prince, and Privy Council, and James took the oath to uphold the articles "in the word of a King." The word of a King in those days meant much, and can, without stretching the imagination, be considered the basis for the assurance or moral certitude on the part of the dispensing party that the agreement would be kept. In addition to the 23 articles the King swore to 4 private ones in favor of the distressed Catholics in England, promising to restore the Church's property and to permit free Catholic services in private houses in England, Scotland, and Ireland. Delays, intrigues, demands, counter-demands, the hesitance of Philip IV of Spain, the death of Pope Gregory XV, all combined to strain the patience of Charles I of England who threw over the match and returned to England. It is of little concern whether the marriage took place or not; the case shows to what detail the *cautiones* were elaborated. The important articles were those which granted freedom in the practice of her religion to the Infanta and which confirmed the promise to rear all the children as Catholics; the others were practical supports to these two.

King James wanted an alliance, so he turned to France, eventually effecting the marriage of his son Charles to Henrietta Maria. A dispensation was obtained from Pope Urban VIII on December 30, 1624, and the marriage took place in the following June, not, however, before the same *cautiones* were secured which were prerequired in the proposed Spanish alliance.[21]

---

[20] Rushworth, *Historical Collections* . . . Beginning the Sixteenth year of King James, *anno* 1618 and ending Fifth year of King Charles, *anno* 1629 (8 vols., London, 1682), I, 86-88.

[21] The *cautiones* or compact in the French case numbered 30 articles, the most important of which are recorded in Roskovány, *De Matrimoniis Mixtis,* II, 10. They refer to the free exercise of the religion of the

On November 11, 1631, Wolfgang Wilhelm (1578-1653), Duke of Neuberg, entered marriage with Catherine Charlotte, heretical daughter of John II, Count Palatinate of Zweibrücken. Moved by a well founded hope for the conversion of Catherine, as well as desiring to avoid greater evils, Pope Urban VIII granted the dispensation in 1633 through the Congregation of the Holy Office.[22] In this case also a contract was demanded of the parties before the Holy See dispensed. The contract contained six major points of agreement and five of lesser moment. All, however, were devised to safeguard the faith and practice of religion for the Catholic party and the offspring as well as to provide in a practical way for Catherine's conversion.[23]

At the beginning of the 18th century Duke Gustave von Zweibrücken married his second cousin, the Protestant Princess Dorothea von Veldenz. While Pope Clement XI refused to dispense from the impediment of mixed religion, he was willing to dispense from the impediment of consanguinity (July 23, 1707) on the condition that Dorothea be converted. The refusal to dispense from mixed religion was due to the absence of a *causa gravis* as well as the patent presence of danger to the faith.[24] Because of

---

princess. To facilitate her devotion to her faith it was covenanted that she was to take with her a bishop and 28 priests for the service of her chapel. Roskovány reports the age of 13 years as the time up to which the children were to remain in the care of the princess. The King did not live up to his promises. Accounts of this marriage and of the *cautiones* involved are found also in Roskovány, *De Matrimoniis Mixtis,* I, 21-22; Carrière, *De Matrimonio,* II, 89; Feije, *De Matrimoniis Mixtis,* p. 10; Albitius, *De Inconstantia in Iure Admittenda vel Non* (Amstelaedami, 1683), *Tractatus de Inconstantia in Fide,* cap. XXXVI, n. 218, typewritten copy used (private); Schenk, *Mixed Religion and Disparity of Cult,* pp. 53-55.

[22] ". . . remittendum hac vice aliquid de rigore canonicae disciplinae, dispensationemque tanto iam tempore ac tanta cum humilitate imploratam, ad evitanda potissimum maiora mala, praelibato Volfgango Neoburgi duci, aliorum potissimum suasionibus prolapso ex paterna SSmi. Nostri benignitate concedendam fore . . ." quoted from Roskovány, *De Matrimoniis Mixtis,* II, 12; Aich, "Ueber die gemischten Ehen . . ."—*AKKR,* XIV (1865), 326.

[23] Roskovány (*De Matrimoniis Mixtis,* II, 12-15) lists the points in agreement; cf. also Feije, *De Matrimoniis Mixtis,* p. 11; also p. 211, footnote.

[24] Aich, "Ueber die gemischten Ehen . . ."—*AKKR,* XIV (1865), 325; Feije, *De Matrimoniis Mixtis,* p. 13.

Dorothea's unwillingness to be converted to the Catholic faith, Gustave broke off the proposed alliance.

In all these marriages there was demanded by the Holy See besides the *cautiones* a cause for the dispensation and not merely a grave cause but also a public cause, a *causa publica.* This is well exemplified in the case of Charles I of England and Henrietta Maria of France for in this alliance the Catholics of England might have gained their freedom to worship had the King been faithful to his word. Because the *causa publica* was wanting in the case of the common people, no dispensations were granted in their regard.[25] For about 150 years (1600-1750) such dispensations were restricted to the nobility.

The demands of the Holy See gradually became mitigated to meet the ever increasing problem of mixed marriages. This problem grew apace with the changing social conditions in which a freer association of Catholics with heretics resulted. The French Revolution, the spread of Protestantism, the loss to the Church of Catholics who simply disregarded the laws forbidding such marriages, the opening of new mission fields in pagan lands where Christians were few in number—all these factors contributed to an inevitable compromise on the part of the Church. Starting with the royalty where the *cautiones* were long and involved, there finally developed the two or three stipulations essential for the safeguarding of the natural divine laws. These safeguards were always required before such marriages were permitted.

Before the Protestant "Reformation" the only condition upon which a mixed marriage was permitted was the promise of conversion. This practice obtained in view of the fact that no other religion was recognized in all of Europe except the Catholic religion and no compromise was required. After the revolt of Luther and Henry VIII, states gave juridic recognition to the Protestant religion and thus social and political changes of great

---

[25] "Quae autem causa sit sufficiens ut Pontifex dispenset ad huiusmodi matrimonia contrahenda: Ego nunquam vidi concessas fuisse similes dispensationes nisi suadente causa boni publici"—Albitius, *Tractatus de Inconstantia in Fide,* cap. XVIII, n. 46.

moment were effected. In the new situation in which the Church found herself, it became apparent that the only expedient thing for her to do was to grant dispensations for Catholics to marry heretics, in order thus to preclude the immediate danger of loss of membership to the Church. To safeguard the faith, however, the *cautiones* were devised, first, as was shown, for the mixed marriages of the royalty, and later for the similar marriages of the common people.

The first *cautiones* were lengthy and involved as demanded of the royalty; later they were simplified in their use for the common people; they were always sufficient, if they were observed, to safeguard the faith and morals and to avert the occasions of sin. It was a long bitter struggle—this progressive compromise on the part of the Church—a struggle which may best be read and understood in the acts and writings of the popes who were involved.

# CHAPTER THREE

## THE PAPAL ACTS ON *Cautiones* AND MORAL CERTITUDE

The present chapter will examine the various papal letters and encyclicals, and the important decrees and instructions of the Roman Curia on the question of the *cautiones* in mixed marriages and of the moral certitude concerning their fulfillment, as issued for the various countries and provinces by the Holy See. These papal acts often constituted ecclesiastical legislation for the whole Church and formed the basis both in letter and in spirit for the specific legislation in the many particular councils which were held in several countries after the Council of Trent. In addition, the pastoral letters which many bishops addressed to their priests were at times directly prompted and inspired by the papal acts. Hence the acts of the popes were in reality a well-spring for the legislation which touched both directly and indirectly on the matter of the *cautiones.* The chapter will be divided into four periods covering the centuries from the year 1600 up to the advent of the present Code.

### I PERIOD: 1600-1800

It has been indicated that the question of mixed marriages throughout the seventeenth and early eighteenth centuries, in the consideration of the causes and conditions prerequired for the granting of a dispensation, was in its practical application concerned exclusively with the royalty and the nobility. A *causa publica* was required before mixed marriages were permitted. The presentation of such a cause had to be accompanied with the furnishing of *cautiones.* These *cautiones* were the agreement or the covenant invoked between the heretical party and the Catholic Church on the point of obtaining assurance that the interests of the faith would not be jeopardized. The intermarriage between the Catholic and the non-Catholic royalty or nobility was a factor of far-reaching public concern in the days when civil governments had adopted the perversely peremptory principle: *Cuius regio, illius et religio.* The religion of thousands of subjects was thus made to hang in the balance with the professed religion of their ruler. The denial of the Holy See to let him enter a mixed marriage when the proper guarantees for his faith and for the faith of his children were forthcoming could in practice have been tantamount to courting the defection of an entire nation from the faith. The Church was averse even passively to invite such a likely disaster.

The situation was different with the common people. They continued to be governed by the statutes of the diocesan synods and by the ordinances of the provincial councils. These regulations for the greater part either unreservedly condemned the marriages of Catholics with heretics, or permitted such marriages only on the condition of the heretic's abjuration of heresy and profession of faith, or in connection with an outright conversion to the Church on the part of the heretic.

There were few papal decrees on the subject from the reign of Gregory XIV (1590-1591) until the time of Benedict XIV (1740-1758). One of the earliest was a resolution of the Sacred Congregation of the Council under date of February 2, 1590 forbidding priests to be authoritative witnesses for the marriages between Catholics and heretics, even though the latter formed the major portion of the population of the Russian border provinces of Pomerania.[1] The resolution was in accord with the mind of the Church as exemplified in a later instruction of the Sacred Congregation of the Council during the reign of Pope Clement VIII (1592-1605) on March 31, 1597. For the cases in which the impediment of mixed religion was conjoined with a diriment impediment of consanguinity or of affinity the bishops were instructed simply to declare invalid the marriages which had been contracted between Catholics and heretics. The removal of the diriment impediment by means of a dispensation would still

[1] "Cum in partibus Russiae et Pomeraniae fere omnes sint haeretici, non licet presbyteris virum catholicum cum haeretica muliere, et e converso, matrimonio conjungere."—Roskovány, *De Matrimoniis Mixtis,* II, 3.

leave the prospective contract of marriage interdicted in view of the extant prohibition of Catholics to enter marriages with heretics, from which prohibition Catholics were in no way to be released through the use of any dispensation even for the diriment impediment. Rather, the bishops were, with the help of the secular power, to procure for such Catholics the legitimately authorized favor of entering marriage with Catholics.[2]

Even at this early date, before the flood of requests for dispensations in mixed religion came upon Rome, there is marked the beginning of two distinct trends in the papal discipline on the problem. The resolution and the instruction mentioned, coupled with a further decision of the Holy Office under Pope Urban VIII (1623-1644) which admitted the lawful contract of marriages with schismatics only on the condition of a prior abjuration of schism and of a concomitant profession of faith,[3] are indicative of one trend, namely, that of a severe and inflexible discipline for such places wherein the faith was well established but was being challenged by the error of heresy. On the other hand, a somewhat mitigated discipline was employed by the Sacred Congregation of the Propagation of the Faith, as is exemplified in an instruction of 1638 which treated the very same problem, but in connection with its appearance in heretical lands where Catholicism was not permitted.[4] Typical of the second discipline wherein the Church

[2] "In matrimonio contracto inter haereticum et catholicam, et e converso, qui essent aliquo gradu cognationis vel affinitatis conjuncti . . . quia tamen etiam legitimo impedimento cessante catholicus cum haeretico contrahere non potest, licet contractum valeat . . . nullo modo videtur dispensandum . . . quin potius partes Ordinarii sunt, talia matrimonia irrita et nulla declarare, et catholicis matrimonia contrahendi legitimam cum catholicis licentiam et favorem impetrare, invocato auxilio brachii saecularis."—Roskovány, *De Matrimoniis Mixtis,* II, 3-4.

[3] S.C.S.Off., 20 iun. 1628: "Matrimonia inter catholicos et schismaticos admittenda non esse, nisi praecesserit abjuratio schismatis et professio catholicae fidei."—Feije, *De Matrimoniis Mixtis,* p. 27; Roskovány, *De Matrimoniis Mixtis,* I, 18. Both authors point to June 20, 1628 as the date of this decision. Feije (*op. cit.,* p. 11) also cites an answer of the Holy Office which under date of August 20, 1671 exacted the same conditions and required that they be fulfilled prior to the marriage.

[4] "In terris haereticorum, ubi haereses impune grassantur maxime, si ibi Catholicae fidei cultus non permittatur, matrimonia cum haereticis per

granted wider powers to vicars apostolic in missionary fields was the concession granted by the Holy Office on September 19, 1671. According to this concession the Catholic spouse who was invincibly ignorant of the impediment of disparity of worship at the time of the celebration of the marriage which took place prior to his or her conversion could be absolved and was not to be put under censure or compulsion to desert the infidel spouse as long as the danger of perversion was not present. This concession to the Catholic spouse naturally implied the intermediate grant of a dispensation from the actually existing diriment impediment and at least a private renewal of matrimonial consent.[5] Such a faculty, however, was to be used by the missionaries with great care and with strict attention to the fulfillment of all the requisite conditions. Thus, when it was seen that the Christian would be forced to take part in superstitious acts, even though remotely, the use of the power to dispense from the impediment of disparity of worship was strictly interdicted.[6] Conditions insisted upon at all times in mission fields and elsewhere looked to the freedom of the Catholic party to practice his religion and to the assurance that all the children would be baptized and reared as Catholics. Formal *cautiones* were not used as yet, and the actual practice invoked for securing the fulfillment of these conditions is not known. It was apparently left to the granter of the dispensation to secure this fulfillment in his own way, for all the decrees of the popes de-

---

exhortationes potius quam per censuras prohibenda."—Roskovány, *De Matrimoniis Mixtis*, II, 9. Cf. also the decree of the Bishop of Chełmno (Kulm), September 9, 1774, for a similar manifestation of tempered discipline—Roskovány, *ibid.*, p. 102.

[5] S.C.S.Off. (Albaniae), 19 sept. 1671, ad 1—*Fontes*, n. 749. For other examples of the Church's indulgence in mission countries, cf. S.C.S.Off. (Tunkin, Orient.), 5 sept. 1736—*Fontes*, n. 790; S.C. Prop. Fide, instr. (ad Vic. Ap. Fokien.), 13 sept. 1760—*Coll. S.C.P.F.*, n. 435; S.C.S.Off. (Vic. Ap. Sutchuen.), 12 ian. 1769—*Fontes*, n. 822. In the last of these documents missionaries were urged to dispense in consanguinity and affinity if they could thus avoid mixed marriages. Cf. also S.C.Prop. Fide, instr. (ad Vic. Ap. Chensi et Chansi), 30 ian. 1807—*Fontes*, n. 4689.

[6] S.C.S.Off. (ad Vic. Ap. Sutchuen.), 15 dec. 1769—*Fontes*, n. 826; S.C.Prop. Fide, 28 iul. 1760, ordered vicars apostolic to suspend from the use of these faculties any missionary who witnessed such marriages without having secured a dispensation—*Coll. S.C.P.F.*, n. 432.

manded the presence of these assurances before any attempt was to be made to use the power of dispensing, but no concrete method for the securing of these assurances was prescribed. Perhaps the civil law custom in the Orient, which granted to the husband full power over the wife, provided a sufficient basis for this security whenever the husband was the Catholic party in the prospective marriage.[7] It is not deducible from the documents which the writer was able to consult just what basis in general was thought to provide a similar assurance if the bride in the prospective marriage was the Catholic party. It appears indicated that in such an instance other factors apart from those which were furnished by the traditional usage of the country had to play a predominant role in supplying the needed assurances concerning the unmolested practice of her faith on the part of the Catholic bride.[8]

Two apostolic letters of Pope Clement XI (1700-1721) show a deep concern for the fulfillment of the condition of conversion or for the abjuration of heresy prior to the admission of erstwhile heretics to the celebration of the Sacrament of matrimony. In a letter to the Bishop of Agen in France, Clement instructs the bishop to admit converts to matrimony only after they have proved themselves sincere in their conversion.[9] He admits, however, that an invariable norm for judging about the sincerity of the nupturients in divers cases cannot be precribed.

In his letter of June 16, 1710, through the Holy Office,[10] Clement insisted that the abjuration of heresy on the part of the heretic

---

[7] S.C. de Prop. Fide, instr. (pro Miss. Sin.), 16 feb. 1795—*Coll. S.C.P.F.*, n. 623.

[8] Vlaming, *Praelectiones Iuris Matrimonii* (3. ed., 2 vols., Bussum in Hollandia: 1919-1921), I, 213-214.

[9] "Hanc regulam servandam esse dicimus et decernimus: eos, de quorum sincera conversione ad religionem Catholicam haud leviter Episcopi suspicantur, non esse admittendos ad Sacramentum matrimonii, ad quod iidem Episcopi pro eorum zelo et prudentia admittere tantum debent eos, qui post ipsorum conversionem seu abjurationem semper se tamquam catholicos gesserunt; in aliis vero casibus in quibus pro eorum diversitate una eademque norma praescribi nequit, iuxta pietatis ac prudentiae dictamen statuendum esse videtur."—litt. apost., 23 feb. 1706—quoted from Feije, *De Matrimoniis Mixtis*, p. 12.

[10] Cited in Feije, *De Matrimoniis Mixtis*, pp. 13-14.

had to precede the marriage with a Catholic and he took occasion to administer a sharp rebuke to those theologians who held a contrary opinion.

This same condition was insisted upon in the famous encyclical *"Magnae Nobis"* of Benedict XIV (1740-1758), written to Poland on June 29, 1748.[11] Strong in his detestation of mixed marriages which he considered a constant threat to the faith, Benedict nevertheless maintained a middle position between those who held that no papal dispensation at all was needed, and those who held that not even the Pope could dispense from the impediment of mixed religion.[12] He declared that mixed marriages even apart from a papal dispensation were valid, but he insisted on the heretic's abjuration of heresy as a safeguard for compliance with the natural divine law. Apparently the encyclical *"Magnae Nobis"* was not fully understood, for on August 8, 1748, Benedict again wrote the Primate Archbishop of Poland, further explaining the discipline to be followed, and again insisting on the abjuration of heresy as requisite before the dispensation would be granted by the Holy See.[13] The Holy See alone was competent to dispense

[11] *Fontes,* n. 387, n. 5. See also n. 6 of this Encyclical according to which the presence of a merely probable cause had to be plainly set forth in the petition for the dispensation. Moreover, the execution of an apostolic rescript of dispensation from some matrimonial impediment had to remain suspended if the executor of the rescript had knowledge that no mention of the heretical status of the one or the other party was made in the application for the dispensation, and the executor had to report to the Roman Curia the cause which underlay the non-execution of the rescript. Cf. Bangen, *Instructio Practica de Sponsalibus et Matrimonio* (IV Partes in 1 vol., Monasterii, 1858-1860), IV, 13-14 (hereafter cited as *De Sponsalibus et Matrimonio*); Esmein, *Le Mariage en Droit Canonique,* II, 257; Gasparri, *Tractatus Canonicus de Matrimonio* (ed. nova, 2 vols., Romae: Typis Polyglottis Vaticanis, 1932), I, 263 (hereafter cited as *De Matrimonio*); Carrière (*De Matrimonio,* II, 85-89) summarizes the conditions required to permit a mixed marriage as contained in the *"Magnae Nobis."* Cf. also Pius VII Breve Apost. (ad Archiep. Moguntin.), 8 oct. 1803—*Fontes,* n. 477; see also Roskovány, *De Matrimoniis Mixtis,* II, 86-90.

[12] Cf. Declaration of Benedict XIV through the Sacred Congregation of the Council on the status of marriages in Belgium and Holland, 4 nov. 1741—*Fontes,* n. 3527; Benedict XIV, *De Synodo Dioecesana* (2 vols., Romae, 1767), Lib. IX, cap. 3, n. 3.

[13] Ep. *"Ad Tuas"*—*Fontes,* n. 389.

in mixed religion and disparity of worship. This did not deter Benedict, however, in accord with missionary policy, to grant faculties for two years to all vicars apostolic to dispense from the inpediment of disparity of worship in mission lands under the following conditions: a) that peaceful cohabitation without contumely and offense to the Creator be insured; b) that all the children be reared as Catholics; c) that the faculties be used only in places wherein infidels outnumbered Catholics.[14] Benedict's Epistle *"Singulari Nobis"*[15] is another of his famous documents in which he defined and explained the impediments of disparity of worship and of mixed religion and also confirmed the fact that the former arose through custom in the Church. He further explained that the impediment of disparity of worship was an impediment to which validly baptized heretics were also subject in their prospective marriage with the unbaptized.

Clement XIII (1758-1769) decried the evils of mixed marriages in his letter to Cardinal de Rohan, Bishop of Strassburg, pointing out the dangers to the faith of the offspring, regardless of whether the mother or the father was the heretical party in the marriage.[16] He laid stress on the evils of religious indifferentism which such inharmonious unions engender in the children,[17] and declared that in spite of precautions such marriages remain a source of danger and an occasion from which unforeseen perversion of the faith may ensue.[18]

Even after faculties to dispense from mixed marriages were granted by the Holy See, Pius VI (1775-1799) ruled that vicars

---

[14] Benedict XIV, 15 feb. 1756—found in Perrone, *De Matrimonio Christiano,* II, 334; cf. S.C.S.Off. (Scutaren.), 9 iul. 1750—*Fontes,* n. 802, wherein reference is made to the former response of the same Congregation given November 18, 1745—*Fontes,* n. 796.

[15] 9 feb. 1749—*Fontes,* n. 394; Planchard, "Dispense de Disparité dc Cult et de Religion Mixte"—*NRT* XV (1883), 393.

[16] Ep. *"Quantopere,"* 16 nov. 1763—*Fontes,* n. 460.

[17] The reader may well compare the Epistle of Clement XIII with the encyclical *Casti Connubii* of Pius XI, December 31, 1930. For the text of the latter cf. *Acta Apostolicae Sedis,* XXII (1930), 539-592, and with relation to the question of mixed marriages and the dangers attendant upon them, pp. 571-572. (Reference to the *Acta* will hereafter be made with the letters *AAS.*)

[18] Ter Haar, *Mixed Marriages and Their Remedies,* pp. 8; 24-25.

apostolic were not to exercise them unless they could assure themselves that the conditions would be fulfilled and that there was some hope of conversion for the heretic.[19] Without compromising these conditions Pius VI struck a note of tolerance in his instruction to the Bishop of Rozsnyó (Rosenau)[20] by allowing mixed marriages to be celebrated in certain places and under certain conditions in order to avoid greater evils. They were simply to be tolerated, but in no way were they to be approved. The same tolerance is noted in his rescript to the Cardinal Archbishop of Malines in Belgium, where mixed marriages continued in spite of the efforts that were made to check them.

If the conversion of the heretic or the abjuration of heresy could not be obtained, then a merely passive or material assistance at the mixed marriage was indicated. Even such an assistance could be given only under stringent conditions. There was to be demanded a written promise, confirmed by oath in the presence of two witnesses, that the heretic would permit freedom for the Catholic to practice his or her religion and to have all the children which were to be born of the union reared as Catholics regardless of their sex. The Catholic party, too, had to sign and swear to a witnessed statement that he or she would not apostatize from the faith, would procure the Catholic education of all the children, and would strive to obtain the conversion of his or her heretic spouse.[21] A material presence in the assistance at mixed marriages, so that pastors *"tamquam inviti audiant dumtaxat utriusque consensum,"* was permitted also in the instruction of the Sacred Congregation of the Propagation of the Faith on September 6, 1785 to the vicar apostolic of Sweden,[22] but only on condition that

[19] S.C.S.Off. (Sutchuen.), 15 feb. 1780; ". . . nisi spem suae conversionis praebuerit, saltem sine contumelia Creatoris et Christiani nominis iniuria sit cum parte fideli cohabitura, nec ullatenus impeditura educationem prolis utriusque sexus in sancta religione."—*Fontes,* n. 840.

[20] S.C.C., Rosnavien., 20 aug. 1780—*Fontes,* n. 3811; Roskovány, *De Matrimoniis Mixtis,* II, 539-542; Feije, *De Matrimoniis Mixtis,* pp. 27; 179; Planchard, "Dispense de Disparité de Cult et de Religion Mixte"—*NRT,* XV (1883), 503.

[21] Cf. S.C.S.Off., instr. (ad Archiep. Quebecen.), 16 sept. 1824, for a similar insistence on the fulfillment of these same conditions—*Fontes,* n. 866.

[22] *Fontes,* n. 4606.

the vicar had moral certitude as to the fulfillment of the *cautiones*.

By the close of the 18th century the celebration of mixed marriages was by no means any longer restricted to the royalty. Apart from missionary countries, however, the popes were reluctant to concede permission to pastors to witness such marriages. A gradual mitigation of the conditions under which they were permitted to do so is noticeable from the time of Benedict XIV onward. He permitted such marriages normally only after the heretic's abjuration of heresy and profession of faith. Pius VI tolerated the heretic's continuance in his or her heretical status, but demanded sworn and witnessed *cautiones* from the heretical as well as from the Catholic party in the marriage. The Catholic was further required to strive for the conversion of the heretic. Never was there any compromise on the two conditions —freedom for the Catholic to practice his religion and assurance for the prospective children to receive Catholic baptism and education. As yet, apart from a few concessions made to missionary vicars, no faculties were given to bishops whereby they were enabled to grant a dispensation from the prohibitive impediment of mixed religion or from the diriment impediment of disparity of worship.

## II PERIOD: 1800-1850

The beginning of a new century witnessed further steps in the gradual lessening of the severe discipline of the Church regarding the tolerated celebration of mixed marriages. For, although Pius VII (1800-1823) branded such marriages as sacrilegious[28] and apart from the valid celebration which distinguished marriages of mixed religion from marriages of disparity of worship which remained invalid in the absence of a dispensation, likened the former to the latter in every other fundamental respect, still the Pontiff employed the phrase *"fere publica"* in his reference to the cause which was prerequired for the granting of a dispensation. Furthermore, perhaps for the first time, if one abstracts from the

[28] Cf. *"Vix nova,"* 17 feb. 1809—quoted in Planchard, "Dispense de Disparité de Cult et de Religion Mixte"—*NRT* XV (1883), 500.

concessions accorded for missionary countries, faculties to dispense from the prohibition of mixed marriages were granted by the Pope to bishops. These faculties were granted by Pope Pius VII in an indult to the bishops of France under date of January 26, 1823.[24] No concession was made, however, regarding the continued strict demand of the stipulated *cautiones*. They were to be demanded in full as outlined in the encyclical *"Magnae Nobis"* of Benedict XIV. If the civil law rendered null the agreement to rear all the children as Catholics as it did in the diocese of Trier, the priests were simply forbidden to assist at the marriage.[25] They were reminded that one "must obey God rather than men." The problem became increasingly acute in Germany, for the civil governments in the Protestant States enacted laws contrary to the practice of the Church in regard to mixed marriages. By the Common Law Code (*preussisches allgemeines Landrecht*) of Prussia (Feb. 5, 1794) boys born of a mixed marriage were to be reared in the religion of the father, girls in the religion of the mother. A royal decree (Nov. 21, 1803) established that all the children had to be reared in the religion of the father, that the banns of marriage had to be published and that pastors had to assist at the marriage. On August 17, 1825, this decree was extended to the Rhineland and Westphalia, which embraced the dioceses of Cologne, Trier, Paderborn, and Muenster.[26] Pope Leo XII wrote an encyclical in 1825[27] to all the bishops of the world decrying and condemning any con-

---

[24] Cf. Planchard, "Dispense de Disparité de Cult et de Religion Mixte" —*ibid.*, p. 528. On this matter one may with particular profit consult Leo XII, const. *"Quo graviora"* 13 mart. 1825—*Fontes*, n. 481, and Carrière, *De Matrimonio*, II, 88.

[25] Litt. (ad Vic. Treviren.), 23 apr. 1817—Roskovány, *De Matrimoniis Mixtis*, II, 164; Feije, *De Impedimentis et Dispensationibus Matrimonialibus* (3. ed., Lovanii, 1885), p. 197 (hereafter cited as *De Imped. et Dispens. Matr.*); Feije, *De Matrimoniis Mixtis*, p. 196; litt. (ad Vic. Treviren.), 31 oct. 1819—Roskovány, *De Matrimoniis Mixtis*, II, 166-168; Feije, *De Matrimoniis Mixtis*, pp. 19; 58; 243.

[26] Knecht, *Handbuch des katholischen Eherechts* (Freiburg im Breisgau: Herder & Co., 1928), pp. 288-289; Bangen, *De Sponsalibus et Matrimonio*, IV, 17-19.

[27] (No further date),—Roskovány, *De Matrimoniis Mixtis*, II, 197.

ventions or pacts between Catholics and Protestants wherein it was agreed to rear all the children or even any of them in any other than the Catholic religion. In more direct remonstrance was the apostolic letter *"Litteris altero"* of Pope Pius VIII (1829-1830), sent to the Archbishop of Cologne and the Bishops of Trier, Muenster, and Paderborn under date of March 25, 1830.[28] The Pope stated that when the *cautiones* were disregarded a grave sin was committed against the natural divine law on which they were based. Such marriages were illicit and gravely forbidden, but the priest was permitted to assist at them *passively* (as a guest) in order to avoid greater evils. Even this could only then be done when circumstances warranted it, that is, when no diriment impediment was present and when at least the Catholic had given due assurance that the required promises would be kept.[29]

The instruction of Cardinal Albani,[30] sent to the same four dioceses two days after the apostolic letter *"Litteris altero,"* explained the one and only position that Pius VIII could assume in the question in the face of the obvious demands of the natural divine law and of the constant tradition of his predecessors, and stated that, while at times circumstances could permit the priest to witness such illicit marriages *passively,* yet the traditionally employed *cautiones* constituted the normal agency for safeguarding and keeping intact the unquestionably righteous demands of the natural divine law.

---

[28] "Nostis autem, Venerabiles Fratres, ipsas omnes *cautiones* eo spectare, ut hac in re naturales divinaeque leges sartae tectae habeantur, quandoquidem exploratum est, catholicas personas seu viros seu mulieres, quae nuptias cum acatholicis ita contrahunt, ut se aut futuram sobolem periculo perversionis temere committant, non modo canonicas violare sanctiones, sed directe etiam, gravissimeque in naturalem ac divinam legem peccare."—*Fontes,* n. 482. Cf. Feije, *De Matrimoniis Mixtis,* pp. 20-21; Bangen, *De Sponsalibus et Matrimonio,* IV, 12-13, and Appendix, nn. 18-19; Feije, *De Imped. et Dispens. Matr.,* p. 208; Ter Haar, *Mixed Marriages and Their Remedies,* pp. 9-10; Planchard, "Dispense de Disparité de Cult et de Religion Mixte"—*NRT* (1883), 507.

[29] Cf. Ayrinhac-Lydon, *Marriage Legislation in the New Code of Canon Law* (New Revised ed., New York: Benziger Bros., 1935), pp. 105-106 (hereafter cited as *Marriage Legislation*).

[30] Secret. Status, instr. 27 mart. 1830—*Fontes,* n. 6451; cf. also Feije, *De Matrimoniis Mixtis,* p. 216.

The opposition to the papal requirements regarding the *cautiones* reached new heights in the pontificate of Gregory XVI (1831-1846). Attention was now centered on Catholic Bavaria, where by edict of June 10, 1803, other religions besides the Catholic faith had been accorded full freedom of exercise by the civil government.[31] On June 16, 1830, the government ordered pastors to be content with the freely entered agreements of the contracting parties regarding the religion of their future children. In October of 1830, Bishop Sailer of Regensburg forbade the publication of the banns and every act of pastoral assistance at the prospective marriage of a Protestant nobleman with a Catholic bride, inasmuch as the contracting parties had come to an agreement that all children were to be reared as Protestants. The civil magistrate ruled that all pastors were to assist at such marriages, even if the *cautiones* had been refused. He furthermore threatened to withdraw all subsidy from pastors who refused to comply with this demand of the state.[32]

The difficulty reached such a pass as to move Gregory XVI to address one of his famous encyclicals to the Archbishops and Bishops of Bavaria.[33] He pointed out the pastoral duties attendant upon the celebration of mixed marriages if a dispensation was rendered obtainable in view of the properly furnished *cautiones*. At the request of the Bishops of Munich, Regensburg, and Passau a further instruction, prepared by Cardinal Bernetti at the order of Gregory XVI, was directed to the bishops of Bavaria.[34] It permitted a purely passive assistance at mixed marriages if other-

---

[31] Knecht, *Handbuch des katholischen Eherechts*, p. 292.

[32] Knecht, *loc. cit.*

[33] Ep. encycl. "*Summo iugiter,*" 27 maii, 1832—*Fontes*, n. 484. Cf. also ep. encycl. "*Commissum divinitus*" (ad ep. Helvetiae), 17 maii, 1835—*Fontes*, n. 490; Roskovány, *De Matrimoniis Mixtis*, II, 212-218; Feije, *De Matrimoniis Mixtis*, pp. 22; 227; Aich, "Ueber die gemischten Ehen. . ." —*AKKR*, XIV (1865), 328.

[34] 12 sept. 1834—*Fontes*, n. 6452; Roskovány, *De Matrimoniis Mixtis*, II, 291-296. As to the question of *cautiones* being demanded of the Catholic party alone in certain cases, cf. Cardinal Lambruschini's instr. Secret. Status (ad omnes ep.), 15 nov. 1858—*Fontes*, n. 6454; S.C.S.Off., 2 mart. 1842—cited in Ayrinhac-Lydon, *Marriage Legislation*, p. 106 and also in Schenk, *Mixed Religion and Disparity of Cult*, pp. 242-243.

wise the marriage would take place before a Protestant minister, but it likewise demanded an assurance from the Catholic party that the children would be reared as Catholics and that every effort would be made to convert the non-Catholic spouse.[85]

These were truly unusual circumstances in which the celebration of mixed marriages was tolerated in *facie Ecclesiae* without the furnishing of formal *cautiones,* on the part of the heretic. Often, in addition to the *cautiones,* the oath and the use of the witnesses were required, as had been stipulated by the Tribunal of the Penitentiary.[86] If passive assistance was permitted without the formal *cautiones,* then it was only after assurance was had, at least from the Catholic party, that the substantial import of the *cautiones* was secured or that the natural divine law was duly safeguarded.

The *cautiones* together with the moral certitude that was required regarding their sincerity and veracity constituted the burden of several acts of Gregory XVI. His letter to the Archbishop of Freiburg[87] is perhaps typical, for it contained a severe prohibition of mixed marriages and exacted both dispensations and *cautiones* when the celebration of the marriage could not be hindered. These represented the normal requirements of the Church. A trying situation arose from time to time in this or that diocese, where greater concessions had to be made. This was true in Germany, as mentioned above, and also in Hungary, as is evi-

---

[85] In this connection one may also consult Cardinal Lambruschini's instr. (ad archiep. et ep. Austriacae ditionis in foederatis Germaniae partibus), 22 maii, 1841—*Fontes,* n. 6453; Roskovány, *De Matrimoniis Mixtis,* II, 820-824, especially 823; cf. also several allocutions of Gregory XVI, wherein he upholds the rights of the Church regarding marriage and defines the rights of the civil government in its civil effects: *Allocut. in consistorio secreto,* 10 dec. 1837—*Acta Gregorii Papae XVI scilicet Constitutiones, Bullae, Litterae Apostolicae, Epistolae* (cura ac studio Antonii Bernasconi, 4 vols., Romae: Ex Typographia Polyglotta, 1901-1904), II, 237-238 (hereafter cited *Acta Gregorii XVI*); *Allocut. in consistorio secreto,* 13 sept. 1838—*Acta Gregorii* XVI, II, 277-279; *Allocut. in consistorio secreto, "Officii memores,"* 5 iul. 1839—*Acta Gregorii* XVI, II, 341-342; cf. also *Fontes,* n. 492.

[86] (Ep. Friburgen.), 19 ian. 1836—Roskovány, *De Matrimoniis Mixtis,* III, 156, footnote.

[87] Ep. *"Dolorem,"* 30 nov. 1839—*Fontes,* n. 493.

denced by Gregory's letter[38] according to which a passive assistance was indeed permitted, but only provided that the demands of the natural divine law were satisfied, even though in the particular case this had to be accomplished without formal *cautiones.*

The formal *cautiones* were directly of ecclesiastical origin, but their valid basis and ultimate foundation were to be sought in the natural divine law.[39] While formal *cautiones* were the normal means to satisfy the requirements of the natural divine law, in unusual circumstances it was left to the bishop to decide whether these requirements were nevertheless met in some particular case without the use of the *cautiones.* But there had to be employed such means as sufficed to produce *moral certitude* in the mind of the granter of the dispensation, and the Holy Office itself determined the criterion of this moral certitude in a response which reads as follows:

> *"Quid accurate et strictissime sumpta significat cautio opportuna?"*
> Resp. *"Talem promissionem, quae in pactum deducta praebeat morale fundamentum de veritate executionis, ita ut prudenter eiusmodi executio expectari possit.*—SSmus. approbavit.[40]

The Holy Father's personal approval of this response of the Holy Office lent full juridic force to the definition of the term *cautio.* It established a criterion for the requisite certitude which had to underlie every dispensation that dealt with the authorized celebration of marriages in cases of mixed religion and disparity of

---

[38] Litt. ap. *"Quas vestro,"* 30 apr. 1841—*Fontes,* n. 497.

[39] Secret. Status, instr. 27 mart. 1830: "Cum enim non ecclesiastica solum, sed naturalis ac divina prorsus lex vetet, ne homo in nuptiis contrahendis se aut futuram sobolem periculo perversionis temere committat; exinde sane manifestum est memoratas omnes *cautiones* idcirco adhiberi, ut naturalis eadem divinaque lex sarta tecta habeatur."—*Fontes,* n. 6451; Ep. *"Non sine gravi,"* 23 maii, 1846—*Fontes,* n. 503; S.C. de Prop. Fide, 25 mart. 1858: *"Cautiones* enim illae ideo naturali divinoque jure exiguntur, . . ."—quoted from Planchard, "Dispense de Disparité de Cult et de Religion Mixte"—*NRT* XV (1883), 582.

[40] S.C.S.Off., 30 iun. 1842, ad 5—*Fontes,* n. 890. See also Pius VI rescript ad Card. Archiep. Mechlinien., 13 iul. 1782—*Fontes,* n. 471.

worship. The criterion which was thus determined received further confirmation and additional corroboration in subsequent official acts of the Roman Curia, and particularly in the responses of the same Holy Office.[41]

The first half of the nineteenth century witnessed two other important changes in the discipline of dispensing from these impediments. Both of them were indicative of a mitigated discipline in the Church on mixed marriages. One was the acceptance of the consideration of a private good as being sufficient to constitute the *causa gravis* requisite for the obtaining of a dispensation. Thus the way was opened for the common people as well as for the royalty in the matter of the possible celebration of a mixed marriage. The other change was the concession of faculties to bishops distant from Rome to enable them to dispense in the cases of mixed marriages. By the middle of the nineteenth century the content of the *cautiones* was well elaborated. Their purpose of rendering secure the conditions and demands of the natural and divine law was well defined. They were recognized as providing an all but indispensable means to that end. The Holy See insisted assiduously upon securing the *cautiones.* Even in unusual cases in which opposition from the civil government made it impossible to obtain written *cautiones* from the heretic, the Church with a view to avoiding more ominous evils as well as for the sake of reconciling the disaffected wills of those whom she was divinely charged to draw into her communion, tolerated a passive assistance at mixed marriages if the indispensable requirements of the natural divine law were rendered secure by means of at least the Catholic party's pledged assurances. The handling of these exceptional cases continued for a time in the fashion here delineated. But with the progress of time there obtained a steady attempt on the part of the Church to effect a uniform procedure in the matters touching upon the problem of mixed marriages, for she had become fully conscious of the perennial character of the problem which confronted her.

---

[41] S.C.S.Off. (ad ep. Aurelianen.), 6 iun. 1879—*Fontes,* n. 1064; Secret. Status, litt. 7 iul. 1890—*Fontes,* n. 6455; S.C.S. Off. (Leopolien.), 18 mart. 1891—*Fontes,* n. 1132. Cf. also Wernz, *Ius Matrimoniale,* pp. 836-837.

## III PERIOD: 1850-1900

### *A. The Pontificate of Pius IX*

At the outset of the reign of Pope Pius IX (1846-1878) a response of the Holy Office to the vicar apostolic of the Sandwich Islands (now commonly known as the Hawaiian group) explicitly determined anew the three *cautiones* which the Holy See was wont to demand in mixed marriages.[42] Insisting on these conditions as the normal requirement, Pius, like his predecessor, Gregory XVI, found it necessary at times to deal separately with this or that country or region, where the civil government had enacted contrary legislation. Such a condition obtained in parts of Hungary, Transylvania, and Switzerland.[43] Pope Pius met these trying situations unflinchingly, deriving his principles of action from the dictates of the natural divine law.[44] In all

[42] S.C.S.Off. (Vic. Ap. Sandwic.), 11 dec. 1850 ad 24: "In mentem . . . revocetur, matrimonia huius generis semper esse detestanda, nunquam a sacerdote catholico benedicenda, et contrahenda extra fores ecclesiae, praemissis prius tribus solitis conditionibus, quae sunt nimirum educatio totius prolis in catholica veritate, liberum exercitium religionis catholicae, et studium catholicae partis pertrahendi scilicet alteram ad verae fidei professionem."—*Fontes*, n. 913; *Coll. S.C.P.F.*, n. 1054.

[43] S.C. de Prop. Fide, instr. (ad Graeco-Rumen.), a. 1858—*Fontes,* n. 4843; *Coll. S.C.P.F.*, n. 1154. In Hungary, if the father was a Catholic, then all the children were to be reared as Catholics, if he was a non-Catholic, then the boys were to follow the father's religion, and the girls the mother's. Cf. Aichner, *Compendium Iuris Ecclesiastici* (11. ed., Brixinae, 1911), p. 181, nota 6; Czibulka, "Ungarische Staatskirchengesetze vom Jahre 1868"—*AKKR,* XXIV (1870), 104-107. The latter provision obtained also for Transylvania. In Switzerland there were localities in which according to civil law all the children were to be reared in the religion of the father. Cf. S.C.S.Off. (Helvetiae), 21 ian. 1863, ad 4—*Fontes,* n. 973.

[44] In the aforementioned instructions and in almost every other Roman document dealing with the problem of mixed marriages, there is the recurring theme of the requirements of the natural and divine law for the satisfaction of which the *cautiones* are to be invoked. Cf. Secret. Status, instr. 15 nov. 1858—*Fontes,* n. 6454; S.C. de Prop. Fide, litt. encycl. 11 mart. 1868—*Fontes,* n. 4872; *Coll. S.C.P.F.*, n. 1324; S.C.S.Off., instr. (ad Archiep. Corcyren.), 3 ian. 1871, ad 6—*Fontes,* n. 1013; *Coll. S.C.P.F.*, n. 1362.

cases he insisted on the *cautiones.* Only rarely did he permit passive assistance at illicit marriages, and then only when there was the founded hope of avoiding a greater imminent evil, or when there was direct promise of some evident good accruing to the Church.

From time to time, as occasion demanded it, the Popes have issued instructions, constitutions, and encyclicals to counteract an abuse, to define a practice, or to clarify a doctrine or discipline. Such was the purpose of Pope Pius IX when his Secretary of State, Cardinal Antonelli issued an instruction to all the bishops of the world, reiterating the Church's position on the entire question of mixed marriages.[45] Again the necessity of the *cautiones* as based on the natural divine law was stressed, but perhaps more important was the fact that the instruction summarized the doctrine and practice of Pius' predecessors in this regard, and outlined the common law of the Church as well as indicated the circumstances which would permit an exceptional and particular discipline.[46]

Following closely upon this instruction were two responses of the Sacred Congregation of the Propagation of the Faith. They sought to correct abuses and to rectify misinterpretations which had arisen. They insisted particularly on the need of a *cause* for the dispensation in addition to the presence of the *cautiones.*[47]

In further determination of the manner for the securing of the *cautiones* (a matter for the greater part left to the discretion of the ordinary), an apostolic letter addressed to the Bishop of the diocese of Rimouski, a suffragan see of Quebec, Canada, per-

---

[45] Cf. instr. Antonelliana (ad omnes ep.), 15 nov. 1858—*Coll. S.C.P.F.*, n. 1169, or also Secret. Status, instr. 15 nov. 1858—*Fontes,* n. 6454. On this matter the reader may well refer to Planchard, "Dispense de Disparité de Cult et de Religion Mixte"—*NRT,* XV (1883), 584-589.

[46] Wernz, *Ius Matrimoniale,* p. 827; Gasparri, *De Matrimonio,* I, 275; Ter Haar, *Mixed Marriages and Their Remedies,* p. 79.

[47] Some were of the opinion that once the *cautiones* were secured, that was all that was necessary. Cf. S.C. de Prop. Fide, 2 dec. 1862—cited in Wernz, *Ius Matrimoniale* p. 827; 25 mart. 1868 (Baltimoren.),—*Concilii Plenarii Baltimorensis II, Acta et Decreta* (ed. altera mendis expurgata, Baltimorae: Murphy, 1894), Appendix n. XX, pp. 308-310; litt. encycl. 11 mart. 1868—*Fontes,* n. 4872 carries the same text.

mitted the oath in support of the *cautiones* to be omitted by the heretic, if without it the ordinary could still have moral certitude that the *cautiones* would be observed.[48] It was stated though, that if such certitude could not be obtained because of the character of the person or in view of other kindred circumstances, then the bishop could by law require the oath in confirmation of the promises made.

Other matters involving the subject of mixed marriages, either directly or indirectly, were treated during the period of the long reign of Pius IX. The importance of the *cautiones* may well be recognized in the fact that they were to be demanded even *in articulo mortis.*[49]

Another point of interest was the demand for the *cautiones* even in the case in which a Catholic wished to marry one who had defected from the faith without joining a heretical sect.[50]

Progress in delineating the moral problem connected with mixed marriages and a constant effort to unify the discipline of the Holy See in their regard seem to have been the characteristics of the reign of Pius IX. Perhaps most of all was emphasized the necessity of the *cautiones* in mixed marriages as requirements answering the normal demands of the natural divine law. The various

---

[48] S.C.S.Off., litt. (St. Germani), 17 feb. 1875—*Fontes,* n. 1039. The Latin text appears in Gasparri, *De Matrimonio,* I, 267-268. Cf. also S.C.S.Off., litt. (ad Ep. Ottawien.), 17 apr. 1879—*Coll. S.C.P.F.,* n. 1517 according to which the *cautiones* must be given in writing in spite of contrary civil law; and if bishops fear that the *cautiones* are not furnished sincerely, then the dispensation must be refused.

[49] S.C.S.Off., instr. (ad Archiep. Corcyren.), 2 ian. 1871—*Fontes,* n. 1013; S.C.S.Off. (Leopolien.), 18 mart. 1891—*Fontes,* n. 1132; S.C.S.Off., 21 iun. 1912—*AAS,* IV (1912), 442-443. Cf. Schenk, *Mixed Religion and Disparity of Cult,* pp. 216-230, esp. 225.

[50] S.C.S.Off. (Leodien.), 30 ian. 1867, ad 1: ". . . dummodo cautum omnino sit catholicae educationi universae prolis, aliisque similibus conditionibus."—*Fontes,* n. 998. The Code refers to this condition as one of "unworthiness" on the part of the fallen-away Catholic, and not technically as one which involves an impediment. Ordinaries may for a grave cause permit the celebration of such a marriage if in their prudent discretion they judge that a proper safeguard has been invoked for the Catholic training and education of all the children and for the obviation of the danger of perversion with regard to the Catholic party. Cf. Canon 1065, § 2.

peculiar problems which presented themselves were solved in the light of that particular approach to the problem.

### *B. The Pontificate of Leo XIII*

During Leo XIII's long reign (1878-1903) the first concession of faculties for dispensing from all matrimonial impediments was granted to all local ordinaries, but its use was restricted to the cases in which one or the other of the parties was in danger of death.[51] If the Holy See became more lenient with regard to conceding faculties for the granting of dispensations, there was no indication in the least of any mitigation in the requirements of the *cautiones.* On the contrary, there was evidence of more exacting demands in some particular localities. Thus in Orleans, France, the *cautiones* had to be signed and attested by oath in the presence of the vicar general of that diocese in the diocesan curia.[52] This response of the Holy Office was given to the vicar general of that diocese upon his inquiring how the words *dummodo cautum omnino conditionibus ab Ecclesia praescriptis* were to be interpreted in a practical way. The opportunity was taken by the Holy See to insist once more that great care must be taken that the dispensation is not granted to those who do not furnish the necessary

---

[51] S.C.S.Off., litt. encycl., 20 feb. 1888—*Fontes,* n. 1109. It is here to be noted, however, that the faculty to dispense from the impediment of mixed religion was not conceded unless a cumulative faculty was enjoyed by the bishop and unless the impediment of mixed religion coexisted with another impediment over which the bishop had the power to dispense. Cf. Wernz, *Ius Matrimoniale,* p. 833. If such was not the case, then recourse had to be made to the Holy See for the necessary faculties. When such faculties were obtained, then their valid application and use presupposed not only the normal procedure required in all other cases of the use of delegated faculties, but also the previous acceptance of the *cautiones* from the parties and the moral certitude that the promises inherent in the *cautiones* would be fulfilled. Cf. S.C.S.Off., 12 apr. 1899—*Fontes,* n. 1219.

[52] S.C.S.Off. (ad Ep. Aurelian.), 6 iun. 1879: ". . . contrahentes curiam episcopalem adire debere ut coram officiali iuratum subscribant promissionem de praefatis conditionibus ab ecclesia praescriptis pro sua quisque parte omnino servandis."—*Fontes,* n. 1064.

basis for moral certitude that they will faithfully fulfill the promises.[53]

Another problem which called for particular attention was the situation that existed in Hungary. This condition of things had lingered on since the time of Pius IX. Regarding the *cautiones* in mixed marriages there, it was explicitly determined that a *mere hope* or a *moral certitude* which was founded solely on the *good will* of the parties was not sufficient.[54]

The *cautiones* were not adequate for their intended purpose when they were given simply by the parents of the Catholic party; they had to be received also from the pagan spouse. This was determined by a response of the Holy Office[55] to a vicar apostolic in Peiping (Peking), China, who had asked whether the parents of a catechumen or of a convert could render a sufficient guarantee relative to the keeping of the promises made by them in behalf of their daughter whom they had espoused to a pagan. If a schismatic, however, refused to observe the *cautiones* once they were given, the Catholic was not to be penalized and could be admitted to the sacraments as long as he promised to the best of his ability to procure both the Catholic education of the children and the conversion of the schismatic spouse.[56] Pastors, however, were admonished regarding their grave duty in conscience to see

---

[53] Ter Haar, *Mixed Marriages and Their Remedies,* pp. 84-85.

[54] S.C.S.Off. (ad Archiep. Strigonien.), 21 iul. 1880: ". . . nulla ratione fieri potest, ut spes illa, quae unice in bona voluntatis contrahentium dispositione fundatur, verarum cautionum locum tenere valeat."—*NRT,* XIX (1887), 5-9. Cf. litt. Secret. Status (ad Archiep. Strigonien.), 7 iul. 1890 ad 2—*Fontes,* n. 6455 wherein it is stated that both the *cautiones* and *moral certitude* are required in the case of a dispensation in spite of the civil laws to the contrary; cf. also for the same text *NRT,* XXIII (1891), 387-388; see also S. C. Negotior. Eccl. Extraord. (ad Archiep. Strigonien.), iul. 1890—*Coll. S.C.P.F.* (Romae: Ex Typographia Polyglotta, 1893), n. 1445; cf. also the Letter of Cardinal Rompolla to the Primate of Hungary, September 26, 1890—*NRT,* XXIII (1891), 388-391, wherein it was established that dispensations were to be refused if it was known that the children already born would be reared as schismatics.

[55] S.C.S.Off. (Pekin.), 29 apr. 1891—*Fontes,* n. 1134.

[56] S.C.S.Off., 10 feb. 1892, ad 2—*Fontes,* n. 1150.

to it that the *cautiones* would be observed when the parties had given them.[57]

Thus, in general constitutions and particular decrees and responses, the discipline of the Church in the matters concerned with mixed marriages shaped itself during the half century comprising the reigns of Pius IX and Leo XIII. These decisions and responses, while they may have constituted the law only in a certain territory, provided the guiding norms for the codifiers of the present law.

### IV PERIOD: THE TWENTIETH CENTURY

During the pontificates of Pius X (1903-1914), Benedict XV (1914-1922) and Pius XI (1922-1939), the ecclesiastical discipline regarding mixed marriages changed very little from the last half of the nineteenth century. If there were accidental changes, they were on the side of leniency, for now the Holy See granted ample faculties to the bishops and vicars apostolic, at least to those whose territories were distant from Rome, for granting dispensations in both mixed religion and disparity of worship, even outside of the cases of danger of death. Important, of course, was the crystallization as a *ius commune* of the major points of the mixed marriage discipline which were already in force either through general or particular legislation during the eighteenth and nineteenth centuries. Moreover, the responses of the Holy Office from the beginning of the present century as well as the Code law itself have been instrumental in clarifying a few points which remained doubtful in their issue in the early years of the twentieth century.

One such problem was that of the observance of the Tridentine form. This point was particularly confusing, for the decree *Tametsi* had not been everywhere promulgated. Hence, there were places where all were bound by the form, places where no one

---

[57] S.C. de Prop. Fide, instr. (ad Archiep. Baltimoren.), 25 iun. 1884, ad 1: "Post celebratas mixtas nuptias, parochi gravi conscientiae onere se gravari sciant invigilandi ut promissae a coniugibus conditiones observentur, et effectum sortiantur."—*Fontes*, n. 4904; *Coll. S.C.P.F.*, n. 1621. Cf. also Canon 1064, 3° in the Code of Canon Law.

was bound, and still other places where only Catholics were bound. The situation led to doubts and also occasioned a considerable number of invalid marriages. An apostolic letter of Pius X sanated the invalid clandestine marriages in Germany and established the Tridentine form for Catholics throughout that country.[58] The concession was extended to Hungary through a decree of the Congregation of the Sacraments.[59]

Then came the famous *Ne temere* decree which went into effect April 19, 1908.[60] It established the Tridentine form for Catholics everywhere, even when they married non-Catholics. It also demanded the pastor's *active* assistance for the valid celebration of marriage. This legislation which barred all merely *passive* assistance was received into the Code. A further decree of the Holy Office[61] permitted pastors to assist *passively* at mixed marriages in which the dispensation from the impediment of mixed religion had not been obtained, and in which the parties obstinately refused to give the *cautiones*. This exception, however, was restricted to cases of *mixed religion* and to those places only where the Holy See had, for one reason or another, permitted passive assistance before the *Ne temere* decree.[62] Hence in most places there was

---

[58] Pius X. litt. ap. "*Provida*," 18 ian. 1906—*Fontes*, n. 670. Cf. also *Analecta Ecclesiastica*, XIV (1906), 149; Cappello, *Tractatus Canonico-Moralis de Sacramentis* (3 vols. in 6, Taurini: Marietti, 1932-1939, Vol. III, Partes I et II [*De Matrimonio*], 4. ed. 1939), III, P. II, 125 (hereafter cited as *De Matrimonio*).

[59] S.C.de Sacr. resol. 23 feb. 1909—*Le Canoniste Contemporain*, XXXII (1909), 389; for the same text cf. *AKKR*, LXXXIX (1909), 717-718.

[60] S.C.S., decr. *Ne temere*, 2 aug. 1907—*Fontes*, n. 4340.

[61] S.C.S.Off. decr., 21 iun. 1912—*AAS*, IV (1912), 443-444; cf. also *Le Canoniste Contemporain*, XXXV (1912), 500-501.

[62] S.C.S.Off. declar., 5 aug. 1916—*AAS*, VIII (1916), 316; cf. also *Le Canoniste Contemporain*, XXXIX (1916), 432. It is to be noted that today even these exceptions have been taken away by force of the rule contained in canon 1102; cf. Response of the Code Commission, 10 mart. 1928—*AAS*, XX (1928), 120, or Bouscaren, *The Canon Law Digest* (2 vols. and Supplement—1941, Milwaukee: Bruce, 1934-1941), I, 546 under canon 1102. For complete doctrinal and historical treatment of the question of passive assistance the reader may consult an article by Oesterle, "Circa Declarationem Authenticam Can. 1102 De Passiva Assistentia"—*Jus Pontificium*, X (1930), 292-314 (hereafter this periodical will be cited *JP*).

required not only the form of the *Ne temere* decree, but also an active assistance on the part of the ordinary, the pastor, or the delegate of either. If passive assistance was employed outside of such territories which enjoyed the privilege of exemption from the required active assistance, then the marriage so celebrated was null and void in its canonical status.

Somewhat allied with the question of the required form was the troublesome problem of interference on the part of civil governments with the Church's demand for the full *cautiones* in mixed marriages, particularly inasfar as these affected the religious education of the children. Instances of this have previously been designated as obtaining during the first half of the past century in certain parts of Germany, Hungary, and Transylvania, whereby the law of the land established that the children were to be reared in the religion of the father, or at least the boys in his, and the girls in their mother's religion. An army regulation in Prussia (June 7, 1853),[63] which forbade officers to sign the *cautiones* under penalty of dismissal from the service, was apparently protracted into the twentieth century for a comparatively recent response of the Holy Office touched that problem directly.[64] If the non-Catholic refused to give the *cautiones* either by oath or simple promise, the faculties for granting a dispensation from the impediment of mixed religion or of disparity of worship could not be used. In answer to whether the sworn assertion of the Catholic, namely, that the non-Catholic party had promised privately to abide by the wishes of the Church, would suffice, the Holy Office allowed the dispensation to be given in extraordinary circumstances, *if the bishop could in conscience obtain moral certitude* of the sincerity of the promise for the present and of the corresponding fulfillment of that promise in the future.

Thus the *cautiones* as demanded by the present Code of Canon Law, have evolved from the erstwhile demand of complicated formal agreements between the Holy See and the Protestant royalty to the few simple requirements now incorporated in the Code law. Though the demands of the Church have been much

---

[63] Cf. Knecht, *Handbuch des katholischen Eherechts*, p. 292.

[64] S.C.S.Off., 10 dec. 1902, ad 2—*Fontes*, n. 1262.

simplified for the expression of the *cautiones,* yet there must be present such safeguards through the *cautiones* that there is an outward manifestation of compliance with the dictates of the natural divine law before the Church will grant a dispensation. It is in the light of their historical development and interpretation that the present-day *cautiones* can be better understood in their full canonical import. Problems of a new kind, particularly as affecting the sincerity of the one who gives the *cautiones* on the one hand, and the necessary moral certitude of the one who grants the dispensation on the other, will be given consideration in the following commentary.

# PART TWO

## Canonical Commentary

## CHAPTER FOUR

### Definitions and Divisions

### I *Cautio*

#### *A. Definition of Cautio*

A philological definition of *cautio* is given by Forcellini[1] while the *Thesaurus Linguae Latinae* is replete with citations as to the use of this term by the Fathers of the Church and by early classical Latin authors.[2] In their spiritual writings and sermons several of the Fathers make use of *cautio* in the sense of *debitum peccati* in which men were held by the devil until Christ by the shedding of His blood paid the price of their redemption.[3] The devil held men, as it were, "in security." This development of *cautio* by the Fathers may have been suggested by the concept of *cautio* as it was used in Roman commercial law.[4]

---

[1] "Cautio significat providentiam qua advertimus ne quid mali nobis accidat. Est cauta agendi, ratio, prudentia; et cautioni opponitur metus. Speciatim est verbum forense, et significat chirographam, fideiussionem, et aliam quamcumque stipulationem qua quis sibi vel alteri cavet, id est se vel alium securum reddit."—*Lexicon Totius Latinitatis* (4 vols., consilio et cura Jacobi Facciolati, Patavii: Th. Bettinelli, 1864-1871), I, s.v. *cautio*. Forcellini cites an example from D. (12. 1) 4.

[2] III (Lipsiae: 1906-1912), s.v. *cautio*.

[3] St. Augustine, *In Epistolam Joannis ad Parthos,* Tractatus, I, 5—*MPL,* XXXV, 1982; *Sermo* CX, V, 5, where he states that the *cautio debitoris* is destroyed by the *fusio sanguinis* of the Redeemer—*MPL,* XXXVIII, 641; *Sermo* CXXXIV, IV, 5—*MPL,* XXXVIII, 745; Joannes Constantinopolitanus: "venit . . . Christus et paternis nos *cautionibus* invenit astrinctos, quas conscripsit Adam . . ."—cited from *Thesaurus,* s.v. *cautio.*

[4] The Roman Law *cautio* concerned monetary contracts exclusively. Cf. C. (2. 12) 1; (4. 5) 4; (4. 30) 6. A true *cautio* or *fideiussio* had to be written in Latin or Greek—(6. 38) 3.

This notion of *cautio* forms a more consistent background to the Code's use of *cautio* in judicial procedure,[5] yet it presents the concept of *security, prudence, chirograph, stipulation* which *cautio* shares both in procedural law and in the ecclesiastical discipline in regard to mixed marriages.

It is not to be suggested, however, that the Patristic use of the word *cautio* can be favored as a canonical definition. For such a definition one must look to the celebrated response of Pope Gregory XVI (1831-1846) to a Bishop in Germany.

> *"Quid accurate et strictissime sumpta significat cautio opportuna?*
> Resp. *"Talem promissionem quae in pactum deducta praebeat morale fundamentum de veritate executionis, ita ut prudenter eiusmodi executio exspectari possit." SSmus. approbavit.*[6]

This definition may well be analyzed.

. . . *in pactum deducta* . . . The *cautio opportuna* here is a general term inclusive of any and all external formalities insisted upon by the Church in her mixed marriage discipline, whether the *cautio* actually be given in writing, by word of mouth, or by some other sense-perceptible sign or act. The last mentioned, indeed, seems incapable of being considered *"in pactum deducta,"* though it may constitute an implicit agreement between the parties, evidence of which can be offered in the external forum.[7] Surely such an implicit *cautio* would not have been admitted in Gregory's

---

[5] Canons 1626; 1631; 1909, § 2.

[6] 30 iun. 1842, ad 5—*Fontes,* n. 890. Modern canonical definitions of *cautio* are substantially the same as that of Pope Gregory. Cf. Payen, *De Matrimonio in Missionibus ac Potissimum in Sinis, Tractatus Practicus et Casus* (2. ed., 3 vols., Zi-ka-wei: in typographia T'OU-SÈ-WÈ, 1935-1936), I, 650 (hereafter to be cited *De Matrimonio*); Noldin-Schmitt, *Summa Theologiae Moralis iuxta Codicem Iuris Canonici* (21. et 22. ed., 3 vols., Oeniponte: Typis et Sumptibus Fel. Rauch, 1932-1934), III, 567 (hereafter cited *Summa Theologiae Moralis*).

[7] A recent response of the Holy Office (May 12, 1941—*AAS,* XXXIII (1941), 294) upheld the validity of a marriage wherein a Catholic married an unbaptized party and *cautiones* were exacted only from the non-Catholic, *as long as the Catholic party gave implicit cautiones.*

time, one hundred years ago. Progressive leniency of the Church's handling of mixed marriages has given rise to forms of the *cautiones* today which can be fitted only with difficulty into the strict meaning of the above definition.

. . . *praebeat morale fundamentum* . . . Not just any kind of promise suffices, but such a serious promise as affords the moral basis for a judgment of the truth of the execution of the promises. Thus the definition shows the intimate relationship between *cautiones* and moral certitude as one approaching that of cause and effect. While the signing of the *cautiones* alone may not produce the required moral certitude, certainly *cautiones* are the principal cause which, taken in consideration with all the other circumstances of the case, will be sufficient to produce moral certitude on the part of the granter of the dispensation.

. . . *de veritate executionis* . . . This phrase embraces rather the sincerity of those giving the *cautiones* than their ultimate fulfillment of the same. Otherwise the following clause would introduce a meaningless repetition.

. . . *ita ut prudenter eiusmodi executio exspectari possit* . . . Hence the word *executio* in the first instance means the giving of the *cautiones,* while in the second it comprehends rather their fulfillment. This clause emphasizes, as the ultimate reason for the *cautiones,* that the one dispensing may prudently foresee that the *cautiones* will be fulfilled in future and that thus the dangers attendant upon mixed marriages will be effectively avoided.

### B. *Divisions of Cautio*

The dangers which consist in the proximate occasion of perversion to the Catholic party and in the failure to baptize and educate all children of both sexes in the Catholic religion must be effectively attended to and provided for through the *cautelae* or *conditiones.* The *cautelae* are required by the natural divine law and are never subject to dispensation.[8]

[8] "Quae quidem cautiones remitti seu dispensari nunquam possunt, cum in ipsa naturali ac Divina lege fundentur, quam Ecclesia et haec Sancta Sedes sartam tectamque tueri omni studio contendit, . . ."—Instr. Secret.

Though the word *cautiones* is often used synonymously with the term *cautelae,* the two are not identical. When certain papal documents state that the *cautiones* can never be subject to dispensation, it is the *cautelae* that are thereby signified. *Cautiones* are of ecclesiastical origin, and sometimes, though rarely, are omitted. Authors speak of the *cautiones* as constituting a *conditio sine qua non.* This manner of speech serves only further to increase the confusion between *cautiones* and *cautelae* or *conditiones.* The *cautiones* are so called because normally no dispensation is obtainable without them. A rare exception will be noted in the *sanatio in radice* case.[9]

*Cautiones* are the formal promises themselves and have for their purpose the securing of the *cautelae.* The *cautiones* are to the *cautelae* as means to the end.[10]

*Cautiones* can be either formal or equivalent (implicit). The formal *cautiones* are solemn public promises expressed in the external forum. They are generally reduced to writing, though this is not necessary to make them formal. They are given to the Church by the parties to the marriage and must be sufficient to establish moral certitude not only of the sincerity of the parties but also of the fulfillment of the pledged word for the future.[11]

---

Stat. iussu Pii PP. IX, 15 nov. 1858—*Coll. S.C.P.F.*, n. 1169. See also Card. Rompolla, litt. (ad Card. Simor), 26 sept. 1890—*NRT,* XXIII (1891), 388-391; instr. S.C.S.Off. (ad Archiep. Corcyren.), 3 ian. 1871, n. 6—*Fontes,* n. 1013; Pius VIII, litt. ap. *"Litteris altero,"* 25 mart. 1830—*Fontes,* n. 482; instr. S.C.S.Off. (ad omnes Ep. Ritus Orient.), 12 dec. 1888, n. 5—*Fontes,* n. 1112.

[9] Canon 1061, § 1, 2°; Cappello, *De Matrimonio,* P. I, 397; Ayrinhac-Lydon, *Marriage Legislation,* p. 103.

[10] De Smet, *Tractatus Theologico-Canonicus De Sponsalibus et Matrimonio* (4. ed., Brugis: Beyaert, 1927), p. 441, nota 3 (hereafter cited as *De Sponsalibus et Matrimonio*); Payen, *De Matrimonio,* I, 650; Cappello, *De Matrimonio,* P. I, 391-392; Wernz-Vidal, *Ius Canonicum* (7 vols. in 8, Romae: Apud Aedes Universitatis Gregorianae, 1923-1938, Vol. V [*Ius Matrimoniale*], ed. altera, 1928), V, 192 (hereafter cited *Ius Matrimoniale*); Wernz, *Ius Matrimoniale,* p. 836, nota 32; Vromant, *Ius Missionariorum* (8 Toms., Tom V [*De Matrimonio*], Louvain: Museum Lessianum, 1931), V, 133 (hereafter cited as *De Matrimonio*); Schenk, *Mixed Religion and Disparity of Cult,* p. 215.

[11] Payen, *De Matrimonio,* I, 650; 654; 821. This does not mean, however, that the *cautiones* themselves are sufficient independently of all other considerations to produce moral certitude in the one who dispenses.

Implicit or equivalent *cautiones*, more common in China than elsewhere, can be used validly in certain circumstances wherein formal *cautiones* cannot be obtained. If formal *cautiones*, even though they be merely oral, cannot be obtained in China from a pagan woman marrying a Catholic, then the vicar or prefect apostolic may decide in individual cases whether implicit *cautiones* will suffice to produce the necessary moral certitude that the dangers are removed. Individual cases are to be weighed by the vicar apostolic or by his subdelegate.[12] Such implicit or equivalent *cautiones* can readily consist in a serious promise on the part of the pagan woman to join the Church or in her actual enrolment among the catechumens. The mere fact that the laws or customs of China concede no power over the education of the children to women is not sufficient, as a general rule, to form an equivalent *cautio*. The missionary must judge the situation carefully and on its own merits in each individual instance.[13]

Further light has been thrown on the *implicit* or *equivalent cautiones* by a recent response of the Holy Office to certain doubts presented by the Archbishop of New York.[14]

---

[12] The possession of this faculty by the vicar apostolic is not made available for him *industria personae*, or with a clause which prohibits it from being shared with others, and hence can be subdelegated by him. Cf. canon 199, § 2.

[13] S.C.S.Off., 5 apr. 1918—quoted in Payen, *De Matrimonio*, I, 823-825; Vromant, *De Matrimonio*, pp. 137-138; Winslow, *Vicars and Prefects Apostolic* (Maryknoll, New York, 1924), pp. 106-107.

[14] I. An validum habendum sit matrimonium celebratum inter partem catholicam et partem acatholicam certe non baptizatam cum dispensatione ab impedimento disparitatis cultus concessa, si sola pars acatholica *cautiones* ad normam can. 1061, § 1, 2° (1071) C.I.C. praescriptas praestiterit?

II. An validum habendum sit matrimonium celebratum inter partem baptizatam et partem certe non baptizatam, cum eadem dispensatione ante Codicis Iuris Canonici promulgationem, si sola pars acatholica *cautiones* praescriptas praestiterit?

Si et quatenus negative ad primum et secundum dubium:

III. Utrum tractandae sint tales causae nullitatis matrimonii ad normam can. 1990-1992 C.I.C., an coram tribunali collegiali ad ordinarium tramitem iuris?

Suprema autem haec S[a]. Congregatio, re mature perpensa, in conventu plenario feriae IV die 7 maii, 1941, respondendum mandavit:

Ad primum et secundum dubium: NEGATIVE, nisi pars catholica

A marriage between a Catholic and one certainly unbaptized, whether before or after the Code, in which the *cautiones* were given by the non-Catholic only, must be considered invalid, unless the Catholic party gave at least *implicit cautiones.* The Holy Office in its *"ad mentem"* declared that if implicit *cautiones* were given by the parties between the time of the petition for the dispensation and its concession, the dispensation is valid. Implicit *cautiones* were described as those acts from which it can be concluded and proved in the external forum that the duty of fulfilling the *cautiones* was known by both parties, and that there was manifest a determined will of the parties to fulfill them.

While the response of the Holy Office came to only one ordinary in the United States, it sets a safe and prudent norm of action in this matter everywhere. Furthermore, the response does not excuse any ordinary from the necessity of securing formal *cautiones.* It will be remembered that a special concession of the Holy Office was needed to make use of *implicit* or *equivalent cautiones* in China. The response is to be considered rather as a *post factum* norm for judging the validity of the dispensation in unusual cases wherein formal *cautiones* were not obtained.

The response states further that a formal judicial process, unless the requisites of canon 1990 manifestly obtain in a particular case, will be needed to determine what acts were placed in the external forum by the parties and whether they were sufficient to constitute *implicit* or *equivalent cautiones* in the case.

An internal division of all *cautiones* is that of their *form* and

---

*cautiones saltem implicite* praestiterit. Ad tertium dubium: NEGATIVE ad PRIMAM partem, AFFIRMATIVE ad SECUNDAM partem, nisi in casu particulari certo constet de requisitis in can. 1990. Et ad mentem: Etsi Sancta Sedes a praxi immemorali exegerit et nunc stricte exigat ut conditionibus adimplendis in quibuslibet matrimoniis mixtis cautum sit per formalem promissionem ab utraque parte explicite requisitam (can. 1061, 1071), tamen usus facultatis dispensandi, sive ordinariae sive delegatae, invalidus dici nequit si utraque pars, inter petitionem dispensationis et eius concessionem, *saltem implicite cautiones* praestiterit, i. e. eos actus posuerit e quibus concludendum sit et in foro externo constare possit eam cognoscere obligationem adimplendi conditiones et manifestasse firmum propositum illi obligationi satisfaciendi."—*AAS,* XXXIII (1941), 294.

*content.* The *form* of the *cautiones* is not to be confused with the *formal cautiones* already considered.

The form of the *cautiones* signifies the manner in which they are given, i.e., in writing, orally, with a supplementary oath, before witnesses, before an ecclesiastical notary, etc.

The Code has laid down a norm by demanding that the *cautiones regularly be exacted in writing,*[15] but the very wording of the canon (*regulariter*) openly admits of exceptions to the rule. The common law in a post-Code decree[16] has further established that wherever the civil law will uphold and enforce ante-nuptial agreements, the *cautiones* for validity must be drawn up in the form recognized and honored by the civil law.[17]

Apart from these two regulations of the common law, the question of the form of the *cautiones* is left to the prudence and decision of local ordinaries in their enactments of particular law. The guiding principle for them will be motivated by their efficacious desire to see the *cautiones* furnished in a form which will beget the requisite moral certitude that the things promised will also be fulfilled. The form that will best promote such certitude is substantially determined by the particular circumstances of place, the specific elements in personal character and the modifying elements inherent in the demands of the time.[18]

Content of the *cautiones,* also called their object,[19] refers to the matter treated in the promises themselves.[20]

---

[15] Canon 1061, § 2.

[16] S.C.S.Off., 14 ian. 1932—*AAS,* XXIV (1932), 25.

[17] Gasparri, *De Matrimonio,* I, 269-270; Chelodi, *Ius Matrimoniale,* p. 69; Ter Haar, *Mixed Marriages and Their Remedies,* p. 185.

[18] Payen, *De Matrimonio,* I, 655-656; Cappello, *De Matrimonio,* P. I, 395-397; Wernz-Vidal, *Ius Matrimoniale,* p. 192, nota 31; Vermeersch-Creusen, *Epitome Iuris Canonici* (3 vols., Vol. I, 6. ed., 1937, Vols. II et III, 5. ed., 1934-1936, Bruxellis: H. Dessain), II, 232; Gasparri, *De Matrimonio,* I, 266-267; De Smet, *De Sponsalibus et Matrimonio,* pp. 441-442; Vromant, *De Matrimonio,* p. 137; Chelodi, *Ius Matrimoniale,* p. 69; Ter Haar, *Mixed Marriages and Their Remedies,* pp. 83-84; Feije, *De Matrimoniis Mixtis,* pp. 212-213; "Questions de science ecclesiastique"—*L'Ami du Clergé,* XLIII (1926), 383-384.

[19] Payen, *De Matrimonio,* I, 656; Wernz-Vidal, *Ius Matrimoniale,* p. 192, nota 31.

[20] A chapter will be devoted to this study later.

The *cause* of the dispensation is also to be clearly distinguished from the *cautelae* and *cautiones.* The cause is identified with the reason for which the dispensation is granted; the *cautiones* are the conditions under which it is granted. Both *cause* and *cautiones* have this in common that they are normal requisites of Canon Law in mixed marriages.[21] Both, too, have at least a foundation in the natural law though the *cautiones* are founded on the natural law in a less proximate manner. Here must be remembered the distinction between *cautiones* and *cautelae,* the latter a requirement of the natural law, the former sharing in that requirement in so far as *cautiones* are the normal means of securing the *cautelae.*

## II MORAL CERTITUDE

### *A. Definition of Certitude*

Certitude is defined as "the firm assent of the mind to one part of a contradictory without fear of erring."[22] The elements associated with certitude are subjective and objective, designating respectively the person knowing or the thing that is known. Yet certitude is primarily and properly a state of the mind, and if certitude is attributed to objects (the thing is certain) it is only by analogy.[23] "Certitude" is more properly linked with the subjective element (the person knowing); "certainty" is more appropriately connected with the objective element (the thing known).[24]

Certitude, however, is neither intuitive nor innate. Exclusion of the fear of error through disregard for or inadvertence to the

[21] O'Mara, *Canonical Causes for Matrimonial Dispensations,* The Catholic University of America Canon Law Studies, n. 96 (Washington, D. C.: The Catholic University of America, 1935), p. 27.

[22] "Firma adhaesio mentis in unam partem contradictoriam sine ulla formidine errandi."—Hickey, *Summula Philosophiae Scholasticae* (3 vols., 1905-1908, I [*Logica et Ontologia*], ed. altera, Dublini: Browne et Nolan, 1908), I, 167; Gredt, *Elementa Philosophiae* (3. ed., 2 vols., Friburgi Brisgoviae: Herder, 1921-1922), II, 44; Coffey, *The Science of Logic* (2 vols., New York: Peter Smith, 1938), II, 211.

[23] St. Thomas Aquinas, *Summa Theologica,* II[a] II[ae], q. 18, 4, c; Joannes a S. Thoma, *Cursus Philosophicus Thomisticus* (ed. nova, 3 Toms., Parisiis, 1883), I, 710; Hickey, *Summula Philosophiae Scholasticae,* I, 168.

[24] "Certainty is either subjective or objective, a state of the believing mind or (in recent years more frequently) a quality of the thing believed;

opposite opinion does not result in certitude. Consequently certitude must be based upon motives, i.e., upon an objective evidence, which constitutes its formal object.[25]

### *B. Divisions of Certitude*

The evidence upon which certitude is based gives rise to various kinds of certitude.[26]

Where evidence is so contained in the intrinsic nature of a thing as to be metaphysically undeniable, it produces a metaphysical certitude.[27] Again, evidence may arise from physical laws and result in physical certitude.[28] Lastly, the evidence may arise from moral laws and result in moral certitude.[29] Metaphysical certitude is absolute; physical and moral certitude are conditioned upon the regularity and inflexibility of physical and moral laws which can suffer change, in the one case only by a miracle,[30] and in the other only by some unusual moral phenomenon.[31]

Moral laws (not ethical laws) upon which is based moral certitude consist in recognized rules which govern the inclinations and actions of people in a given set of circumstances. Thus it may be set down as a moral law that men love truth and hate falsehood, that parents love their children. Consequently judgments based upon such laws are morally certain.[32]

---

certitude is almost exclusively subjective, and suggests especially the assurance of the one who believes."—Webster's *New International Unabridged Dictionary,* 1941, see words, *certitude, certainty.*

[25] Gredt, *Elementa Philosophiae,* II, 77.

[26] Account is taken here solely of natural certitude, which embraces objects of which knowledge can be acquired by the intellect, and not of supernatural certitude whose motives rest on divine authority. Cf. Hickey, *Summula Philosophiae Scholasticae,* I, 172; 180.

[27] The following will serve as examples: A circle is necessarily round; the whole is greater than its constitutive parts; the mind has an aptitude for knowing truth. Hickey, *Summula Philosophiae Scholasticae,* I, 169-172.

[28] Thus, fire burns; water is wet. Cf. Hickey, *op. cit.,* I, 173-174.

[29] "Certitudo moralis est firmus assensus praestitus ex motivo, cum quo contradictorium moraliter repugnat." Cf. Hickey, *op. cit.,* I, 173-174.

[30] E.g., the passage through the Red Sea—*Exodus,* XIV.

[31] E.g., a mother who kills her own child.

[32] Gredt, *Elementa Philosophiae,* II, 46-47; Bittle, *Reality and the Mind* (3. ed., Milwaukee: Bruce, 1940), pp. 23; 293.

Since these moral laws embrace phenomena which for the greater part are dependent upon the will of men, the possibility of error cannot be entirely removed. Men are free agents and have been known, in exceptional cases, however, to act contrary to these fundamental moral laws. Strict or perfect moral certitude, however, will not admit any prudent doubt, whether actual or possible, that the opposite of the judgment be true. Yet, situations may arise in which strict, philosophical moral certitude cannot be had, for some possible prudent doubt of error remains and some light reasons for the truth of the opposite judgment can still be entertained. But the evidence for the truth of the judgment in such cases is sufficient for the assent of prudent men.

This slight latitude in the degree of assurance has called for a further distinction in moral certitude. The moralists and canonists have considered such prudent judgment as moral certitude in the wide sense (*in sensu lato*). Hickey[33] calls it "prudent opinion," while Gredt[34] calls it imperfect moral certitude and adds that it is not strictly certitude. St. Thomas in the *Summa Theologica*[35] describes it when he says that it embraces the truth in most instances, but in a very few instances it fails to do so. Nevertheless, moral certitude in the wide sense has been adopted by the moralists as a sufficient rule of moral action in an individual and concrete case, and as such it is a practical judgment of conscience. It is the licitness rather than the veracity of a given fact or statement in accordance with the norms of morality that forms the basis for the judgment of the moralists.[36]

---

[33] *Summula Philosophiae Scholasticae,* I, 177.

[34] *Elementa Philosophiae,* II, 47; cf. also Donat, *Summa Philosophiae Christianae* (8 vols., Innsbruck: Verlag Felizian Rauch, 1933-1936, Vol. II [*Critica*], 7. ed., 1933), II, 77.

[35] IIa IIae, q. 70, a. 2.

[36] Tanquerey, *Synopsis Theologiae Moralis et Pastoralis* (3. ed., 3 vols., New York: Benziger Bros., 1907), I, 211-212; Noldin-Schmitt, *Summa Theologiae Moralis,* I, 220; Sabetti-Barrett, *Compendium Theologiae Moralis* (27. ed., Neo-Eboraci: Pustet, 1919), p. 37; Ferreres, *Compendium Theologiae Moralis* (14. ed., Barcinone: Eugenius Subirana, 1928), I, 49; Slater, *A Manual of Moral Theology* (3. ed., 2 vols., New York: Benziger Bros., 1909), I, 59-60; Génicot-Salsmans, *Institutiones Theologiae Moralis* (10. ed., 2 vols., Bruxellis: Alb. Dewit, 1922), I, 42.

# CHAPTER FIVE

## Mixed Marriages and the Law

### I THE POSITIVE DIVINE LAW

#### *A. Old Testament*

The danger of defection from the moral code and the Jahwistic worship on the part of the chosen people was always attendant upon their close association with the pagan tribes about them. Marital unions with the members of such tribes were so destructive of Jewish morality as to form the remote cause of the flood and to move Almighty God to "repent of having made man."[1]

There were not wanting explicit prohibitions in the Jewish Theocracy against such marriages. The Lord God speaking to Moses on Mount Sinai enjoined the chosen people: "Neither shalt thou take of their daughters a wife for thy son, lest after they themselves have committed fornication, they make thy sons also to commit fornication with their gods."[2] Similarly there was the prohibition for the chosen people not to intermarry with the seven pagan nations of Cana: "Thou shalt make no league with them nor show mercy to them. Neither shalt thou make marriages with them. Thou shalt not give thy daughter to his son nor take his daughter for thy son: for she shall turn away thy son from following me, that he may rather serve strange gods. . . .[3] This unequivocal condemnation of such marriages was a juridical precept and hence affected only the Jews, but because of its moral implication, Bellarmine[4] considers it to have passed with full vigor into the Christian dispensation.

---

[1] Genesis, VI, 2-7.

[2] Exodus, XXXIV, 16.

[3] Deuteronomy, VII, 1-4.

[4] *De Sacramento Matrimonii,* Lib. I, cap. 23—*Opera Omnia* (12 vols., ex editione Veneta, iterum edidit Justinus Favre, Parisiis, 1870-1874), V, 119; cf. also Sanchez, *De Sancto Matrimonii Sacramento,* Lib. VII, disp. 71, n. 2 et 5; St. Thomas Aquinas, *Summa Theologica,* Iª IIªª, q. 99, a. 3-4.

The Old Testament shows plainly that the reason for the prohibition of mixed marriages was to be found in the danger of perversion from the Mosaic ceremonial law, which in turn led to idolatry.[5] In fact, the entire Old Testament history of the Jewish people affords ample evidence that their many defections from the true worship of the God of Israel were caused chiefly by their intermarriage with pagan tribes. Even those in high places among the people of Israel fell victims to this ruinous snare, as is witnessed, for example, by the tragic defection of King Solomon.[6]

The juridic status of these mixed marriages of the Jewish people labors under an obscurity which no internal or external evidence can entirely remove. One text from Esdras[7] perhaps suggests their invalidity, but Benedict XIV[8] interpreted this text in the light of the strong prohibition contained in Deuteronomy, VII, 1-4, and further declared that the separation which was demanded by Esdras contemplated only a separation from bed and board. What parallelism can be drawn between this text and that of Math. I, 19; XIX, 3-8; Deuteronomy, XXIV, 1? If "to put away" signified a complete divorce or dissolution of the bond, permitted to the Hebrews because of the hardness of their hearts, then the validity of the intermarriage mentioned in the text of Esdras remains unquestioned, inasmuch as there is no room for a complete divorce in a marriage which is contracted invalidly. On the other hand, "to put away" may have been Esdras' command to the Jews to dismiss those who were not joined with them in valid union, and thus he would postulate the invalidity of these marriages. The apparent cogency of either interpretation increases the obscurity of the juridic status of those marriages. Even were it possible to remove this obscurity, it is

---

[5] "They shall be a pit and a snare in your way and a stumbling block at your side, and stakes in your eyes . . ." Josue, XXIII, 12-13.

[6] Cf. III Kings, XI, 1-11; cf. also III Kings, XVI, 31-32; Numbers, XXV; Judges, III, 5-7; I Esdras, IX; Malachias, II, 11-12.

[7] "Let us make a covenant with the Lord our God to put away all the wives and such as are born of them, according to the will of the Lord . . ." I Esdras, X, 3; ". . . separate yourselves from the people of the land, and from your strange wives." I Esdras, X, 11.

[8] Ep. *"Singulari"* 9 feb. 1749—*Fontes,* n. 394.

to be remembered that the text of Esdras consisted in a juridical decree extending only to the marriages of Jews and pagans in the land of Cana, and did not carry its juridic force into the new dispensation.[9]

### B. New Testament

The New Testament, unlike the Old, is not susceptible to abrogation in its juridical enactments. The juridic and moral force of the gospels and epistles embraces all peoples and will last to the end of time. The Old Testament written for the chosen people was unmistakably direct, even blunt, in its prohibition of Jewish marriages with pagans. The New Testament, while not less forceful, expresses the same prohibition to Christians by emphasizing rather the incongruity of such unions in the face of the mystical union of the Christian with Christ. Such description and expression of that higher union are found particularly in the Pauline epistles. Thus in II Corinthians, VI, 14-16, St. Paul said: "Do not bear the yoke with unbelievers. For what has justice in common with iniquity? Or what fellowship has light with darkness? What harmony is there between Christ and Belial? Or what part has the believer with the unbeliever? And what agreement has the temple of God with idols?"

A number of the Fathers and exegetes consider the words "Do not bear the yoke with unbelievers" as a prohibition against marrying pagans.[10] Another opinion holds that St. Paul merely reminded the Corinthians that as Christians they had been purified from their former pagan vices and were never to return to them.[11]

---

[9] Schenk, *Mixed Religion and Disparity of Cult*, p. 9.

[10] St. Cyprianus, *Ad Quirinium*, Lib. III, cap. 62—*CSEL*, III, P. I, 166; St. Hieronymus, *Adversus Jovinianum*, Lib. I, n. 10—*MPL*, XXIII, 225; Estius, *In Quatuor Libros Sententiarum Commentaria* (2 vols., Parisiis, 1696), *ad vers. cit.*; cf. also such commentators as Wernz, *Ius Matrimoniale*, p. 760, nota 9; Cappello, *De Matrimonio*, P. I, 514, nota 31; Blat, *Commentarium Textus Codicis Iuris Canonici* (5 vols. in 6, 1921-1927, Vol. III, P. I. [*De Rebus*], 2. ed., Romae: Typographia Pontificia in Instituto Pii IX, 1924), III, P. I, 575 (hereafter cited as *De Rebus, P. I*).

[11] St. Thomas Aquinas, *In Omnes D. Pauli Apostoli Epistolas Doctissima Commentaria* (restituit F. Remigius Florentinus, Venetiis, 1562), II Cor.

This opinion, of course, renders the reference to marriage very remote.

St. Paul permitted widows to marry again but added the prescription, ". . . only let it be in the Lord."[12] Here again there is some dispute as to the true meaning of the words. It is construed to mean that she may marry only a Christian,[13] though the interpretation that the passage refers to the purported intention in the marriage, namely, that the marriage be sought with honorable motives, has some support.[14]

There are other statements in the Pauline epistles which are not subject to such an alternative interpretation. On one occasion the Christians are commanded not even to take food with one who is called a brother, if he is immoral, or covetous, or an idolater, etc.[15]

The intimate union of the Christian with Christ in the mystical body and the close relationship of husband and wife in marriage causes the Apostle to exclaim: ". . . Shall I then take the members of Christ and make them the members of a harlot? By no means!"[16]

St. Paul insisted that the Christians were not so much as to associate with those who were not of the faith,[17] and St. John[18] forbade the faithful to greet or extend any hospitality whatsoever to false teachers. Thus in view of the danger of perversion to their newly found faith the Christians were bidden to abstain from all social intercourse with those who were not of their own faith. Much more was it incumbent upon them to refrain from

---

Cap. VI, Lectio III; Cornely, *Commentarius Scripturae Sacrae—Cursus Scripturae Sacrae,* II, *Prior Epistola ad Corinthios,* III, *Epistolae ad Corinthios Altera et ad Galatas* (Parisiis, 1890-1892), ad II Cor., VI, 14.

[12] I Cor., VII, 39.

[13] Tertullian, *Liber de Corona,* Cap. XIII.—*MPL,* II, 96; Thomas Aquinas, *In Omnes D. Pauli Epist. Comment.,* I Cor., VII, Lectio VIII; Cappello, *De Matrimonio,* P. I., 514, nota 31.

[14] Calmet, *Commentarius Literalis in Omnes Libros Veteris et Novi Testamenti* (8 vols., ed. Latina, A. J. D. Mansi, Venetiis, 1754-1756), VIII, *ad vers. cit.*

[15] I Cor. V, 11.

[16] I Cor. VI, 15-16.

[17] Titus, III, 10.

[18] II John, 10-11.

intermarrying with pagans and heretics, for such unions would of necessity involve an association of the most intimate kind for a life-long duration.

Nevertheless it must be admitted that such marriages were considered juridically valid, for there is no evidence to the contrary. St. Paul's determined condemnation indeed implied a grave prohibition of such unions, and in the moral order this prohibition was sanctioned under pain of a serious sin of disobedience, but to all appearances these marriages enjoyed the juridic status of a valid union. Sanchez, after reviewing the evidence in the Scriptures concerning such marriages, affirmed their validity on the grounds that they were not contrary to the prime purpose of marriage, even though they were attended with grave obstacles to the Christian education and training of the offspring.[19]

The diriment impediment of disparity of worship, which presupposes the fact of baptism in the one, but the absence of baptism in the other party, still awaited its determination in the realm of diriment matrimonial impediments through the agency of a long continued ecclesiastical custom to that effect. Hence, though they were forbidden, still the marriages with pagans entered into by the early Christians prior to the crystallization of the ecclesiastical impediment were unquestionably valid. One may point, for example, to the marriage of St. Monica with Patrick, of St. Cecilia with Valerian, of St. Clotilde with Clovis, as unions whose validity was never called into question in any way by the authority of the Church.[20]

## II THE NATURAL DIVINE LAW

### *A. Principles*

The highest and most comprehensive of all laws is the Eternal Law which, in the last analysis, is the attribute of Divine Wisdom

[19] *De Sancto Matrimonii Sacramento,* Lib. VII, disp. 71, ad 7, n. 1.

[20] Cf. Sanchez, *De Sancto Matrimonii Sacramento,* Lib. VII, disp. 72, ad 7, n. 2; Sabetti-Barrett, *Compendium Theologiae Moralis,* pp. 888-889; cf. also *NRT,* XV (1883), 394, which furnishes a list of the names of saints who upon their marriage sanctified their pagan spouses.

itself and embraces in its scope the government of all created things, guiding and directing them to their proper ends.[21]

The natural divine law is a proximate application of the eternal law for man in this that it guides him to his proper end. It is true law, for it is founded upon human nature and is promulgated by human reason, and thus all men of all times and in all places are subject to the natural law. The natural law embraces the entire moral order and constitutes the objective code of morality in all of man's actions in relation to God, to himself, to his fellow-man, and to creatures about him.[22]

There is a gradual division of the natural law in accordance with the degree of force or efficacy needed to preserve the moral order. This gives rise to the primary and the secondary precepts of the natural law. The primary precepts are so necessary that the moral order could not endure without them; the secondary precepts are of such importance that, were they not observed, the moral order would suffer distortion and be rendered less perfect.[23]

---

[21] St. Thomas Aquinas, *Summa Theologica*, Iª IIªᵉ, q. 93, a. 1-6; Noldin-Schmitt, *Summa Theologiae Moralis*, I, 119; Arregui, *Summarium Theologiae Moralis* (12. ed., Bilbao: El Mensajero del Corazón de Jesús, 1934), p. 42; Cathrein, *Cursus Philosophicus*, Pars VI, *Philosophia Moralis* (15. ed., Friburgi Brisgoviae: Herder, 1929), p. 150 (hereafter cited *Philosophia Moralis*); Lehmkuhl, *Theologia Moralis* (4. ed., 2 vols., Friburgi Brisgoviae: Herder, 1887), I, 123.

[22] St. Thomas Aquinas, *Summa Theologica*, Iª IIªᵉ, q. 91, a. 2; Cathrein, *Philosophia Moralis*, pp. 152-153; Noldin-Schmitt, *Summa Theologiae Moralis*, I, 120-121; Vermeersch, *Theologia Moralis* (ed. altera, 3 vols., Romae: Università Gregoriana, 1926-1927), I, 229.

[23] That God must be worshipped is an absolute precept; that vows and oaths must be observed exemplifies conditioned precepts. Cf. Noldin-Schmitt, *Summa Theologiae Moralis*, I, 122. This division of the natural law is not to be confused with the division *ratione cognitionis*. The latter embraces three classes of precepts of the natural law: a) universal precepts known immediately by all, e.g., do good, avoid evil; b) precepts immediately derived from the first, e.g., the decalogue except the determination of the Sabbath; c) all the precepts which can be derived from the first and second by discursive reasoning, e.g., a thing found must be returned to its owner. These are subjective considerations of the natural law as to the manner in which it is known by man and are recorded by most authors. Cf. Noldin-Schmitt, *Summa Theologiae Moralis*, I, 121; St. Thomas Aquinas, *Summa Theologica*, Iª IIªᵉ, q. 94, a. 6; Cathrein, *Philosophia Moralis*, p. 171; Morrison (*Marriage* [Milwaukee: Bruce, 1934], p. 11) gives a practical diagram of the three classes of precepts *ratione cognitionis*.

Since man's actions can be good or bad, and correspondingly promote or disturb the established moral order, both positive and negative aspects of the natural law must be given due consideration.[24] The negative phase of the natural law which forbids evil actions has a universal application and extension. Hence the precept to avoid evil binds all men at all times and everywhere enjoins the shunning of all kinds of evil. On the other hand, the positive phase of the natural law to do good is universal in affecting all men, but it does not comprise in its command the performance of all possible good. Hence no one is bound to the performance of all the good of which he is capable.[25] This is not to say that all negative precepts of the natural law are primary and absolute. Negative precepts fall into the primary or secondary class in accordance with the harmful effect their non-observance would have upon the moral order. A threefold division of negative precepts from the viewpoint of their objects may well serve to determine their obligatory force in view of the primary and secondary precepts of the natural law.

1. Objects which are evil both in themselves (*in se*) and *on their own account* (*propter se*) can never become good or licit.

2. Objects which are evil in themselves, not, however, on account of an evil intrinsic to themselves, but rather because of some extrinsic danger, can become "not evil" when that danger is removed or at least made remote, thereby rendering these objects licit.

3. Objects which are evil both in themselves and on account of themselves because they violate the right of a third party (*ius alienum*), can become licit when the third party voluntarily yields his right, for then there is no violation of the natural law which forbids the injuring of the rights of others.[26]

---

[24] "Ratio divina vel voluntas Dei ordinem naturalem conservari iubens, perturbari vetans."—St. Augustine, *Contra Faustum,* Lib. XXII, c. 27—*CSEL,* XXV, P. I, 621.

[25] All evil, if it be such intrinsically, even independently of any prohibition in positive law, is forbidden by the natural law. But with reference to that which is good the natural law enforces no command and urges no claim outside of the realm which defines man's status and condition in respect to God, to himself and to his neighbor. Cf. Ballerini-Palmieri, *Opus Theologicum Morale* (7 vols., Prati: Giachetti, 1889-1893), I, 267.

[26] Lehmkuhl, *Theologia Moralis,* I, 125.

It goes without saying that the first class of objects forbidden by negative precepts is to be considered as partaking of the character of primary absolute precepts of the natural law which affect all men at all times. Thus, for example, it is always wrong to blaspheme or to lie.

The second class of objects is considered a secondary conditional precept of the natural law. It is hypothetically necessary for the fulfillment of the natural law and for the good of the moral order. The fulfillment of the natural law in the second class of prohibitions is imperilled by the connected danger. If the danger of evil which accompanies the objects in the second class is removed or diminished, the moral order is not harmed and consequently the natural law is not disturbed. As long as the danger of evil remains acute in the second class of objects, the natural law forbids all acts by which it is intended to attain these objects. One is bound to avoid occasions and dangers of sin just as one is bound to avoid the sin itself.[27]

### B. *Application of Principles*

The application of the above principles of the natural divine law to the question of mixed marriages, whether of mixed religion or disparity of worship immediately points to two definite conclusions.

First, the prohibition of mixed marriages falls into the second class of negative precepts listed above. Hence mixed marriages are forbidden by the secondary precepts of the natural divine law. An immediate corollary may be submitted to the effect that even the impediment of disparity of worship, which is of a diriment character in the Church's law, is by the natural divine law to be regarded as not transcending the status of a prohibitive impediment. All modern authors are in accord with earlier writers on the point of assigning the origin and the invalidating effect of the impediment of disparity of worship respectively to ecclesiastical custom and ecclesiastical law.[28] Only those hindrances of or

---

[27] Noldin-Schmitt, *Summa Theologiae Moralis,* I, 320.

[28] Cappello (*De Matrimonio,* P. I, 504-505) writes: "[Disparitas cultus] non irritat profecto iure naturali, quia prolis generatio atque educatio, etiam

impediments to marriage are of a diriment character by reason of the natural law which involve a substantial defect of consent or an absolute or relative disability of the person to enter marriage. Thus, violent force, overpowering fear, and substantial error constitute absolute hindrances to the making of a valid matrimonial contract. Thus also impotence, an extant sacramental bond which has become maritally consummated, consanguinity in the direct line, and possibly also consanguinity in the first degree of the collateral line exist as diriment impediments inherently in the natural divine law.[29]

The basic deformity of mixed marriages in the moral order and the consequent prohibition of them by the natural law results from the presence of the moral dangers which are connected with such marriages. These dangers arise from the intimate relationship and communication of Catholics with heretics and infidels[30] and are reducible to three heads: a) the *communicatio in sacris* which can never be entirely avoided; b) the danger of loss of faith and the impending detriment to the morals of the Catholic party of the marriage; and c) the like danger of perversion which impends for the offspring.

Since the prohibition of mixed marriages constitutes a negative precept of the natural divine law, it may here be examined whether its force and application touch all sincere Christian believers alike. Must *bona fide* heretics comply with the precept and in consequence abstain from marriage with Catholics for the same reason that Catholics must abstain from marriage with heretics? There can be no doubt that this precept must be followed by all men in accordance with the direction which the light of their conscience points out to them, for even an erroneous conscience—granted that its error is invincible—must be followed under pain of sin.[31]

---

eo exstante, haberi potést; scil. matrimonii naturae eiusque fini non repugnat." Cf. also Payen, *De Matrimonio,* I, 798-800; Gasparri, *De Matrimonio,* I, 259. Among the earlier writers, cf. Bellarmine, *Opera Omnia,* III, cap. 23, p. 835; Sanchez, *De Sancto Matrimonii Sacramento,* Lib. VII, disp. 71, ad 6 ss.

[29] Perrone, *De Matrimonio Christiano,* II, 133-135.

[30] St. Thomas Aquinas, *Summa Theologica,* I[a] II[ae], q. 10, a. 9; Ferreres, *Compendium Theologiae Moralis,* I, 175-176.

[31] Lasting invincible ignorance of the proximate conclusions of the primary principles of the natural law (decalogue) is generally not ad-

The duty of *bona fide* heretics to forego marriages with Catholics does not, of course, rest upon any objective basis, but the fact that this duty stands vindicated by the testimony of their own conscience makes it none the less compelling. Of themselves the objective realities within the faith of the Catholic Church precludes any and every right on the part of even *bona fide* heretics to exact *cautiones* from Catholics in deference to and for the protection of their own sincere but erroneous beliefs. These realities, however, do not rule out the possible fact of an invincibly erroneous conscience which would demand from such heretics obedience to and compliance with it in opposition to the actual but unknown demands of the positive divine law. Under the circumstances here assumed, it is true that to remain faithful to their conscience, these *bona fide* heretics would from their honest viewpoint have to make the same kind of demand upon Catholics by way of *cautiones* as Catholics by the force of the positive divine law as well as by the dictates of their own conscience must make upon heretics.

While the natural divine law does not embrace all truths of the positive divine law,[82] for the latter contains many truths which are supernatural, yet the natural law remains in force in its own right whenever it coincides with the positive law of God. The supernatural is based upon the natural, going beyond it and rising above it, but never contradicting it. The natural law cannot contradict the positive divine law, for both have God as their author. The former conforms with and is rightly subject to the latter. Thus the natural law in demanding safeguards for the faith and morals of a Catholic who contemplates a mixed marriage is consistent with the positive divine law. Such consistency would be lost if compliance with the natural law in abstraction from the positive divine law were urged in defense of those who even apart from all guilt lack knowledge of and therefore sense no subjection to the positive divine law. It would be nothing

mitted by theologians. Cf. St. Thomas Aquinas, *Summa Theologica*, I$^{a}$ II$^{ae}$, q. 94, a. 4 ad 2; Noldin-Schmitt, *Summa Theologiae Moralis*, I, 122; 212. Infidels warrant no consideration here, for they have no supernaturally revealed faith to protect.

[82] St. Thomas Aquinas, *Summa Theologica*, I$^{a}$ II$^{ae}$, q. 94, a. 4, ad 1.

short of absurd to consider it obligatory or even permissible to honor the claims of the natural law which abstracts from the positive divine law in the same measure in which one must respect the demands of the natural law which is leagued with the positive divine law. Were this possible, a well-meaning heretic might demand safeguards from the Catholic in protection of his own sincere belief and of all the moral consequences flowing therefrom in the same measure in which a Catholic can, not only with equal piety, but also with unassailable reason, demand safeguards for the divinely true faith which he holds and which is to come to his children.[83] It is, further, a matter of observation that the farther a man is removed from a knowledge of the primary precepts of the natural law, the more prone he is to error and defection from truth and rectitude. Passion, depraved customs, vices, bigotry—at least in regard to secondary precepts—all play a part in blunting the knowledge of that law or even of eradicating it from the human heart.[84] The natural law cannot be urged in such a man's favor; it stands against him. The natural law must always be urged in favor of him who respects its dictates after the manner in which they are corroborated by the force of the positive divine law.

The ultimate conclusion, derivable from the theory of the permissible private interpretation of the Bible, as proposed in Protestant circles, and from the contention that all religions are of equal value, leads one to the conviction that in reality few Protestants will be found who in good faith could venture to make reciprocal demands upon Catholics in the matter of the *cautiones.*

The *communicatio in sacris* can be of two kinds, the one entailing Catholic participation in non-Catholic ceremonies, the other a participation of non-Catholics in Catholic rites.[85] Active par-

---

[83] Wernz-Vidal, *Ius Matrimoniale,* pp. 200-201.

[84] St. Thomas Aquinas, *Summa Theologica,* Iª IIªᵉ, q. 94, a. 4 et 6.

[85] One author calls Catholic participation in non-Catholic rites *communicatio activa,* and non-Catholic participation in Catholic rites *communicatio passiva.* Cf. Noldin-Schmitt, *Summa Theologiae Moralis,* II, 34. But it is to be remarked here that more generally this terminology is used to designate respectively on the part of Catholics the taking of an active part and the assuming of a passive role in non-Catholic ceremonies. Cf. canon 1258, § 2. The latter terminology is adopted here.

ticipation in non-Catholic rites is a sacrilege on the part of Catholics. It is forbidden by the positive divine law, since it involves at least an implicit profession of heresy or schism.[36] On the other hand, the active participation of non-Catholics in a Catholic rite can not necessarily, but only incidentally, be regarded as interdicted to Protestants, for it is only at the sincere dictate of an erroneous conscience that such an action could involve any transgression of law, namely, of the law which binds all men to follow their conscience. In mixed marriages an active participation in the rite forms a necessary concomitant, for the parties necessarily perform an act which constitutes a contract, one and indivisible in its juridical effects for both parties. Between baptized persons such a contract is always a sacrament,[37] and between a Catholic and an unbaptized person such a contract, though it is not sacramental in character, still constitutes a sacred union effected *in facie Ecclesiae.*[38]

The specific danger of harm to the Catholic religion which is inherent in the semblance of an adherence to a condemned sect, as well as the imminence of scandal, is at times very pronounced in the participation of Catholics with non-Catholics in a religious rite. The difference of status between Catholics and non-Catholics in the reciprocal participation of a religious rite which is alien to their own beliefs has been sufficiently outlined to indicate that what is frequently permissible for Protestants cannot with equal reason or justifying cause be considered as permissible for Catholics.[39] But if such a participation on the part of Catholics does not entail even an implicit adherence to heresy, Gasparri holds that this participation is not interdicted by the natural law, but forbidden simply by the ecclesiastical law.[40]

---

[36] S.C.S.Off. instr. (ad omnes Ep. Ritus Orient.), 12 dec. 1888, n. 7—*Fontes,* n. 1112; Benedict XIV, *De Synodo Dioecesana,* Lib. VI, cap. 7, n. 2; Cappello, *De Matrimonio,* P. I, 403-404.

[37] Canon 1012; Payen, *De Matrimonio,* I, 658; Gasparri, *De Matrimonio,* I, 259.

[38] Pius XI, litt. encycl. *"Casti connubii,"* 31 dec. 1930—*AAS,* XXII (1930), 539-541.

[39] Ferreres, *Compendium Theologiae Moralis,* I, 176.

[40] *De Matrimonio,* I, 259-260; see also Vermeersch, *Theologia Moralis,* II, 42-44.

The danger to the faith and morals of the Catholic party in the marriage, as well as the danger of perversion for the offspring, unquestionably underlies the prohibition of the natural divine law.[41] The danger to the faith and morals of the Catholic contracting party has ever been considered the primary cause for concern, for it becomes a reality immediately upon the celebration of the marriage. The danger of perversion of the offspring is not so immediately present.[42] In the cases wherein mixed marriages remain without the issue of offspring this particular danger is not present at all. But wherever it is present in view of any justified assumption that children will issue from the marriage, the Church must exercise solicitude for the faith of the future children. Questions touching upon religious belief and education, as well as factors which deal with the moral aspect of an adopted way of life, will inevitably arise for a Catholic who lives in the close relationship of the bond of matrimony with a non-Catholic. The ensuing differences of mental outlook and of moral attitude can not but furnish the occasion of disastrous consequences for the children. If there be engendered in them a state of doubt and bewilderment over the lack of religious unity between their parents, such a state of mind can easily lead to religious indifferentism, if not to actual apostasy.[43]

From the principle that the danger to faith and morals underlies the prohibition of the natural law relative to the contracting of mixed marriages, there follows the second necessary conclusion. As long as this danger to the Catholic party and to the future

---

[41] Gasparri, *De Matrimonio,* I, 259-260; Aichner, *Compendium Iuris Ecclesiastici,* p. 646; Bangen (*De Sponsalibus et Matrimonio,* IV, 3) gives a thorough appreciation of the dangers to faith and morals inherent in mixed marriages. Cf. also Ter Haar, *Mixed Marriages and Their Remedies,* pp. 17-28; Kelly et Geniesse, *Efficax Antidotum ad Matrimonii Mixta Praecavenda* (Romae: Pustet, 1923). Almost all papal letters and decrees on the subject of mixed marriages eloquently stress the insidious imminence of these dangers. Cf. examples in Gregory XVI, ep. encycl. "*Summo iugiter,*" 27 maii, 1832—*Fontes,* n. 484; S.C.S.Off. instr. (ad omnes Ep. Ritus Orient.), 12 dec. 1888, n. 2—*Fontes,* n. 1112.

[42] Payen, *De Matrimonio,* I, 650.

[43] Ayrinhac-Lydon, *Marriage Legislation,* p. 101; Ter Haar, *Mixed Marriages and Their Remedies,* pp. 17-28.

offspring remains imminent in character, the mixed marriage is prohibited not only by ecclesiastical law, but by the natural law itself. Before this prohibition of the natural law can in any way be relaxed, this danger must either be obviated or at least rendered remote. Only then can a mixed marriage be undertaken so as to come within the realm of satisfying the substantial demand of the immutable natural law.

Consequently the strictest guard must be set against the likely or even possible occurrence of the forbidden *communicatio in sacris* by Catholics on the occasion of a mixed marriage. The connected but dissociable dangers to faith and morals, regardless of their portent for prospective parent or forthcoming offspring, must form a matter of profound concern when mixed marriages are to be contracted. It is left to positive ecclesiastical legislation to invoke the necessary practical precautions against these potential evils. Whatever measures the Church may appropriate, they will have their basis in the natural divine law. The *cautelae* which denote the actual removal of the imminent dangers attendant upon mixed marriages, are the essential requirements of the natural law apart from any extant ecclesiastical legislation.

If the *cautiones* can in unusual circumstances be foregone, as is true in the case of the *sanatio in radice,* this procedure is never allowable at the expense of the natural law, for the *cautelae* must always be present inasmuch as they are necessary to afford assurance for the Catholic party that all imminent dangers to faith and morals are removed and that the non-Catholic party will not interfere to make them imminent in the future. Thus a *cautio* is had even in this case, though it be only negative. Indeed, for a grave public cause a mixed marriage could be permitted even though the grave danger of perversion be present provided that the Catholic reflects a firm will against its eventual realization in actual harm. In such a case the grave public cause for the celebration of a mixed marriage is attendant with a positive safeguard which is recognized as providing satisfactory assurance that the grave danger is at least counterbalanced or neutralized by the positively sincere and efficacious will of the Catholic party.[44]

---

[44] Lehmkuhl, *Theologia Moralis,* II, 501.

## III THE ECCLESIASTICAL LAW

The natural law provides the foundation for the superstructure of every rightful positive law. It is the root with which every positive law which can command rightful obedience must be joined in its pristine origin, in its continued development, and in its ultimate character of a binding enactment. The very obligation of obedience to the will of a legitimately established superior as expressed by law can strike its roots nowhere else than in the soil to which the natural law itself is indigenous. Positive legislation, whether it be of a civil or an ecclesiastical character, must be concordant, or at least not discordant with the natural law, for there can be no law which is truly and justly a law if it runs counter to the inborn demands of human nature or the innate claims of human destiny. The natural law, as a mirror, must reflect in some fashion the traits of its own likeness when positive laws are brought within the range of its own prospect; otherwise these laws, in their lack of all authentic likeness, are deprived of their intended legal efficacy and force.[45]

The positive legislation of the Code of Canon Law follows the natural law step for step in the question of mixed marriages. The Code makes a distinction, however, which is not explicitly contemplated in the natural law, namely, between the impediments of mixed religion and of disparity of worship. The first of these impediments is prohibitive,[46] while the second is diriment in character,[47] that is, nullifies the marriage if it is contracted without a valid dispensation. The basis of the distinction between the two impediments inheres, on the one hand, in the modal difference of a profession of faith in mixed religion which still leaves possible

---

[45] Noldin-Schmidt, *Summa Theologia Moralis,* I, 121; Lehmkuhl, *Theologia Moralis,* I, 122.

[46] Canon 1061: Severissime Ecclesia ubique prohibet ne matrimonium ineatur inter duas personas baptizatas, quarum altera sit catholica, altera vero sectae haerticae seu schismaticae adscripta; quod si adsit perversionis periculum coniugis catholici et prolis, coniugium ipsa etiam lege divina vetatur.

[47] Canon 1070, § 1: Nullum est matrimonium contractum a persona non baptizata cum persona baptizata in Ecclesia catholica vel ad eandem ex haeresi aut schismate conversa.

the contracting of a *matrimonium ratum,* and, on the other hand, in the radical difference between the baptized and the unbaptized in disparity of worship which excludes the possibility of contracting a *matrimonium ratum.*[48]

Canon 1060 makes explicit mention of the natural law in such terms as to invite the conclusion that some individual cases of mixed religion may be free of the natural law impediment—"*. . . quod si adsit perversionis periculum. . . .*" This phrase does not disturb the general presumption of the presence of such dangers in all cases. It does indicate, however, that while the natural law impediment may not be present in a given case, the ecclesiastical impediment remains. While the ecclesiastical impediment, therefore, takes its rise from the natural law and the universal presumption of danger,[49] it is nevertheless separable and independent of it.[50]

The technical determination of the words "*Catholica*" and "*altera vero sectae haereticae seu schismaticae adscripta*" has received ample treatment by several authors, particularly by Schenk.[51] The only addition to be made on this score is to draw attention to the response of the Code Commission which is dated 30 July, 1934. The Commission was asked:

> "An ad normam Codicis iuris canonici qui sectae atheisticae adscripti sunt vel fuerunt, habendi sint quoad

---

[48] Schenk, *Mixed Religion and Disparity of Cult,* pp. 80-81.

[49] If a positive law is founded on a *praesumptio facti,* and if truth to the contrary can be established in a particular case, the law ceases to bind in that case. If, however, a law is founded on a *praesumptio periculi universalis,* then the law still binds even if in a particular case it is established that the danger has ceased, for it then rests on the supposition of a common danger, which continues to exist in its nature of a common peril even if exceptional or isolated cases do not reveal the presence of any such danger.—Ballerini-Palmieri, *Opus Theologicum Morale,* I, 417; Noldin-Schmitt, *Summa Theologiae Moralis,* I, 172-173; Feije, *De Matrimoniis Mixtis,* p. 57, n. 6, 8. This principle is unmistakably enunciated in canon 21 of the Code of Canon Law: "Leges latae ad praecavendum periculum generale, urgent, etiamsi in casu particulari periculum non adsit."

[50] De Smet, *De Sponsalibus et Matrimonio,* p. 439.

[51] *Mixed Religion and Disparity of Cult,* pp. 83-90; cf. also Aichner, *Compendium Iuris Ecclesiastici,* p. 646; De Smet, *De Sponsalibus et Matrimonio,* p. 437.

> omnes iuris effectus etiam in ordine ad sacram ordinationem et matrimonium, ad instar eorum qui sectae acatholicae adhaerent vel adhaeserunt."
> Resp. AFFIRMATIVE.[52]

According to the words *"ad normam Codicis iuris canonici"* the response of the Code Commission is to be considered not as an extensive but as simply a declarative interpretation of the words of the Code; hence it needs no promulgation and has retroactive effect.[53] The response, of course, does not affect the status of the canonical diriment impediment of disparity of worship or of the prohibitive impediment of mixed religion if the respective conditions for these impediments be present. Since atheistic sects are put on a par with non-Catholic sects, all the canonical interpretations and implications of the one are equally applicable to the other. The canonists[54] are almost unanimous in requiring actual membership in a heretical or schismatical sect at the time of the marriage before the canonical impediment of mixed religion can be truly said to bind. This seems to be the obvious sense of canon 1061. Hence actual membership in an atheistic sect at the time of the marriage is a like requirement. Vermeersch-Creusen[55] seem to stand alone in opposing this view. Consequently Payen[56] considers the words *"qui adscripti sunt vel fuerunt"* in the question proposed to the Code Commission as referring to sacred ordination,[57] while only the words *"adscripti sunt"* refer to matri-

---

[52] *AAS,* XXVI (1934), 494; for an English translation of this query, cf. Bouscaren, *Canon Law Digest,* II, 110, under canon 1065.

[53] Canon 17, § 2; Vermeersch, "Annotationes"—*Periodica de Re Canonica et Morali, Pars Altera (Monumenta),* XXIII (1934), 145-147.

[54] Cappello, *De Matrimonio,* P. I, 389; Chelodi, *Ius Matrimoniale,* p. 67; Wernz-Vidal, *Ius Matrimoniale,* p. 183, nota 1; De Smet, *De Sponsalibus et Matrimonio,* p. 437; cf. also Schenk, *Mixed Religion and Disparity of Cult,* p. 88; Payen, *De Matrimonio,* I, 642-643.

[55] *Epitome Iuris Canonici,* II, 231; cf. Vermeersch, "Annotationes"—*Periodica, Pars Altera (Monumenta),* XXIII (1934), 145-147.

[56] *De Matrimonio,* I, 643.

[57] Canon 2314, § 1, 3°, compared with canon 984, 5°. Those who have joined atheistic sects, whether *present* or *past* members, cannot validly enter a religious novitiate. Cf. canon 542, 1°. The response of the Code Commission however relative to the meaning of the words *"qui sectae acatholicae adhaeserunt"* as referring to those who fell away from the

mony. The prohibitive impediment arising from actual membership in an atheistic sect is sanctioned in addition by the divine law itself, as expressed in the final clause of canon 1060. Past membership, but now terminated, in such societies, may, in the prudent judgment of the ordinary, also be contained in the ambit of that clause.[58]

Participation on the part of Catholics in the rite and ceremonies of non-Catholics has been seen to be a matter forbidden by the natural law. As a consequence of and in harmony with the natural law, such participation in heretical rites is forbidden by the positive law of the Code as well.[59] A specific determination of this prohibition as it affects the marriage ceremony is stated in canon 1063, § 1,[60] wherein Catholics, even though a dispensation from mixed religion or disparity of worship had been obtained in their favor, are forbidden personally or through proxy to give or renew their matrimonial consent before a non-Catholic minister acting in his ministerial capacity. A further sanction to this specific prohibition is seen in the law of the Code which imposes a *latae sententiae* excommunication upon Catholics who disobey, and reserves the absolution from this censure to the ordinary.[61]

Participation on the part of non-Catholics in Catholic rites, on the contrary, is inescapable in a mixed marriage. But since it is

---

Church and then joined a non-Catholic sect, finds like application to our present case, and hence one falling away from the Church and joining an atheistic sect, could not validly enter a religious novitiate. Cf. Bouscaren, *Canon Law Digest,* I, 298, under canon 542.

[58] Canestri, in *Apollinaris,* VIII (1935), 54; for further comment on the response of the Code Commission, cf. *JP,* XIV (1934), 222; *Irish Ecclesiastical Record,* 5th Series, XLIV (1934), 637 (hereafter cited *IER*); *Ecclesiastical Review,* XCI (1934), 498 (hereafter *ER*).

[59] Canon 1258, § 1 : Haud licitum est fidelibus quovis modo active assistere seu partem habere in sacris acatholicorum.

[60] "Etsi ab Ecclesia obtenta sit dispensatio super impedimento mixtae religionis, coniuges nequeunt, vel ante vel post matrimonium coram Ecclesia initum, adire quoque, sive per se sive per procuratorem, ministrum acatholicum uti sacris addictum, ad matrimonialem consensum praestandum vel renovandum."

[61] Canon 2319, § 1, 1° : Subsunt excommunicationi latae sententiae Ordinario reservatae catholici : Qui matrimonium ineunt coram ministro acatholico contra praescriptum can. 1063, § 1.

not intrinsically evil and consequently not condemned by the natural law, it receives the same tolerance of positive ecclesiastical law as does the passive participation of Catholics in non-Catholic rites.[62]

The other two dangers attendant upon mixed marriages, namely, that of perversion for the faith and morals of the Catholic party and the danger that the offspring may be deprived of Catholic baptism and education, receive adequate attention in the Code of Canon Law. Thus Canon 1061, § 1, 2°, demands the *cautiones,* a formal promise from the non-Catholic party not to interfere with the religious practices of the Catholic and a formal promise from both parties to the marriage that all the children of their marriage will be baptized and educated in the Catholic religion alone. These *cautiones,* while they are of ecclesiastical origin, are a natural outgrowth of the essential demands made by the natural law. They are the practical precautions established by positive law for the purpose of satisfying the demands of the natural law. Furthermore, moral certitude on the part of the dispensing agent is so intimately connected with the question of the furnished *cautiones* as to share with them an identical status relative to their mediate derivation from the natural law. Consistently, therefore, moral certitude of the fulfillment of the *cautiones* is a positive requirement by the Code of Canon Law for the validity of the dispensation.[63]

All the positive legal effects attendant upon the dispensation from mixed religion, inclusive of *cause, cautelae, cautiones, moral certitude* and the *avoidance of active participation by Catholics in non-Catholic rites* are applicable as well to the impediment of disparity of worship by virtue of canon 1071.[64]

---

[62] Canon 1258, § 2: Tolerari potest praesentia passiva seu mere materialis, civilis officii vel honoris causa, ob gravem rationem ab Episcopo in casu dubii probandam, in acatholicorum funeribus, nuptiis similibusque solemniis, dummodo perversionis et scandali periculum absit.

[63] Canon 1061, § 1, 3°: Ecclesia super impedimento mixtae religionis non dispensat nisi moralis habeatur certitudo de cautionum implemento.

[64] The Catholic's obligation to strive for the conversion of the non-Catholic (Canon 1062) as well as the further obligation of ordinaries and pastors to watch over and care for the fulfillment of the *cautiones* (canon 1064, 3°) will be given attention in a later chapter of this dissertation.

Thus a marked consistency with the requirements of the natural law runs through positive legislation of the Code of Canon Law. It may be justly declared that the Code offers the practical application in positive law of the principles and precepts of the natural law.

## IV CESSATION OF IMPEDIMENT

### *A. Relaxation of the Natural Law*

Since the natural law answers to the needs and exigencies of the religious, sensitive-rational, and social character of man, it is as changeless as human nature. Hence the immutability of the natural law is a consistent thesis of the moral philosophers and theologians.[65] One must distinguish, however, between internal and external change of the natural law. An internal change would presuppose a change of human nature itself. Hence it is not admitted. An external change consists in a dispensation with the normal demands of the natural law through divine or human power. Furthermore, a dispensation may declare the obligation of the law to cease in a particular case while the object matter of the law remains the same. This is a dispensation properly so called (*proprie*).[66] On the contrary, a dispensation may declare the obligation of the law to cease because the object matter of the law has suffered a change. This is an indirect method and is called a dispensation improperly (*improprie*). In the first instance the obligatory force of the law is suspended for a particular case; in the second the obligatory force of the law remains, but the object is removed from the pale of the law and consequently the subject is not bound.[67]

What power has the Church to dispense in matters of this kind? St. Peter was given ample power to interpret and declare

---

[65] St. Thomas Aquinas, *Summa Theologica*, Iª IIªᵉ, q. 94, a. 5; Lehmkuhl, *Theologia Moralis*, I, 122; Noldin-Schmitt, *Summa Theologiae Moralis*, I, 123; Hickey, *Summula Philosophiae Scholasticae*, III, 131; Cathrein, *Philosophia Moralis*, pp. 159-161.

[66] Canon 80.

[67] Noldin-Schmitt, *Summa Theologiae Moralis*, I, 124; O'Mara, *Canonical Causes for Matrimonial Dispensation*, p. 7; Joyce, *Christian Marriage* (Heythrop Series: I, London: Sheed & Ward, 1933), pp. 26-27.

infallibly and authoritatively the meaning and extent of the natural and positive divine law.[68] This gave him in effect the power to superintend, moderate, and temper the application of that law, though not to dispense from it in the strictly accepted sense.[69]

With regard to the natural law, no power, whether human or divine, can dispense either properly or improperly from the primary principles. Hence, to blaspheme is always wrong and not even God can make it right, for that would imply His contradiction of Himself. God can, however, abstract from urging the application of the secondary principles of the natural law at all times, for under conceivable circumstances such a non-application will not give rise to acts which are intrinsically and absolutely wrong.[70]

As in matters of the positive divine law, so in the natural law, the power which the Church exercises in authoritative interpretation can result in dispensation in the improper sense. Thus the Church can and does dispense in matters pertaining to vows and oaths[71] by declaring that the object matter has changed and is no longer contemplated as being within the scope of the natural divine law. Furthermore, by a magisterial and vicarious power,

---

[68] "And I will give thee the keys of the kingdom of heaven; and whatsoever thou shalt bind on earth shall be bound in heaven; and whatsoever thou shalt loose on earth shall be loosed in heaven."—Matt., XVI, 19. Abundant evidence of the Pope's power to determine the divine law is seen throughout the Code. Cf. cc. 339, § 1 compared with declar. S.C.C., 13 iul. 1918—*AAS,* XI (1918), 48; 727, § 1; 1012, § 1; 1038; 1060; 1068, § 1; 1139, § 2; 1322, § 2; 1405, § 1; 1509, 1°; 1513; 1529; 1926; 1935, § 2; 2364.

[69] "Nequit Papa dispensare in Jure Divino, quamvis illud interpretari possit atque declarare quod id ob certas circumstantias hic et nunc per seipsum obligare cesset."—Reiffenstuel, *Ius Canonicum Universum,* Lib. I, tit. 2, n. 455; cf. also Schmalzgrueber, *Ius Ecclesiasticum Universum* (12 vols., Romae, 1843-1845), Lib. I, tit. 2, nn. 56, 76-79; Suarez, *Opera Omnia* (ed. nova, 26 vols., Parisiis, 1856-1866), V (*De Legibus*), Lib. II, cap. 13-14. The application of this truth to matrimonial impediments is expressed in canon 1038, § 1. The limits of this power are mentioned by Noldin-Schmitt, *Summa Theologiae Moralis,* I, 129.

[70] Noldin-Schmitt, *Summa Theologiae Moralis,* I, 124; Joyce, *Christian Marriage,* pp. 30-31.

[71] Canons 1309-1313; 1320.

the Holy Father exercises the power of dispensation over the *matrimonium ratum et non consummatum*[72] and the *vinculum naturale.*[73]

Presupposed requisites of the positive and natural divine law which exist as absolute demands are not subject to cancellation through any papal dispensation. Thus no human power can in the absence of marital consent supply for that defect,[74] for consent is of the very essence of marriage. Also the impediments of impotence, of an extant sacramental and maritally consummated bond, of consanguinity in the direct line and probably in the first degree of the collateral line are not subject to dispensation by the Pope. Substantial error, violent force, and overpowering fear are likewise so absolute as hindrances in their relation to the essence and end of marriage as to render the Pope unable to dispense in their regard.[75]

The impediments of disparity of worship and of mixed religion, as has been pointed out, are prohibitory impediments of the natural divine law because of the connected dangers to faith and morals. Hence they are not absolute but conditioned impediments. If the dangers no longer remain, or if they are effectively precluded, the impediment of the natural law ceases. The Pope, whose prerogative it is to interpret infallibly the positive and natural divine law, is within his competence to determine when these dangers have ceased to exist. The history of the mixed marriage problem which outlines the policies of the various papal acts from the time that dispensations from these impediments were first conceded down to the time that the law became crystallized in the Code of Canon Law, evidences both a deep concern regarding these dangers and a definite consciousness on the part of the Pope of his competence to evaluate them juridically.

---

[72] Canons 1119; 1985.

[73] S.C.S.Off., 5 nov. 1924—*Periodica,* XIV (1925), 19—the decision on the Helena case; see also, "Dispensation from Natural Marriage 'in favorem fidei'—An Important Decision"—*ER,* LXXII (1925), 186-188.

[74] Canon 1081, § 1.

[75] Wernz, *Ius Matrimoniale,* pp. 872-873; De Smet, *De Sponsalibus et Matrimonio,* pp. 633-634; Perrone, *De Matrimonio Christiano,* II, 133-135; Feije, *De Imped. et Dispens. Matr.,* p. 500; Cappello, *De Matrimonio.* P. I, 272-275; Gasparri, *De Matrimonio,* I, 165.

Thus the Pope cannot be said to dispense from these impediments of the natural law except improperly, namely, by declaring and establishing under what circumstances these dangers to the observance of the positive divine law have been effectively eliminated.

Indeed, there are those who say that these dangers never really cease even with the furnishing of the *cautiones*.[76] This opinion is not without its support in pastoral experience, for many attest the fact that mixed marriages, perhaps more than any other single factor, are a cause of great leakage from the Church.[77]

Yet it is conceivable that the dangers to the faith and morals of the Catholic party and of the offspring may in a given case be offset or neutralized even without the use of the *cautiones*. In such cases, rare though they be, the natural law impediment does not urge.[78] But because of the universal presumption of the presence of such dangers the ecclesiastical law does not cease, even in this case, until the *cautiones* are furnished, a just and grave cause obtains, and the dispensation has been properly executed. Indeed without these effects a marriage undertaken in the face of the impediment of disparity of worship would be null and void even though the natural law impediment had ceased.

### B. *Dispensation from the Ecclesiastical Law*

Thus far it has been deduced that the requirement of the *cautiones* and of the accompanying moral certitude of their fulfillment in marriages which are contracted with a dispensation from the impediment of mixed religion or of disparity of worship strikes its taproot in soil provided by the natural divine law, even though the requirement as a juridical demand is of ec-

[76] Payen, *De Matrimonio,* I, 644-646; Reiffenstuel, *Ius Canonicum Universum,* Lib. IV, tit. 1, n. 362; Bangen, *De Sponsalibus et Matrimonio,* IV, 3-5; Ter Haar, *Mixed Marriages and Their Remedies,* p. 52.

[77] Ter Haar, *Mixed Marriages and Their Remedies,* pp. 31-46.

[78] By the conversion of the non-Catholic party both the natural law and the ecclesiastical law impediment cease *ipso facto.* There is no longer a question of mixed marriage. Aside from this contingency, the circumstances of a case may argue the cessation of the natural law impediment while the ecclesiastical law impediment remains.

clesiastical origin. The furnishing of the *cautiones* and the conscious possession of moral certitude relative to their fulfillment together constitute a prerequired condition for the lawful granting of the dispensation, for a dispensation from an ecclesiastical matrimonial impediment can not be granted licitly as long as assurance is not had that the natural law demands are substantially satisfied. It further has been established that after the prohibitory impediment of the natural law has ceased to exist, normally through the furnishing of the *cautiones* by the parties, the ecclesiastical impediment, whether it be that of mixed religion or that of disparity of worship, still remains and consequently calls for the needed dispensation.[79] When such a dispensation is granted by the competent ecclesiastical authority, it is implied that the natural divine law no longer binds in the case and thereby also obviates the ecclesiastical impediment so that the contemplated marriage can be contracted both validly and licitly. What is required for the granting of this ecclesiastical dispensation? The answer is to be found in canon 1061 of the Code, and it applies equally well for the impediment of disparity of worship by virtue of the particular mention to this effect as contained in canon 1071.

### § 1 *Ecclesia super impedimento mixtae religionis non dispensat, nisi:*

The word *nisi* has the same kind of juridic force as *si* or *dummodo* and hence must be recognized as introducing *essential* conditions for the dispensation.[80] If it were to be argued that the application of canon 39 must be restricted to rescripts and that therefore it has no bearing on canon 1061, then, nevertheless, the phrase *dummodo cautum omnino sit conditionibus ab Ecclesia praescriptis,*[81] as contained in the Apostolic faculty issued to bishops to enable them to dispense in these impediments, places

[79] Canon 21; cf. also Wernz-Vidal, *Ius Matrimoniale,* p. 187; Ballerini-Palmieri, *Opus Theologicum Morale,* I, 417.

[80] Canon 39; cf. Van Hove, *Commentarium Lovaniense,* IV (*De Rescriptis*), p. 123.

[81] Formula D, art. 3 et 4—Konings-Putzer, *Commentarium in Facultates Apostolicas* (3. ed., Ilchestriae: Typis Congregationis Sanctissimi Redemptoris, 1893), pp. 335; 344; 15. Cf. also Beste, *Introductio in Codicem* (Collegeville: St. John's Abbey Press, 1938), Appendix, p. 974.

the essential requirements of the conditions introduced by the word *nisi* beyond further contention. This applies to all three conditions so introduced. The use of the colon after *nisi* in canon 1061 further delineates the extent of the essential conditions. Paragraph two of this canon, set off from paragraph one, is free of the dependence to which nn. 1, 2 and 3 in paragraph one are subject in relation to the opening conditional clause in the canon. The word *regulariter* in paragraph two, suggesting implicitly the very probability of exceptions, further frees this paragraph of all dependence upon the earlier conditional clause in paragraph one.

> 1° Ecclesia super impedimento mixtae religionis non dispensat nisi *urgeant iustae ac graves causae.*

The emphasis in this clause is on the just and grave character of the cause. The conclusion need not be adopted that more than one cause is required in every case. It is the curial practice in this country to grant a dispensation even if only one cause be given as long as it can be considered a sufficient cause and just and grave. Obviously, a recognized canonical cause which affects the case must be indicated in the application for the dispensation.[82] The causes themselves are not to be found in the Code but in two separate documents emanating from the Holy See. The one, a list of sixteen causes in an instruction of the Sacred Congregation of the Propagation of the Faith,[83] and the other, a list of twenty-eight causes given through the Apostolic Datary,[84] have received a more thorough consideration and canonical investigation by several authors than is contemplated in this treatise.[85]

---

[82] Schenk, *Mixed Religion and Disparity of Cult,* p. 194, note 36. Mixed Religion, though it is but a prohibitive impediment, may not be considered a *minor* impediment and hence does not enjoy the favor of canon 1054. Cf. Augustine, *Rights and Duties of Ordinaries according to the Code and Apostolic Faculties* (St. Louis: Herder, 1924), p. 274.

[83] 8 maii, 1877—*Coll. S.C.P.F.*, n. 1470.

[84] *Acta Sanctae Sedis,* XXXIV (1901-1902), 34-35 (hereafter cited as *ASS*).

[85] Payen, *De Matrimonio,* I, 648-649; Cappello, *De Matrimonio,* P. I, 401-402; De Smet, *De Sponsalibus et Matrimonio,* pp. 681-692; O'Mara, *Canonical Causes for Matrimonial Dispensation;* Schenk, *Mixed Religion and Disparity of Cult,* pp. 186-207.

Suffice it to say that a grave and just cause is a categorical requirement of the positive ecclesiastical law for the validity of the dispensation.

A consideration of the relative seriousness of the dangers which threaten the Catholic spouse and the future offspring has led authors to demand a more impelling cause for the needed dispensation if the man be the non-Catholic who jeopardizes the faith of the Catholic spouse and if the woman be the non-Catholic who compromises the spiritual welfare of the future offspring.[86] It is in such relative situations that the first and second dangers become relatively emphasized. The faith and morals of the Catholic spouse are considered more in jeopardy if the non-Catholic be the husband, while the danger of perversion of the offspring seems more acute if the non-Catholic be the wife. In most mixed marriages both dangers are present and may be considered serious.

Is a just and grave cause demanded also by the natural divine law? It has been contended that the dangers to faith and morals connected with mixed marriages are not entirely removed even though they have been rendered sufficiently remote by *cautiones* to permit the contracting of the marriage. The *communicatio in sacris* which connotes the participation of a non-Catholic in Catholic rites is a necessary and ever-present concomitant. There is also the added consideration of scandal which must be precluded. Now, according to the moral principle that one may expose himself only with a reasonable cause to a light or remote danger of sinning gravely, it would appear conclusive that a just and grave cause for permitting a mixed marriage is required also by the natural law.[87] The authors concur in the application of this principle to mixed marriages.[88]

In consequence of the need of a *just* and *grave* cause for granting the ecclesiastical dispensation, an ordinary would dispense

---

[86] Gasparri, *De Matrimonio,* I, 264; Cappello, *De Matrimonio,* P. I, 402.

[87] Noldin-Schmitt, *Summa Theologiae Moralis,* I, 321.

[88] Pius IX, litt. encycl., 11 mart. 1868—*Fontes,* n. 4872; *Coll. S.C.P.F.*, n. 1324; cf. also Wernz-Vidal, *Ius Matrimoniale,* p. 191; Chelodi, *Ius Matrimoniale,* p. 68; De Smet, *De Sponsalibus et Matrimonio,* pp. 439-440 and esp. pp. 442-443; Ter Haar, *Mixed Marriages and Their Remedies,* pp. 60-61.

both invalidly and illicitly if in virtue of his Apostolic faculties he were to grant a dispensation from the impediment of mixed religion or of disparity of worship without the presence of such a cause. This is explicitly declared in canon 84, § 1, and can be further deduced from canon 40. Moreover, if the dispensation were granted by the Holy See in a case wherein error was induced by falsely assigned causes, the dispensation would be invalid in view of the rule contained in canon 42. But, if the Holy See were to dispense knowingly from these impediments without a just and grave cause (a hypothetical case), the dispensation would have to be acknowledged as valid in the positive law of the Church, although of course the grant would have been made illicitly.[89] While Gasparri admits the validity of such a dispensation in the positive law of the Church, he distinctly is of the opinion that as far as the natural law is concerned, the dispensation is invalid.[90]

The opinion of Gasparri is intriguing. We have already seen that the ecclesiastical dispensation in mixed marriages performs a double office; it declares implicitly that the natural divine law no longer binds, and it dispenses in the proper sense from the ecclesiastical impediment. Since there is but one dispensation granted to cover both laws, we are forced, in accepting Gasparri's opinion, to accept the unusual and seemingly inconsistent conclusion that a dispensation can be both valid and invalid at the same time. The contradiction is only apparent, however, for we cannot say that a dispensation, properly so called, is granted with regard to the impediment of the natural law. Furthermore, the two impediments, one of the natural law, the other of the ecclesiastical law, while one in intent and purpose, are really distinct and separable. Hence a dispensation can effectively remove the impediment of the ecclesiastical law, and yet remain ineffective, and, as Gasparri says "invalid" as regards the implicit declaration concerning the impediment of the natural law. Now

[89] O'Mara, *Canonical Causes for Matrimonial Dispensation*, pp. 40-41.

[90] *De Matrimonio*, I, 265; cf. also *ibidem*, p. 181 where he states that such a dispensation would *more probably* be null by the natural law. Wernz-Vidal, (*Ius Matrimoniale*, p. 192) agree to the validity and illicitness of the dispensation as regards the ecclesiastical law, but make no mention of the natural divine law.

since the natural law sets up only a prohibitive impediment in both mixed religion and disparity of worship, the marriage consequent upon such a dispensation would indeed be valid in positive ecclesiastical law, though it would remain gravely illicit because the requirements of the natural law remain unsatisfied. If the natural law impediments against marriages of mixed religion and disparity of worship were diriment impediments, a marriage celebrated in the given hypothesis would be both illicit and invalid. In reverence to the Holy See it must be repeated that the discussion here undertaken is purely theoretical, lacking any application to known or recognized jurisprudence.

> 2° Ecclesia super impedimento mixtae religionis non dispensat nisi *cautionem praestiterit coniux acatholicus de amovendo a coniuge catholico perversionis periculo, et uterque coniux de universa prole catholice tantum baptizanda et educanda;*

This is the second essential condition for a valid dispensation from the ecclesiastical impediments of mixed religion and disparity of worship. The *cautiones* are of ecclesiastical origin and hence can be, though rarely are, dispensed with by the Church. It has been seen that the *cautelae* which the natural law demands can never be overlooked in their absolute requirement. If the formal *cautiones opportunae* are not required in a given *sanatio in radice* case, or if they are not demanded from both parties in certain rare instances in which *equivalent* or *implicit cautiones* are recognized as being sufficient, there must nevertheless always be present along with the *cautelae* the moral certitude that the natural law no longer prohibits the celebration of the marriage.

The content or object of the *cautiones* will receive detailed investigation in a separate chapter.

The phrase *perversionis periculo* mentioned in canon 1061, § 1, 2° and also in canon 1060 and 1065, § 2, contemplates first and foremost a danger to the *faith* of the Catholic party and of the offspring. The many defections from the faith as a result of mixed marriages are ample proof of that danger. The phrase, however, does not exclude from its comprehension *moral perversion* as well. Indeed, it would seem that the latter is implicitly contained in the former. Ter Haar[91] draws attention to the moral dangers inherent in mixed marriages.

> 3° Ecclesia super impedimento mixtae religionis non dispensat nisi *moralis habeatur certitudo de cautionum implemento.*

This is the third essential condition for the ecclesiastical dispensation. It shares with the *cautiones* an intimate dependence on the natural law. This requirement will be given thorough consideration along with its juridic aspects in the following chapter.

> Canon 1061, § 2: *Cautiones regulariter in scriptis exigantur.*

It has been stated that this is not an essential condition for the dispensation. Thus, in exceptional circumstances other forms of the *cautiones* will satisfy, e.g. in danger of death. The practice in our dioceses is to send the written *cautiones* to the Chancery with the application for the dispensation where they may be kept on file.[92]

---

[91] *Mixed Marriages and Their Remedies,* p. 18.

[92] Cf. Cappello, *De Matrimonio,* P. I, 394-395; Payen, *De Matrimonio,* I, 655; cf. also De Smet, *De Sponsalibus et Matrimonio,* p. 442, note 3.

# CHAPTER SIX

## MORAL CERTITUDE AND THE *Cautiones*

### I MORAL CERTITUDE IN CANON LAW

On the question of certitude and its use in the Code of Canon Law, particularly in procedure, one can immediately eliminate metaphysical and physical certitude. Nowhere are they demanded; nowhere do they find application by way of indispensable requirement. Even the absolute and unreserved use of the word *certo* in canon 1069, § 2,[1] which canon requires that a *certain* and legitimate proof of the nullity or of the dissolution of the prior marriage be had before a second matrimonial union is permitted, does not in itself point to anything more than the need of *moral certitude* both in its historical background[2] as well as among present-day canonists.[3] In commenting on canon 1069 Wernz-Vidal explicitly exclude the need of metaphysical or physical certitude as a means of proof, but they also point out that a mere probability does not suffice.[4] Indeed one instance has been cited wherein a *defensor vinculi* was rebuked for insisting on metaphysical certitude rather than moral certitude of the death of a former spouse before he acknowledged freedom for the celebration of a second marriage.[5]

---

[1] "Quamvis prius matrimonium sit irritum aut solutum qualibet ex causa, non ideo licet aliud contrahere, antequam de prioris nullitate aut solutione legitime et *certo* constiterit."

[2] S.C.S.Off., instr. 13 maii, 1868, n. 6—*Fontes,* n. 1002; cf. Sanchez, *De Sancto Matrimonii Sacramento,* Lib. II, disp. 46, n. 6.

[3] "Certitudo de nullitate aut solutione prioris vinculi moralis sit oportet."—Vermeersch-Creusen, *Epitome Iuris Canonici,* II, 240; Gasparri, *De Matrimonio,* I, 346; Ayrinhac-Lydon, *Marriage Legislation,* pp. 131-132; Chelodi, *Ius Matrimoniale,* p. 89; Cappello, *De Matrimonio,* P. I, 487; Noldin-Schmitt, *Summa Theologiae Moralis,* III, 580.

[4] "Hinc quamvis certitudo metaphysica vel physica non requiratur, tamen mera probabilitas quae ad omne dubium prudens excludendum non pertingat, nullo modo sufficit."—*Ius Matrimoniale,* p. 294.

[5] Cf. Rice, *Proof of Death in Pre-Nuptial Investigation,* The Catholic University of America Canon Law Studies, n. 123 (Washington, D. C.: The Catholic University of America Press, 1940), p. 106.

The insistence of the canonists in these cases on excluding the need of metaphysical and physical certitude on the one hand, and on stressing the insufficiency of mere probability on the other, leads normally to the necessity of moral certitude for a licit declaration of freedom to marry. The identification of *maxima probabilitas* with moral certitude in *ligamen* cases,[6] far from implying any kind of contradiction, simply argues for the admission of such moral certitude which in the *wide sense* is commonly called *imperfect moral certitude.* While positive arguments are required to prove the alleged death of a former spouse, it is significant that the Church deems the summary trial of canon 1990, with the sole intervention of the *defensor vinculi,* sufficient as a means to attain the required moral certitude. If the value of the arguments can conscientiously be called into question, then the *defensor vinculi* must appeal the case for a reconsideration in a second instance.[7]

In formal ecclesiastical trials, no matter what be the case, the judge must have moral certitude before passing his sentence. This is the explicit requirement of the Code of Canon Law.[8] Inasmuch as canon 1869 of the Code determines the acts and proofs of the case as the source from which the judge is to acquire his moral certitude, it is conclusive that imperfect moral certitude (*in sensu lato*) will suffice. Such certitude, therefore, which excludes every serious and prudent doubt of error, even though it does not preclude every possibility of error, suffices as a basis for the judge's eventual sentence. Indeed some admitted slight reason for the opposite's being true does not debar the judge from passing sentence as long as the weight of proof for his side is such as to move prudent men to act. This is undoubtedly conformable with the opinions of the canonists and with the exigencies of human affairs.[9]

---

[6] Wernz-Vidal, *Ius Matrimoniale,* p. 294, nota 52; Cappello, *De Matrimonio,* P. I, 491.

[7] Canon 1991.

[8] Canon 1869, § 1: Ad pronuntiationem cuiuslibet sententiae requiritur in iudicis animo *moralis certitudo* circa rem sententia definiendam.

§ 2: Hanc certitudinem iudex haurire debet ex actis et probatis.

§ 3: Probationes autem aestimare iudex debet ex sua conscientia, nisi lex aliquid expresse statuat de efficacia alicuius probationis.

[9] "Ad sententiam ferendam certitudo moralis, *saltem late dicta,* requiritur, id est non quaelibet seria probabilitas, sed is saltem probabilitatis gradus

Thus the moralists and canonists for all practical purposes have admitted also as a norm of action moral certitude in the wide sense rather than simply the strict or perfect moral certitude of which the philosophers speak. And if this may be noted in the opinions of the commentators, it is also clearly evidenced in the jurisprudence of ecclesiastical tribunals, particularly, of the Sacred Roman Rota.[10]

### II MORAL CERTITUDE AND THE *cautiones*

> Canon 1061, § 1, 3°: Ecclesia super impedimento mixtae religionis non dispensat, *nisi moralis habeatur certitudo de cautionum implemento.*

If moral certitude in the *wide sense,* which some authors specifically identify with the "utmost of probability" suffices for the judge to pass sentence in an ecclesiastical tribunal, and has moreover the sanction of the Holy Office as a recognized means for establishing full acceptance of the alleged death of a former

qui in negotiis magni momenti omne dubium serium excludit."—Vermeersch-Creusen, *Epitome Iuris Canonici,* III, 109; Coronata, *Institutiones Iuris Canonici* (5 vols., Taurini (Italia): Marietti, Vol. III [*De Processibus*], 1933, Vol. IV [*De Delictis et Poenis*], 1935), III, 307-308 (hereafter cited as *De Processibus* or *De Delictis et Poenis*); "Quae ratiocinatio excludit probabilitatem sed non possibilitatem errandi; quia materia moralis talis est quod non est ei conveniens perfecta certitudo."—Roberti, *De Processibus* (2 vols. in 1, Romae: Officina Tipografica Ausonia, 1926), II, 24; Noval, *Commentarium Codicis Iuris Canonici,* Lib. IV, *De Processibus* (2 vols., Augustae Taurinorum et Romae: Marietti, 1920), I, 409 (hereafter cited *De Processibus*); "Haec certitudo moralis non est absoluta et perfecta sed relativa, pro subiecta materia excludens probabilitatem erroris."—Lega-Bartoccetti, *Commentarius in Iudicia Ecclesiastica* (3 vols., Romae: Anonima Libraria Cattolica Italiana, 1938-1942), II, 934.

[10] Cf. *Thesaurus Resolutionum Sacrae Congregationis Concilii* (167 vols., Romae, 1718-1908), CXXVIII (1869), 686-687 (hereafter cited as *Thesaurus Resolutionum*). Cf. also *votum in causa Parisiensi,* 11 aug. 1894—*Thesaurus Resolutionum,* CLIII (1894), 900; *votum in causa Massilien.,* 20 apr. 1899—*Thesaurus Resolutionum,* CLVIII (1899), 277; *causa nullitatis matrimonii,* 21 maii, 1892—*Thesaurus Resolutionum,* CLI (1892), 274-275; *Causa nullitas matrimonii,* 6 iun. 1918, coram R.P.D Pietro Rossetti, dec. VI—*Sacrae Romanae Rotae Decisiones seu Sententiae quae . . . prodierunt anno 1909-1932* (24 vols., Romae: Typis Vaticanis, 1912-1940), X (1918), 44, ad 5 (hereafter cited as *S.R.R. Decisiones*).

spouse, then the same moral certitude or eminent degree of probability is also sufficient to satisfy the requirement of canon 1061, § 1, 3°.[11] In the case in which proof is sought for the alleged death it is the validity of a marriage that is directly involved; in the present consideration, the question of moral certitude regarding the fulfillment of the *cautiones* involves directly the validity of a dispensation, and indirectly the validity of a marriage, but the latter only then when the diriment impediment of disparity of worship figures in the case for which the needed dispensation is given. It has been pointed out that the requirement of moral certitude, in addition to being an essential demand of ecclesiastical law for a valid dispensation, also enjoys a foundation in the natural law along with the required *cautiones* themselves.[12]

The faculties granted to bishops in the United States and other countries far from Rome leave no doubt as to who must have the moral certitude with regard to the fulfillment of the *cautiones*.[13] Though the one who dispenses is the bishop, and though the Apostolic faculties demand moral certitude in him, in actual practice it is the pastor who deals directly with the contracting parties and who therefore must assure himself of their sincerity in making the promises and thus in the light of all the various circumstances of places and persons, must form his judgment regarding the fulfillment of the promises in the future. Upon the pastor, therefore, devolves the necessity of acquiring moral certitude before the granted dispensation will be valid.[14]

[11] "Requiritur ergo certitudo qua quis, omnibus perpensis, positive indicat, *etsi cum prudenti quadam formidine*, utrumque coniugem, cum catholicum tum acatholicum, *cautiones* seu promissiones in futurum fideliter esse impleturum."—Vromant, *De Matrimonio*, p. 136, nota 1. Cf. also, Ter Haar, *Mixed Marriages and Their Remedies*, pp. 86-87; Payen, *De Matrimonio*, I, 836.

[12] "Haec certitudo tam necessaria videtur ad validitatem dispensationis, quam necessariae sunt ipsae *cautiones*. Ex definitione cautionum, satis constat."—Payen, *De Matrimonio*, I, 836.

[13] ". . . dummodo . . . ipse R.P.D. Ordinarius moraliter certus sit easdem [conditiones] impletum iri . . ."—Beste, *Introductio in Codicem*, 974; cf. also S.C.S.Off., litt. (S. Germani), 17 feb. 1875—*Fontes*, n. 1039; *Coll. S.C.P.F.*, n. 1433; Gasparri, *De Matrimonio*, I, 267, nota 3.

[14] Schenk, *Mixed Religion and Disparity of Cult*, pp. 249-250. Whether the pastor's office be considered an extension of the episcopal office in the

Canon 1061, § 1, 3° makes no explicit mention of the requirement of moral certitude concerning the *sincerity* of the parties in making the promises. This may seem to introduce a departure from pre-Code legislation, for more than one papal document made specific mention of such requirement.[15] But to say that the need of moral certitude with regard to the sincerity of the accompanying promises is no longer implied in present law would be uncanonical, temerarious, and illogical. The silence of the Code in this matter has no telling significance.[16] Nor can canon 6 be advanced to challenge this contention. Number 6 of canon 6[17] which may appear to threaten this stand, can, on closer scrutiny, be advanced rather in support of the retention of the pre-Code clause than for its rejection. Moral certitude of the fulfillment of the *cautiones* necessarily includes in it a moral certitude of the present sincerity of the parties who furnish the *cautiones.* Hence the pre-Code clause is *implicitly* contained in canon 1061, § 1, 3°. In the very nature of things one could hardly be said to be morally certain of the future fulfillment of a promise when he lacks such certitude of the present sincerity of those making the promise.

---

various parts of the diocese, or whether the bishop be said to enjoy *vicarious* moral certitude through the pastor, it is difficult to explain the seeming incongruity between the rigid demand of the Apostolic faculties and the actually obtaining practice in various dioceses. More probably the bishops base their moral certitude upon the facts presented in the application for the dispensation and especially upon the recommendation of the worthiness of the case given by the pastor. Cf. Ayrinhac-Lydon, *Marriage Legislation,* p. 107; De Smet, *De Sponsalibus et Matrimonio,* p. 732, nota 5.

[15] S.C.S.Off., litt. (ad Card. Simor), 21 iul. 1880: ". . . moralis certitudo sive de cautionum sinceritate *pro praesenti,* sive de eorum adimplemento pro futuro . . ."—*NRT,* XIX (1887), 7; Litt. Secret. Status (ad Archiep. Strigonien.), 7 iul. 1890: "Altera conditio est, ut moraliter certi sint Episcopi de *sponsionum sinceritate* eorumque implemento, non obstantibus litteris circularibus a gubernio datis."—*Fontes,* n. 6455; *Coll. S.C.P.F.,* n. 1731; S.C.S.Off., 12 apr. 1899—*Fontes,* n. 1219; S.C.S.Off., 10 dec. 1902—*Fontes,* n. 1262.

[16] Schenk, *Mixed Religion and Disparity of Cult,* p. 249, footnote 154.

[17] "Si qua ex ceteris disciplinaribus legibus, quae usque adhuc viguerunt, nec explicite nec implicite in Codice contineatur, ea vim omnem amisisse dicenda est, nisi in probatis liturgicis libris reperiatur, aut lex sit iuris divini sive positivi sive naturalis."

The former is very much a part of the latter. Even when moral certitude of the present sincerity of the parties furnishing the *cautiones* is had, it is recognized that factors outside of and beyond the control of the parties themselves may interfere with the eventual fulfillment of these promises. It is this acknowledged fact that underlies the very tone of the decree of the Holy Office issued in 1932.[18] But what assurance can a bishop who dispenses have of the future fulfillment of the *cautiones,* regardless of external factors, if he cannot assure himself that the parties themselves are sincere in their promises? Recognized present insincerity of the parties making the promises will not beget moral certitude of their future fulfillment even if outside factors of civil law, custom, precedent, etc. all point to a favorable expectation of their fulfillment. Law will not accomplish in this respect what the perverse will and intention of the parties themselves will not permit. Furthermore, the need of moral certitude along with that of the *cautiones* is founded, if only indirectly, in the natural law. Since moral certitude of the fulfillment of the *cautiones* is bound up so intimately with moral certitude of the present sincerity of the parties, they may both be said to have at least an indirect foundation in the natural law. It is in this way that paragraph 6 of canon 6 may be advanced in favor of the retention of the pre-Code clause in the present law.

If indeed any doubt could remain regarding the retention or rejection of the pre-Code clause in the present Code law, then the rule of paragraph 4 of the same canon—that the former law continues intact when the present law reveals at most a doubtful discrepancy—would argue its retention. The omission in the Code is not even noted by some of the modern authors, who, in commenting on canon 1061, § 1, 3°, speak of the required moral certitude regarding the sincerity of the contracting parties in the same manner as they insist on certitude concerning the fulfillment of the *cautiones,* without adverting to the silence of the Code.[19]

---

[18] S.C.S.Off., decr. 14 ian. 1932—*AAS,* XXIV (1932), 25.

[19] Cappello, *De Matrimonio,* P. I, 393; Gasparri, *De Matrimonio,* I, 265; Payen, *De Matrimonio,* I, 655; Blat, *De Rebus,* P. I, 560; Vromant, *De Matrimonio,* p. 136; Chelodi, *Ius Matrimoniale,* p. 68.

### III MORAL CERTITUDE AND INSINCERE *cautiones*

The bishop's moral certitude regarding the sincerity of the promises of the parties in furnishing the *cautiones* is one thing; the parties' actual sincerity is another. Parties have been known to furnish the *cautiones* fraudulently in order to obtain a dispensation from the Church. They had no intention to fulfill the promises. Do such insincere promises invalidate the dispensation for mixed religion or for disparity of worship even though the deceived bishop possesses moral certitude regarding the sincerity of the promises and of their future fulfillment? Canonists have debated this question, and particularly so in recent years. They have advanced an array of strong arguments on either side. No question of invalidity arises relative to the marriage itself, if the marriage was celebrated simply with a dispensation from the impediment of mixed religion, for this impediment is exclusively prohibitive in character and therefore does not involve the marriage in an invalid status. It is different, however, when the dispensation is needed to remove the diriment impediment of disparity of worship, for if the dispensation be invalid, then the diriment impediment remains, and the subsequently contracted marriage is null and void.

#### *A. Invalidity of the Dispensation*

A search of the authors has revealed a number of canonists who hold that the furnishing of *insincere cautiones* does invalidate the dispensation, regardless of the presence or absence of moral certitude on the part of the one who grants the dispensation.[20]

---

[20] Woywod, *A Practical Commentary on the Code of Canon Law* (2 vols., New York: Jos. F. Wagner, 1925), I, n. 1056; Petrovits, *The New Church Law on Matrimony* (Philadelphia: McVey, 1921), p. 178; W. H. O'Neil, *Papal Rescripts of Favor,* The Catholic University of America Canon Law Studies, n. 57 (Washington, D. C.: The Catholic University of America, 1930), p. 115, n. 60; Nau, *Manual of the Marriage Laws of Canon Law* (New York: Pustet, 1933), p. 72; White, *Canonical Ante-Nuptial Promises and the Civil Law,* p. 36; Donovan (*The Pastor's Obligation in Pre-Nuptial Investigation,* The Catholic University of America Canon Law Studies, n. 115 [Washington, D. C.: The Catholic University of America, 1938], pp.

These authors maintain that for the valid granting of the dispensation there must be present sincere *cautiones,* either in the sense that they were sincere when they were given and then continued as such up to the time of the dispensation, or in the sense that they were sincere at least when the dispensation was granted, although at first they had been given insincerely.

In consequence, if it were later juridically proved and determined that the *cautiones* in a marriage of disparity of worship were not sincerely given and thereupon continued insincere up to the time of the granted dispensation, or that they were indeed sincerely given but were rendered insincere before the granting of the dispensation, then the marriage itself would have to be considered invalid as a necessary result of the invalidly granted dispensation. On the other hand, if neither of the two assumptions can be established by means of conclusive proof, then the marriage must be regarded as valid, inasmuch as the validity of the dispensation stands acknowledged.

The arguments employed in the defense of this contention may be summarized thus:

1. *Cautiones* given insincerely and in bad faith are the equivalent of no *cautiones* at all. An insincere *cautio* is a contradiction in terms. A fictitious act is no act, for the intention of the agent determines the nature of his free acts. The sincerity of the *cautiones* is so much an essential part of the *cautiones* as to be a constitutive element of them. Hence the nullity of the *cautiones* in such a case is derivable from the very

---

243-245) seems to lean to this side of the controversy; Woywod, "Insincere Promises and Validity of Dispensation from Impediment of Disparity of Cult"—*The Homiletic and Pastoral Review,* XXXIV (1933-1934), 518-520 (hereafter cited *HPR*); Harrington, "The Importance of the Cautiones in Disparity of Worship"—*ER,* LXV (1921), 257-262; Foley, "Sincerity of the Promises before Mixed Marriages"—*HPR,* XXXIII (1933), 742-743; cf. also *idem,* "Insincere Ante-Nuptial Guarantees"—*ER,* XCII (1935), 72-73; Oesterle, "De Cautionibus Matrimonialibus"—*JP,* XIV (1934), 270-276; XV (1935), 64-81; 191-195; cf. also Oesterle, "Quaestio de Cautionibus in Missionibus"—*Commentarium pro Religiosis et Missionariis,* XIX (1938), 101-109; P. O'Neil, "Disparity of Worship and Fictitious Guarantees"—*IER,* 5th Series, XLI (1933), 630-635.

norm of canon 1680, § 1.[21] Furthermore, if the final motive advanced for a dispensation is false, then the dispensation itself remains without valid effect according to canon 45. *A fortiori,* in the present case wherein a dispensation from the demand of the divine law is in question, false *cautiones* do invalidate the dispensation.[22]

2. The dispensation is granted on condition that the *cautiones* be true, ". . . si preces veritate nitantur. . . ."[23] Hence it is stated that the Church cannot be accused of intending to dispense if she has been deceived by false promises. If the Church demanded no more than the mere fact of the promises, she would be placing a premium on dishonesty. It would be tantamount to encouraging fraud in order to procure a dispensation. It may not be assumed that the Church would be ready to jeopardize the spiritual welfare of her children by sanctioning and legalizing bad faith in the *cautiones.*[24]

3. Foley, writing in *The Ecclesiastical Review*[25] considers it "far more probable" that the dispensation is invalid if it be granted when the *cautiones* are insincere. He argues that the moral certitude which is demanded on the part of the bishop gives rise to a corresponding necessity of sincerity on the part of the promissor.

4. Woywod[26] presents an interesting marriage case in which it was discovered that the parties who had obtained a dispensation

---

[21] "Nullitas actus tunc tantum habetur, cum in eo deficiunt quae actum ipsum essentialiter constituunt, aut sollemnia seu conditiones desiderantur a sacris canonibus requisitae sub poena nullitatis."

[22] Harrington, "The Importance of the Cautiones in Disparity of Worship"—*ER,* LXV (1921), 257-262; Foley, "Insincere Ante-Nuptial Guarantees"—*ER,* XCII (1935), 72-73; cf. *idem.* "Sincerity of the Promises Before Mixed Marriages"—*HPR,* XXXIII[2] (1933), 742-743; P. O'Neil, "Disparity of Worship and Fictitious Guarantees"—*IER,* 5th Series, XLI (1933), 630.

[23] Canon 40.

[24] Woywod, "Insincere Promises and Validity of Dispensation from Impediment of Disparity of Cult"—*HPR,* XXXIV (1933-1934), 518-520.

[25] "Second Marriage Ceremony before a Minister"—*ER,* XC (1934), 173-175.

[26] "Dispensation From Disparity of Cult and Secret Agreement of the Parties to Raise Children Non-Catholic"—*HPR,* XXXI (1930-1931), 630-631.

from the impediment of disparity of worship had had a secret agreement between themselves not to rear any of their children as Catholics. In reality, however, all the children were baptized as Catholics and received a Catholic education. The writer of the article, in answer to the question whether the marriage was invalid, replied that, as long as the bishop had moral certitude of the sincerity of the *cautiones* and of their fulfillment, the marriage was valid in the external forum of the Church. Because of the secret pact, however, he adjudged the *marriage invalid* in conscience and before God. Consequently his advice to the inquiring pastor was to obtain a new dispensation and a secret renewal of consent according to the norm of canon 1135, § 2.

5. The contention is made that the dependence of the validity of a marriage upon the internal intention of the parties in giving the *cautiones* does not place the marriage in jeopardy any more than a similar dependence on the internal intention of the parties in the exchange of matrimonial consent according to the requirement stated in canon 1081, § 1.[27]

6. Perhaps no one has given more attention and support to the proposition that *insincere cautiones* invalidate the dispensation than Oesterle.[28] In an article in the *Jus Pontificium* he opposes the view of Toso,[29] and bases his conclusion on 1) the interpretation of canon 1071 and 1061; 2) the exposition of the decrees of the Holy Office; and 3) the doctrinal authority of canonical jurisprudence.

1) Oesterle's interpretation of canons 1071 and 1061 clarifies the status of the impediment of disparity of worship as *diriment* in ecclesiastical legislation, *prohibitive* in the natural divine law. As long as the *cautiones* are given in direct deception of ecclesiastical authority, so he maintains, the Church does not intend to dispense in the face of the natural divine law, which still prohibits the marriage. Furthermore, a strict analysis of the term *cautio* in canon 1061, § 1, 2°, is emphasized as denoting *sincere* and *firm* promises and a similar treatment of the phrase *moral certitude* in

[27] O'Neil, "Disparity of Worship and Fictitious Guarantees"—*IER*, 5th Series, XLI (1933), 630-635.

[28] "De Cautionibus Matrimonialibus"—*JP*, XIV (1934), 270-276; XV (1935), 64-81; 191-195.

[29] "De Cautionibus Matrimonialibus"—*JP*, XIII (1933), 207-214.

canon 1061, § 1, 3°, is stressed as implying such certitude as necessarily can derive only from the presence of sincere *cautiones*.[80] Finally, the contractual nature of the *cautiones* necessitates a basis of good faith and sincerity in the *cautiones*. The historical antecedents of the presently required firm and sincere *cautiones* are reflected in the erstwhile *cautiones* which demanded at least the probable hope of the non-Catholic's conversion before the marriage was permitted.

2) After examining the terms of the rescripts of the Holy Office conceded to bishops to enable them to grant a dispensation from the impediments of mixed marriage, Oesterle observes that they are given in *forma commissoria voluntaria*, by which it is left to the prudent judgment of the ordinary either to grant or not to grant the dispensation according to whether the conditions have or have not been fulfilled. Thus the power of granting a dispensation is committed to the ordinary in such a manner that he can grant the dispensation only if in his conscientious knowledge and prudent judgment the *preces* are true and the *cautiones* will be fulfilled. In consequence Oesterle insists on the objective veracity of the *cautiones* as a requirement stipulated by the norm of canon 40. Several decrees and responses of the Holy Office are turned back upon Toso who offers them as arguments in favor of the opposite position.[81]

3) Oesterle then cites several authors in support of his position, and concludes his article by opposing Toso's stand that sincerity or

---

[80] Oesterle (*op. cit., JP,* XV (1935), 66-67) justifies his insistence on the use of such phrases as *vera cautio* and *opportunae cautiones* by appealing to the following text in a response of the Sacred Congregation of the Propagation of the Faith under date of March 11, 1868: "Profecto novit Eminentia tua, Ecclesiam nunquam permittere, imo neque permittere posse mixtarum nuptiarum celebrationem nisi . . . *opportunae exhibeantur cautiones,* quarum virtute a coniuge catholico amoveatur perversionis periculum, et provideatur catholicae institutioni ac educationi prolis universae."—*Fontes,* 4872; *Coll. S.C.P.F.,* n. 1324.

[81] S.C.S.Off. (Cochinchin.), 1 aug. 1759—*Fontes,* n. 810; S.C.S.Off., instr. (ad Archiep. Corcyren.), 3 ian. 1871, ad 3—*Fontes,* n. 1013; S.C.S.Off. (Victoriae Nyanzae), 22 dec. 1887, ad 1 et 5—*Fontes,* n. 1106; S.C.S.Off., instr. (ad omnes Ep. Ritus Orient.), 12 dec. 1888, ad 5—*Fontes,* n. 1112; S.C.S.Off., 10 dec. 1902, ad 1 et 2—*Fontes,* n. 1262.

insincerity constitutes an imperceptible element which does not enter the purview of positive legislation. In pursuing his view the author points out that the positive law of the Code in several canons renders acts juridically null in view of some *internal defect* provided only that such a defect stands proved in the external forum.[82]

Thus Oesterle rests his case. His summary reemphasizes his position: 1) that insincere *cautiones* do not answer to the condition demanded by canon 1061, § 1, 2° ; and 2) that the requirement of canon 40, which demands "truth" as a condition in all *preces* for the obtaining of an effective rescript, is by no means satisfied by insincere *cautiones.*

### B. *Validity of the Dispensation*

The position taken by the above cited authors has not gone unchallenged. A number of canonists have examined the question and are satisfied that the dispensation from the impediments of mixed marriage is valid even though the *cautiones* be insincere, provided only that the dispensing ordinary justifiably possesses a moral certitude that the *cautiones* are to be adjudged sincere and that their fulfillment is reliably assured.[83] The juridic arguments advanced by these canonists seem to carry more weight than the arguments of their opponents. First, they successfully meet the

---

[82] Cf. canons 40; 92; 104; 169, § 1; 214; 556, § 1; 572, § 1; 586; 644, § 3; 728; 729; 1136; 1965; 1684-1686. Several ordinations were declared invalid in consequence of a defect of intention. Cf. S.C.C., Milevitana, 26 nov. 1791, et 18 iun. 1792—*Fontes,* nn. 3873, 3880; S.C.S.Off. (Angliae), 2 mart. 1842—*Fontes,* n. 887; S.C.S.Off., 28 nov. 1900—*Fontes,* n. 1248.

[83] De Smet, *De Sponsalibus et Matrimonio,* pp. 441; 517; 731-732, esp. 731, nota 3; Ayrinhac-Lydon, *Marriage Legislation,* p. 108; Cappello (*De Matrimonio,* P. I, 399) distinguishes between those fictitious *cautiones* which are manifest and those which are occult; Doheny, *Canonical Procedure in Matrimonial Cases* (Milwaukee: Bruce, 1938), p. 450; Payen, *De Matrimonio,* I, 656, nota 4; Vromant, *De Matrimonio,* p. 136; Schenk, *Mixed Religion and Disparity of Cult,* pp. 248-254; Ter Haar, *Mixed Marriages and Their Remedies,* p. 95, n. 4; Toso, "De Cautionibus Matrimonialibus"—*JP,* XIII (1933), 207-214; Park, "Insincere Ante-Nuptial Guarantees"—*ER,* XCI (1934), 446-459; O'Donnell, "Mixed Marriage Guarantees"—*IER,* 5th Series, XVIII (1921), 411-418.

objections by the opponents against the present thesis. Secondly, the jurisprudence of the Sacred Roman Rota seems to favor their view, though it forms as yet but a negative argument in so far as no case on record turns on the exact point at issue. Thirdly, the concept of moral certitude as demanded in canon 1061, § 1, 3°, seems more consistently explained according to this view.

### C. *Review of Objections*

1. *Cautiones* given insincerely and in bad faith are the equivalent of no *cautiones* at all. The writer in *The Homiletic and Pastoral Review* in advancing this argument writes: "Before 1912 there were theologians who maintained that the guarantees were not a condition of validity, but the Holy See definitely declared that they were in a decision given on June 21 of that year."[84]

What the Holy See in the quoted decree actually declared was that a dispensation from the impediment of disparity of worship is invalid when granted by a delegate of the Holy See, if the guarantees were not demanded or if they had been refused (*non requisitis vel denegatis praescriptis cautionibus*). The decree, therefore, concerns a juridic fact and does not contemplate the intent behind the fact, namely, the sincerity or insincerity of the petitioner. Moreover, the decree of the Holy Office of January 14, 1932,[85] to which Foley appeals in seeking support for his view concerning the need of actually sincere *cautiones* is irrelevant, for the language of the decree is unmistakable in its import. The decree has no reference to the sincerity of the parties giving the *cautiones*. It is concerned primarily with the moral certitude of future fulfillment required by the one dispensing and it declares invalid a dispensation granted in the face of known and recognized opposition to the fulfillment of the *cautiones*. Thus a dispensation would be invalid if it were granted in a country where the civil law took a hostile attitude to such pre-nuptial agreements and

[84] *AAS,* IV (1912), 443—The quoted argument is from Foley, "Sincerity of the Promises Before Mixed Marriages"—*HPR,* XXXIII[0] (1933), 742-743.

[85] *AAS,* XXIV (1932), 25.

rendered them ineffective. It would also be invalid if a dispensation were granted to a couple who intended after their marriage to make their home in a place where such antagonistic laws were in force.[86]

Canon 1680, § 1, quoted above by the opponents as defining the nullity of acts, does not have application to insincere *cautiones*. To say that *sincere* CAUTIONES are conditions which are required by the canons under pain of nullity is but a begging of the question. It is just this that needs to be proved by definite canonical texts. Is the sincerity of the guarantor's intention so essential an element of the act that without it the *cautio* is simply non-existent? If the natural divine law simply prohibits, but does not nullify the granting of a dispensation in the face of insincere promises, then the dispensation which is granted in violation of that law does indeed connote the presence of a sinful act, but it remains a dispensation of which the effect is not one of invalidity, but notably one of sin, inasmuch as that which is not invalidated by the natural divine law is also not invalidated by the ecclesiastical law, unless the latter enacts an express invalidating sanction over and above the solely moral sanction of the natural divine law. Just as the impediment of disparity of worship is not of a diriment character in the natural divine law, but by the same law implies the presence of an extremely strict prohibition against entering a disparate marriage, so also the need of sincere promises does not in the natural divine law rule out the possibility of a valid dispensation from the impediments of mixed religion or of disparity of worship even though the need is so imperatively stressed by the same law that any act which denotes a wilful disregard of it must be considered as being most severely forbidden. In either case the flaunting of the prohibition of the natural divine law does not entail invalidity for the violative act.[87] And if it is thus patent that the natural divine law does not necessitate *sincere promises* as a

[86] False interpretations of this decree in the United States were set right by an article by Bernardini, "The Decree of the Holy Office respecting Ante-Nuptial Agreements in Mixed Marriages"—*ER*, LXXXVIII (1933), 185-190; cf. also Schaaf, "In How Far Does the Recent Decree Regarding the Cautiones Apply to the United States"—*ER*, LXXXVI (1932), 408-411.

[87] Suarez, *De Legibus*, Lib. V, cap. 27, nn. 2 et 9.

condition for a valid dispensation, then the question simply remains whether ecclesiastical law has done so. Canon 1680, § 1, which is invoked by the opponents as proof that the Church has enacted such a requirement simply mentions two conditions: The presence of the essential constituents of an act, and the observance of such formalities as are required under invalidating sanction. Now, the demands of *sincere* CAUTIONES cannot be brought under either of these two conditions. It should appear rather evident that sincerity is not an element essential to the existence of a *cautio,* for the opponents themselves speak of *fictitious* as well as of *sincere* CAUTIONES, and this they could not logically do if indeed all insincere promises were the equivalent of no *cautiones* at all. It should also seem evident that the furnishing of *sincere* CAUTIONES may not be regarded as a legal formality which the law of the Church requires under pain of nullity. For, one may ask, in what canon, or decree, or enactment, has the Church set up the presence of *sincere* CAUTIONES as a formality in the absence of which the grant of the dispensation from the impediment of mixed religion or of disparity of worship is expressly or equivalently designated as null and void? Inasmuch, therefore, as canon 1680, § 1, does not touch the question of the *sincerity* of the *cautiones* either as an essential element or as an indispensable formality for the validity of the dispensation, one may well assume that its canonical import for the question under consideration has been unduly magnified, if not in reality distorted, by those who bring this canon in such intimate relation to the canonical doctrine on the *cautiones.*[88]

If the final motive advanced for a dispensation is false, so state the opponents, then the dispensation itself remains without valid effect according to canon 45. *A fortiori,* so they argue, false *cautiones* invalidate the dispensation when there is question of dispensing, not from ecclesiastical law, but from the demand of the divine law.

In answer to this objection it hardly seems necessary to state that all canonists are agreed that the Church can not dispense from a divine law. The opponents' implication by that very fact loses its force. For, when the Church dispenses from an invalidating ec-

[88] Park, "Insincere Ante-Nuptial Guarantees"—*ER,* XCI (1934), 455.

clesiastical enactment which by divine law stands simply as a prohibition, the question of a *valid* dispensation relative to the demand of the divine law would by no means require any attention, for the simple reason that the question is not an actual one as long as the divine law in this case does not contain any invalidating sanction over and above its moral sanction of a severe prohibition. But there is need here of a distinction the importance of which the opponents seem to overlook. *Causa* and *cautio* are two different considerations. One may not universally apply to the one what is applicable to the other. Canon 45 does not make mention of *cautiones*. Unless one can somewhere find as definite a statement about the *cautiones* as the one that canon 45 makes about the *causa*,[39] no mutual interchange in the application of canonical principles should be attempted. To do so implies a confusion of separate and independent issues.[40]

2. The same distinction between *causa* and *cautio* renders ineffective the argument of number 2 indicated above based on canon 40. The *preces* in the application for a dispensation embrace the *cause* for the dispensation and not the *cautiones,* which constitute the condition under which the dispensation is granted. O'Donnell admits the *cautiones* within the consideration of canon 40 but understands *verae cautiones* as referring to *cautiones* that are not based on vague, casual or ambiguous statements, or on the supposed character of the parties, or in fact on anything that gives rise to conjecture rather than to moral certitude.[41]

What is to be said of the argument that the Pope has no intention to dispense if the *cautiones* are not sincere? It can readily be conceded that if the Pope has no intention under such circumstances to grant the dispensation, then the dispensation is certainly invalid. But it must first be equally certain that he has actually withheld his intention to grant the dispensation in such an event.

---

[39] Canon 45: Cum rescriptis ad preces alicuius impetratis apponitur clausula: Motu proprio, valent quidem ea, si in precibus reticeatur veritas alioquin necessario exprimenda, non tamen si falsa *causa* finalis eaque unica proponatur, salvo praescripto can. 1054.

[40] Park, *ibid.,* p. 455.

[41] O'Donnell, "Mixed Marriage Guarantees"—*IER,* 5th Series, XVIII (1921), 411-418.

The external act which betokens the granting of a dispensation must also be accepted as reflecting the internal intention to grant it, unless this natural and reasonable presumption is counteracted by compelling proof to the contrary. One may not argue that a forthright intention to grant a dispensation upon a previous investigation of the causes and conditions, when such a scrutiny has rightfully begotten a prudent moral certitude, implies at the same time one's unwillingness to grant the dispensation should his morally certain judgment prove erroneous. Nor does it argue a willingness to offend against God's law. The first of all laws for rational beings is to follow the light and direction of their intellect. When that is done, the law of God is fully obeyed. If it should incidentally happen that certain elements or factors, over which man has no control, will nevertheless cause an unwilled factual contravention in a purely material sense, then one cannot ascribe such a consequence to any perverseness in man's will or argue that his intention was nullified thereby. Rather, it comes as a result of his very desire to live in accordance with the *obsequium rationale,* which God acknowledges as the prime consideration of all faithful service in the keeping of His law.

"The opinion that a dispensation is not vitiated by the bad faith of the parties in giving the *cautiones* as long as it was not manifest to the Ordinary, does not put a premium on vice any more than the recognition of the gravity of causes for dispensation which have their ultimate source in a grave sin of the parties. It does not sanction fraud any more than canon 1054, which upholds the validity of a dispensation from a minor impediment even though the causes alleged for dispensation were fraudulent."[42]

3. The argument advanced in number 3 above noted, stresses the essential condition of moral certitude on the part of the bishop.[43]

It is quite true, and everybody must be ready to grant, that the Church expects and desires the promissors to be sincere. There is a grave obligation on their part to furnish the guarantees seri-

---

[42] Schenk, *Mixed Religion and Disparity of Cult,* p. 254.

[43] Foley, "Second Marriage Ceremony before a Minister"—*ER,* XC (1934), 173-175.

ously and to fulfill them conscientiously. This arises from the natural divine law for the safeguard of which the Church has instituted the *cautiones.* Against the non-observance of these promises the Church invokes the punishments prescribed in canon 2319 which visits a *latae sententiae* excommunication the absolution of which is reserved to the ordinary, upon those who enter marriage with an agreement to have any of their children baptized or educated in any religion other than the Catholic faith. Furthermore, should the non-Catholic refuse to attend to his promise to have all the children baptized and educated as Catholics, the Church will sanction for the Catholic party a separation from bed and board according to canon 1131, and will promote the Catholic education of the children, in the best possible way according to canon 1132. Hence, the Church beyond all doubt expects sincerity of those who make the promises, and in her legislation she has provided both punitive and administrative measures to the end that the *cautiones* be fulfilled.[44] But despite all this, the sincerity of the promissors is not an essential condition for the validity of the dispensation. There still is to be found any clear canonical text that so provides. The absence of any such text of law strongly supports and confirms the position held by the second group of canonists, for canon 11 stoutly affirms that an invalidating effect attaches to the violation of only that law which incorporates the sanction of nullity in an express or equivalently manifest manner.

4. On what grounds does the writer in *The Homiletic and Pastoral Review* consider the marriage in the case presented in number 4 above invalid in conscience and before God? Because the dispensation was invalid in positive ecclesiastical law? If so, then the marriage also was invalid in the external forum of the Church even though no proof was at hand to establish that fact. Because of the demand of the natural divine law? But the natural divine law establishes nothing more than an *impedimentum prohibens* even in the case of disparity of worship. By defect in the consent? There is no evidence in the case that true matrimonial consent was either withheld or in any way exchanged in a substantially deficient manner. Perhaps on the basis that the

[44] Canon 1064, 3°.

marriage was entered with an intention *contra bonum prolis?* It is rather unanimously agreed today that sinful pacts to rear the children in heresy are simply invalid agreements, but do not in and of themselves invalidate the marriage. The *bonum prolis* is a concept which is restricted in its application to the question which deals with the procreation of children, and hence is a notion which has no application *extra ordinem physicum.*[45] Such a sinful pact gives rise to the incurrence of the penalty specified in canon 2319, § 1, 2°.[46] The pointed wording of this canon (*matrimonio uniuntur*) argues the necessity of the celebration of a *valid* marriage before the censure is incurred.[47] Now, since a sinful pact described in the canon unquestionably results in *insincere* or *fictitious cautiones* in a mixed or disparate marriage, it will be necessary for the opponents of the present thesis to square their position with canon 2319, § 1, 2° which connotes a valid marriage even in the face of false promises. If insincere *cautiones* invalidate the dispensation, the subsequent marriage of disparity of worship would be invalid. This hypothesis would force one to the very questionable conclusion that the censure of canon 2319, § 1, 2° could never find application in a marriage of disparity of worship.

[45] Cf. Feije (*De Matrimoniis Mixtis,* pp. 161-169) who offers a thorough treatment of the present question in his rejection of the doctrine which connects the *bonum prolis* with the spiritual and moral as well as with the physical order.

[46] "Subsunt excommunicationi latae sententiae Ordinario reservatae catholici qui matrimonio uniuntur cum pacto explicito vel implicito ut omnis vel aliqua proles educetur extra catholicam Ecclesiam."

[47] The unqualified use of the word "*matrimonio*" connotes a valid union, for elsewhere in the Code the word *matrimonium* when used to designate an invalid union receives explicit or contextual qualification which renders that meaning unmistakable. The necessity of a valid marriage as pre-required for the incurrence of this censure receives the support of a number of canonists. Cf. Beste (*Introductio in Codicem,* p. 939) who says: "Ad poenam incurrendam requiritur: 1. ut matrimonium ineatur *verum* seu *validum* . . ."; Cappello, *Tractatus Canonico-Moralis De Censuris iuxta Codicem Iuris Canonici* (3. ed., Augustae Taurinorum et Romae: Marietti, 1933), p. 320: "Intelligitur matrimonium *verum* seu religiosum, sive mixtum sit, sive non."; cf. also, Coronata, IV (*De Delictis et Poenis*), 313; Chelodi, *Ius Poenale et Ordo Procedendi in Iudiciis Criminalibus iuxta Codicem Iuris Canonici* (4. ed., Tridenti: Libreria Moderna Editrice A. Ardesi, 1935), p. 80.

5. In answer to argument number 5 listed above, it is submitted that there is a real and characteristic difference between the antecedents which constitute a condition for the granting of a matrimonial dispensation and the essential internal factor of the will which effects matrimonial consent. The internal consent of nupturients is of the essence of marriage, and is explicitly required by canonical text.[48] There is no *a-pari* argument from this to the internal intention to fulfill the *cautiones.* The law on matrimonial consent is a declaration of the divine law, while the law on the guarantees is of ecclesiastical origin exclusively, even though it rests upon the foundation of the natural law inasmuch as it provides for the practical means wherewith the necessary *conditiones* or *cautelae* are to be recognized as present.[49]

6. The arguments advanced by Oesterle (above, n. 6) may in part be evaluated from the discussion contained under the previous five numbers. But there remain a few arguments which demand closer consideration here.

Oesterle argues that *sincere guarantees* are canonically required in view of the contractual nature of the *cautiones.* The true nature of a contract, he says, demands sincerity on the part of those who are the parties of the contract. Without true consent based on sincerity there can be no contract.[50]

To this is opposed the doctrine that the validity of a contract is conditioned upon the contractual nature of the guarantees and upon the attendant solemnities or formalities required by law, and not upon the good or bad faith of the contracting parties. The security of the *cautiones* cannot be based upon so intangible and imperceptible an element as that of internal sincerity. Monetary contracts cannot be set aside upon the allegation or even proof of insincerity of intention in one of the parties. In positive law the external act is considered, not the internal intention.[51]

---

[48] Canon 1081, § 1: Matrimonium facit partium consensus inter personas iure habiles legitime manifestatus; qui nulla humana potestate suppleri valet.

[49] Park, "Insincere Ante-Nuptial Guarantees,"—*ER,* XCI (1934), 446-459.

[50] "De Cautionibus Matrimonialibus," *JP,* XV (1935), 68-69.

[51] Cf. Toso, "De Cautionibus Matrimonialibus,"—*JP,* XIII (1933), 213.

Oesterle[62] and Toso[63] agree that the dispensation granted by the Holy Office in the case of an impediment of mixed religion or disparity of worship is executed *in forma commissoria.* Thus the effect of the dispensation according to the clear text of canon 38 is had at the moment of its execution. Oesterle and Toso do not see eye to eye upon the manner of action and the extent of action on the part of the executor. Oesterle seems to favor the opinion of Cappello who holds the dispensation from mixed religion and disparity of worship is granted *in forma commissoria voluntaria* whereby the execution or non-execution of the dispensation is left to the prudent and conscientious judgment of the executor himself (Canon 54, § 2). Thus, according to Oesterle, the effect of the dispensation is suspended until it is made operative by the executor. Toso, on the contrary, holds that when the dispensation is granted by the Holy Office, it is granted *in forma commissoria necessaria* and the executor must grant the dispensation with the few exceptions mentioned in canon 54, § 1. The distinction of the manner of execution, however, is of little moment, for canon 55 prescribing attention to the fulfillment or veracity of the essential clauses in the rescript is equally applicable to both methods of execution. Hence the executor who must execute the rescript as well as the free executor who sees it fit and proper to do so, must follow the norms of the rescript (canon 55) and observe the conditions set forth therein. But normally the conditions set forth in the rescript are simply the regular requirements of canon 1061. Not a word concerning the sincerity or insincerity of the promises in the nature of an essential condition for the validity of the dispensation is to be found. Moral certitude on the part of the executor is indeed required but not moral certainty which of necessity would imply the subjective sincerity of the promissors as a basis for the objective veracity of the outwardly manifested *cautiones.*

In concluding his article Oesterle offers a list of canons of the Code wherein the Church takes cognizance of internal defects. He thus seeks to prove that the Church herself does not consider the intention and sincerity of a man to be intangible and imper-

---

[62] *Art. cit.,* pp. 74-75.

[63] *Art. cit.,* pp. 210-211.

ceptible elements. It is significant, however, that no like canon which insists with equally decisive and expressive language on sincerity and good faith with regard to the giving of the *cautiones* can be advanced. If Oesterle's argument, then, is to have any value, it can be accepted only on his own implied assumption that the law of the Church suffers a *lacuna* in an all-important matter. To the present writer it appears that Oesterle's assumption does not correspond to actuality, for the simple reason that the profound solicitude of the Church in the matter of mixed marriages could not have found its full expression apart from the indication of a definitely perceivable norm regarding *all* the conditions and factors governing the concession of a *valid* dispensation from the impediments of mixed religion or of disparity of worship. The lack of an express indication correspondingly points to the lack of any requirement for subjective sincerity as a prerequired condition for the *validity* of the dispensation.

### D. *Argument from Jurisprudence*

Attention to the decisions given by the Holy See can provide but a negative proof, i.e., an argument *ex silentio,* that insincere *cautiones* do not of themselves invalidate the dispensation. "In the jurisprudence of the Holy Office mention is sometimes made of the moral certainty which both the one dispensing by delegated power and the executor *in forma commissoria* of the rescript of dispensation must acquire concerning *the sincerity of the guarantors pro presenti* and the faithful *fulfillment of the obligations pro futuro.* But nowhere is this *sincerity* said to be *objectively* necessary for the *validity of the dispensation.* Hence it is not required for validity (canon 19)."[54] The cases referred to by Park and Toso are contained in the following responses of the Holy Office: 1 aug. 1759; 22 dec. 1887; 29 apr. 1891; 22 dec. 1916; 14 ian. 1932.[55] The argument from these responses consists in noting

[54] Park, "Insincere Ante-Nuptial Guarantees,"—*ER,* XCI (1934), 458. Cf. also Toso, "De Cautionibus Matrimonialibus,"—*JP,* XIII (1933), 211-212.

[55] S.C.S.Off. (Cochinchin), 1 aug. 1759, ad 4—*Fontes,* n. 810; S.C.S.Off. (Victoriae Nyanzae), 22 dec. 1887, ad 1 et 5—*Fontes,* n. 1106; S.C.S.Off. (Pekin.), 29 apr. 1891, ad 2—*Fontes,* n. 1134; S.C.S.Off., decr. 22 dec. 1916, ad 1—*AAS,* IX (1917), 13; S.C.S.Off., decr. 14 ian. 1932—*AAS,* XXIV (1932), 25.

the silence of the Holy Office on the matter of *insincere* CAUTIONES. Indications pointed to possible and even probable insincerity in the guarantees; yet the Holy Office in no case pressed the question of sincerity, but disposed of the case *post factum* through the recommendation of remedies at law, through separation from bed and board, etc., but never through a dissolution of the marriage by a declaration of nullity in view of the probably or even certainly extant insincerity in the promises.

Oesterle[56] reviews the case of August 1, 1759, and attempts to show that there was no question of insincere guarantees at the start, but simply a change of will years later. The responses of the Holy Office (cited above in Oesterle's arguments) are offered by Oesterle in confirmation of his thesis. The object of the responses, however, in every instance concerns not *sincere* CAUTIONES, but *cautiones* as such, and the required moral certitude that they be sincere.

O'Donnell makes reference to a reply of the Holy Office[57] which, while not exacting an oath of the parties at all times, nevertheless demanded a serious promise (*promessa seria*) in order that the bishop might be able to acquire moral certitude (*certezza morale*). O'Donnell argues that moral certitude is the object to be gained; the serious promise must be one which reflects such gravity in the external forum as to warrant that certitude. To say that the reply contemplates the internal intention of the promissor is to add something without warrant to the reply itself.

The position which maintains that *insincere* CAUTIONES do not invalidate the dispensation has the strong support of at least one observation of the Sacred Roman Rota. The decision *"non constat de nullitate"* was rendered in a marriage case tried on the grounds of conditional consent. If the matrimonial consent was conditioned upon the existence of *true and sincere* CAUTIONES, then surely that condition had to be present if the marriage was to be

---

[56] "De Cautionibus Matrimonialibus,"—*JP,* XV (1935), 76-81.

[57] S.C.S.Off. (S. Germani), 17 feb. 1875—*Fontes,* n. 1039; cf. "Mixed Marriage Guarantees,"—*IER,* 5th Series, XVIII (1921), 411-418.

valid. Lacking the determination of such condition, the insincere *cautiones* alone did not invalidate the marriage.[58]

### *E. Argument from Concept of Moral Certitude*

Sincerity of the *cautiones* in mixed marriages is certainly what the Church wants and expects when she grants dispensations. There is no intention to underemphasize its importance. But is this sincerity required as an essential condition for a dispensation, so that the dispensation would have to be considered null if that sincerity was lacking? There is no canonical text upon which the contention of invalidity can be based. It is of little value to point to canons elsewhere in the Code simply because they legislate for the internal forum of conscience. This merely emphasizes the fact that, without a definite canon to require sincerity in the guarantees as a condition for a subsequent valid dispensation, insincere guarantees ought not to be considered as barring the way for a possible valid dispensation.

Canon 1061, § 1, 3° requires moral certitude that the guarantees will be fulfilled in the future. It is at least an implicit requirement that the same kind of moral certitude be present concerning the sincerity of the promises, for this sincerity is a primary consideration in its character of a means to achieve the desired fulfillment of the guarantees. But beyond this the law makes no additional demand for safeguarding the dictates of the natural divine law. The nature of moral certitude, its requirement in the bishop who dispenses, the common law requirement that "regularly" the *cautiones* are to be given in writing as well as the practical indications which the canonists offer on how one may acquire such moral certitude—a matter which will be given consideration later—all point rather to the issue of the ordinary's judgment upon the facts revealed to him or to the pastor, than to the objective correspondence of the internal intention of one

---

[58] "Quare, etiamsi pars acatholica ficte promittat, peccat utique, sed quia consensus alterius partis his promissionibus non subiicitur tanquam conditioni sine qua non, matrimonium validum nihilominus est." S.R.R. Nullitas Matrimonii, 11 aug. 1921, *coram* R.P.D. Francisco Solieri, dec. XXIII—*S.R.R. Decisiones,* XIII (1921), 214.

or both of the parties to the externally manifested *cautiones*. "The fundamental question concerning the validity of the dispensation is not whether fictitious promises are real promises or not, but whether the character of the parties, the circumstances of the case, and the very character of the promises given (in writing, orally, with an oath, etc.) justifies the judgment as to the sincerity and fulfillment of the *cautiones*."[59]

There is scarcely any question whether the word *certitudo* in canon 1061, § 1, 3° has the significance of "certitude" in English. The word denotes a subjective state of the mind rather than an objective status in fact. The latter notion attaches rather to the word "certainty." It is precisely for this reason that "certainty" is sometimes spoken of as an analogous certitude. Objective truth, ontological truth, the correspondence of a thing to the notes contained in its idea—all this is objective truth or *certainty*. Certitude, of course, must have some basis in reality. All those circumstances of place, time, person, event, character, etc., in a word, whatever prudent men take into consideration for the forming of a judgment—these are the criteria of moral certitude. In these a man may err inasmuch as he must base his judgment on considerations which in human nature are not absolutely constant but relatively variable, yet by way of general rule he will be correct. It has been seen that moral certitude in the wide sense, *in sensu lato* (imperfect certitude), which allows some latitude for error, nevertheless suffices for a prudent man to act and proves sufficient in the matter of certifying the character of the guarantees.

This doctrine is surely consistent with the demands of the Church in her discipline of the sacraments. The Church is satisfied to have moral certitude of the death of a former spouse to permit another marriage. Moral certitude provides a sufficient basis for the Holy See to grant a dispensation which makes possible the celebration of a new marriage when an existing union is recognized to be a *matrimonium ratum et non consummatum.* It is of course true that the parties are warned about the invalidity of the new marriage if the earlier union was in

[59] Schenk, *Mixed Marriages and Disparity of Cult*, pp. 250-251.

fact a ***matrimonium ratum et consummatum.*** The need of this is apparent from the fact that a Christian and sacramentally consummated marriage is beyond all possibility of dissolution through any declaration or dispensation that the Church may employ, for the natural law itself precludes every possibility of a new marriage while such a consummated union perdures.

Moral certitude of baptism guarantees the recognized validity of a later ordination. Moral certitude of the firm purpose of amendment on the part of a penitent establishes all needed authorization for an approved confessor to absolve in the sacrament of penance.

The question of the *cautiones* in mixed marriages is not unlike the question of the interpellations in the Pauline privilege case. Both factors are of ecclesiastical origin but both also rest upon a foundation supplied by the divine law. In both cases there must be present a moral certitude in the one who dispenses, lest the natural divine law be insufficiently safeguarded. Concerning the sincerity of the *cautiones* it is moral certitude, and not objective certainty, that the law demands; no further requirement is set up by the law of the Code as a condition intermediate to the moral certitude that the *cautiones* will be respected and fulfilled. The moral aspects of the problem, inasfar as they touch conscience and inasmuch as they connote the presence of sin, constitute separate considerations and involve distinct factors which lie outside of the scope of the present study.

## CHAPTER SEVEN

### CONTENT OF THE *Cautiones*

When formal *cautiones* were first introduced by the Church in order to protect the faith and morals of Catholic spouses and of their offspring against the dangers which threatened in the mixed marriages of the royalty, the promises themselves were lengthy contracts which resembled the diplomatic agreements of courts. With the extension of dispensations which implied the toleration of mixed marriages for the common people, these promises were simplified to hew closer to the bare essentials that would normally procure the requisite *cautelae* demanded by the natural divine law. A continued mitigation through papal decrees, letters, etc., of the number and kind of promises demanded of the non-Catholic as well as of the Catholic party to the marriage has finally resulted in the crystallization in the Code of Canon Law of the few essential promises exacted today by the common law.

Over and above the specifications of the *cautiones* contained in the Code, can faculties which are granted to ordinaries by the Holy See for the sake of empowering them to dispense from the impediments of mixed religion and disparity of worship further extend the content of the promises? Can particular law exact additional promises? What is the limit for such legislation? These and other allied questions will be considered in this chapter.

A methodical exposition of the content of the *cautiones* will be used in the treatment of the subject: 1) as it affects the Catholic party alone; 2) as it affects the non-Catholic party alone; and 3) as it affects both the Catholic and the non-Catholic parties conjointly in the promises which are required of both.

#### I PROMISE FROM THE CATHOLIC PARTY ALONE

Prior to the Code the Catholic party to a mixed marriage had to promise expressly that he would strive according to his best possible efforts (*pro viribus*) to procure the conversion of the non-Catholic party.[1] This promise was considered to be of such serious importance in the eyes of the Church that the granting of the dispensation was conditioned upon it. It was a strict *cautio*.[2]

Cappello indeed cites an instance in ecclesiastical law wherein the Church, due to opposition of the civil law in Prussia, refrained from exacting this promise from Catholics who entered mixed marriages in that country.[3] But the fact that the pastor and confessor, in lieu of a formal promise, were enjoined to warn Catholics of their grave obligation to seek the conversion of their consorts, and thus could substantially circumvent the purpose in the civil law of Prussia, signalizes this instance as an exception in method and form rather than in substance.

Since the Code this exception has become the law. No longer does the common law include the express promise of the Catholic to make an effort to procure the conversion of the non-Catholic among the *cautiones* as a condition for the validity of the dispensation. Hence no mention of it is to be found in canon 1061, which enunciates the various required conditions, but the reference to it is relegated to the following canon, wherein this effort on the part of the Catholic party is stressed in its nature of an obligation.[4]

The present law also introduces a significant change in its statement of the manner in which the conversion is to be sought.

---

[1] S.C. de Prop. Fide, litt. encycl., 11 mart. 1868: ". . . Catholicus ipse coniux teneri se sciat ad acatholicum *pro viribus* ab errore retrahendum."—*Fontes*, n. 4872; instr. (ad Archiep. Corcyren.), 3 ian. 1871, ad 3: ". . . et suscipiatur a parte catholica omnes curandi ut alteram acatholicam partem ad veram fidem unitatemque catholicam perducat."—*Fontes*, n. 1013; Gregorius XVI, litt. ap. "*Quas vestro*," 30 apr. 1841, n. 2: ". . . non modo ut coniux catholicus ab acatholico perverti non posset, quin potius ille teneri se sciret ad hunc pro viribus ab errore retrahendum . . ."; cf. also S.C. de Prop. Fide, instr. (ad Vic. Ap. Sveciae), 6 sept. 1785—*Fontes*, n. 4606.

[2] Feije, *De Imped. et Dispens. Matr.*, p. 446.

[3] *De Matrimonio*, P. I, 393, nota 12; cf. also S.R.R. *Nullitas Matrimonii*, 30 iun. 1910, *coram* R.P.D. Lega, dec. XXIII—*Rotae Decisiones*, II (1910), 219-237; Gasparri, *De Matrimonio*, I, 270.

[4] Canon 1062: Coniux catholicus obligatione tenetur conversionem coniugis acatholici prudenter curandi.

It stresses a prudent procedure (*prudenter*) for the fulfillment of this obligation in place of the more outright inculcation of duty (*pro viribus*) as expressed in the former law.[5] The new emphasis seems not only to be in accord with the result of tried methods of missionary activities and with the successful advance of pastoral apologetics, but appears also to harmonize more effectively than the stark expression of the former law with the express and pointed principle that no one be constrained to embrace the faith apart from his own direct desire to do so.[6]

The exclusion of the requirement of this promise on the part of the Catholic party from the enumeration of the conditions mentioned in canon 1061 does not mean that the obligation has ceased. It is a profound obligation of Christian charity arising from the natural law that men share with their neighbor the saving doctrine of Christ's Church, outside of which the Lord has not prepared any way that leads to salvation. This obligation remains constant despite the present change of legislation regarding the formerly required promise for the fulfillment of the obligation. It binds directly the conscience of the Catholic who lives in the close association of marital bonds with one who is not a member of the true faith. Since the time of the Code canonists have consistently noted the exclusion of the demand of this promise on the part of the Catholic from the canonically required *cautiones*, but they have also invariably insisted upon the retention of the obligation as it is found expressed in canon 1062, for the legislation of the Code on this point constitutes but the positive expression of a demand which is inherent in the natural law itself.[7] While the common law of the Code no longer exacts an

---

[5] "Quod praesertim praestabit vitae exemplo, caritate mansueta, precibus, consiliis monitisque opportunis."—Vromant, *De Matrimonio*, p. 139; ". . . it is an obligation which must be fulfilled 'prudently' that is, by good example, kindness and charity, prayer and advice given at the proper time."—Ter Haar, *Mixed Marriages and Their Remedies*, p. 78; cf. also Petrovits, *The New Church Law on Matrimony*, p. 119; Ayrinhac-Lydon, *Marriage Legislation*, p. 111.

[6] Canon 1351: Ad amplexandam fidem catholicam nemo invitus cogatur.

[7] Cappello, *De Matrimonio*, P. I, 393 and 403; Gasparri, *De Matrimonio*, I, 270; De Smet, *De Sponsalibus et Matrimonio*, pp. 444, 732; Blat, *De Rebus*, P. I, 561; Chelodi, *Ius Matrimoniale*, p. 69; Petrovits, *The New Church Law on Matrimony*, p. 119; Schenk, *Mixed Religion and Disparity of Cult*, p. 237.

express promise from the Catholic to seek the non-Catholic's conversion as an essential condition intermediate to the dispensation, an apostolic indult by virtue of which a bishop is enabled to dispense from the impediments of mixed religion and of disparity of worship may well do so.[8] Hence it is necessary to attend carefully to the clauses which are contained in the *formula* of the general indult or of the particular Apostolic rescript. The use of such words as *"si"* or *"dummodo"* when they appear in such *formulae,* are to be understood as introducing conditions upon the fulfillment of which depends the *validity of the dispensation.*[9]

In general the faculties which are granted to ordinaries exact only those conditions which are expressed in the common law as essential for the validity of the dispensation. Consistently the pre-Code indult for dispensations from disparity of worship included within the ambit of its *dummodo* clause the condition of the express promise of the Catholic to strive for the non-Catholic's conversion.[10]

Since the Code the demand of the same express promise as a condition requisite for the dispensation is excluded from the wording of the faculties granted by the Holy Office to ordinaries in the United States in order to enable them to dispense from the impediments of mixed religion and disparity of worship. While the express promise is no longer a part of the requirements, the

---

[8] A number of the canonists make the unconditional statement that particular indults or rescripts may call for such an express promise on the part of the Catholic. Cf. e.g., De Smet, *De Sponsalibus et Matrimonio,* p. 444, nota 2; Ayrinhac-Lydon, *Marriage Legislation,* p. 105.

[9] Canon 39: Conditiones in rescriptis tunc tantum essentiales pro eorundem validitate censentur, cum per particulas, *si, dummodo,* vel aliam eiusdem significationis exprimuntur.

[10] ". . . *dummodo* cautum omnino sit conditionibus ab Ecclesia praescriptis . . . de conversione conjugis infidelis pro viribus curanda . . ."—Cf. Konings-Putzer, *Commentarium in Facultates Apostolicas,* p. 335, and *ibid.,* p. 344, where the same condition is mentioned as qualifying the faculty to dispense from the impediment of mixed religion; Cappello, *De Matrimonio,* P. I, 400, where is quoted the decree of the Holy Office, June 21, 1912—*Fontes,* n. 1293. Chelodi (*Ius Matrimoniale,* p. 57) places both the Catholic's obligation to strive for the non-Catholic's conversion as well as the prohibition to give the matrimonial consent before a non-Catholic minister within the scope of the *"dummodo"* clause.

faculties do impose, relative to the one who dispenses, the necessity of bringing the knowledge of this obligation to the Catholic party. Since the faculties express this last condition by the use of the *ablative absolute,* the question naturally arises whether this form is to be considered in the same significance as *"si"* or *"dummodo,"* and consequently whether it introduces an essential condition for the validity of the dispensation.[11]

The statement of Gasparri that this latter obligation, namely, the necessity to inform the Catholic party of his duty to strive to convert the non-Catholic, is to be considered along with the *cautiones* themselves under the conditions introduced by the *dummodo* clause is somewhat disturbing.[12]

Since the Code the interpretation regarding the force of the ablative absolute has been greatly modified. Today the presumption stands that its use does not regularly imply the same significance as do the particles *"si"* and *"dummodo."* Consequently its use cannot invariably be regarded as introducing an essential condition. This doctrine without doubt reflects the common opinion of the authors who treat the first book of the Code.[13]

But this does not mean that the ablative absolute cannot, or is not used to express an essential condition, for the fact is well

---

[11] After indicating within the ambit of its *dummodo* clause the *cautiones* of which canon 1061 makes mention, the rescript of faculties continues: "*declarata* insuper parti catholicae *obligatione,* qua tenetur, prudenter curandi conversionem coniugis ad fidem catholicam."—Beste, *Introduction in Codicem,* Appendix (Allegatum I), p. 974. Cf. also Gasparri, *De Matrimonio,* II (Allegatum V), 437-441, for samples of *formulae* according to which the Holy Office grants dispensations in individual cases from the impediments of mixed religion and disparity of worship.

[12] "In formulis quae in Alleg. V referuntur, verbo *conditionum* comprehenduntur et *cautiones* de quibus supra, et *haec obligatio* coniugis catholici."—*De Matrimonio,* I, 270.

[13] Vermeersch-Creusen, *Epitome Iuris Canonici,* I, 145; Cicognani, *Canon Law,* p. 708; Van Hove, *Commentarium Lovaniense,* IV (*De Rescriptis*), 123; Ojetti, *Commentarium in Codicem Iuris Canonici* (4 vols., Romae: Apud Aedes Universitatis Gregorianae, 1927-1931), I, 215-216; Beste, *Introductio in Codicem,* p. 108; Michiels (*Normae Generales Juris Canonici,* 2 vols., Lublin, Polonia: Universitas Catholica, 1929, II, 211) states: ". . . communius tenetur formam ablativi absoluti *ex se* nunquam sufficere ad exprimendam conditionem pro validitate rescripti necessario servandam."

known that some essential conditions are thus expressed. While each indult or rescript, therefore, must bear the closest scrutiny in text and context, it is safe to accept the following norms on the use of the ablative absolute regarding the essential or accidental character of the condition it expresses: a) if the ablative absolute embraces a condition which is necessary in the very nature of the case, then the condition is of the same essential force as that which is inherent in the nature of the case; b) if the ablative absolute expresses a condition already prescribed by the common law, this condition derives its character from that of the common law and will be either essential or accidental in accordance with that law; c) finally, the ablative absolute may introduce a new condition, and then inasmuch as it is not expressed by such a particle as canon 39 prescribes, and insofar as there is no known *stylus Curiae Romanae* in its regard, this condition is to be considered accidental in character. These norms are recognized and approved by most of the canonists already cited when they treat the matter contained in the Code under the subject of rescripts.

Immediately one may apply the second norm to the question of the character of the condition placed in the ablative absolute in the faculties granted to ordinaries relative to dispensation from the impediments of mixed religion and disparity of worship. Since the obligation to pursue prudent measures for the conversion of the non-Catholic is not an essential condition of the common law for a valid dispensation (canon 1062), the expression of that condition by the form of the ablative absolute is not an essential but only an accidental condition.

In the exemplification of essential conditions the authors significantly leave unmentioned the condition under consideration when they speak about the faculties of ordinaries to dispense in the cases of mixed marriages. Michiels mentions only those conditions which are controlled by the use of the particle *"dummodo,"*[14] as also does Van Hove,[15] while Ojetti raises a doubt as to the true character of the condition that calls for the previous declaration to

[14] *Op. cit.*, II, 212.

[15] *Op. cit.*, IV, 125.

the Catholic party of his obligation prudently to bring about the conversion of the non-Catholic partner.[16] O'Neil reviews the entire phrase in the faculties, both the *dummodo* clause and the ablative absolute clause which is appended immediately after the semicolon within the sentence, but he points to only those conditions as essential which stand in relation to the particle *dummodo* that introduces them.[17] De Smet clearly states that the injunction of this obligation upon the Catholic no longer constitutes an essential condition for the dispensation.[18]

Additional confirmation of the position upholding the non-essential character of the ablative absolute clause in the faculties is had from a consideration of canon 66. This canon likens habitual faculties, which are conceded perpetually, or for a definite time, or for a certain number of cases, to privileges *praeter ius*.[19] Hence faculties of this kind do not fall under the restriction of a strict interpretation according to the demands of canon 50,[20] nor can canon 85 be advanced against a wide interpretation, for that canon is concerned explicitly with faculties conceded *for a certain case* and not with the habitual faculties here contemplated.

Thus it seems conclusive that the apostolic faculties granted to ordinaries for dispensing from impediments in mixed marriages are to receive a broad interpretation. Certainly the obligation to advise the Catholic party of his duty to strive for his consort's conversion to the faith would unduly restrict those faculties, were that obligation considered essential for a valid dispensation. Though the condition is expressed in the form of the ablative absolute, this fact alone is not a sufficient basis for so stringent an interpretation. Were the condition expressed by the particles

---

[16] *Op. cit.*, I, 129. Unfortunately the author did not live to treat this question more thoroughly in his proposed commentary on the sacraments.

[17] *Papal Rescripts of Favor*, pp. 114-115.

[18] *De Sponsalibus et Matrimonio*, pp. 444, 732.

[19] Canon 66: Facultates habituales quae conceduntur vel in perpetuum vel ad praefinitum tempus aut certum numerum casuum, accensentur privilegiis praeter ius.

[20] "In dubio, rescripta quae . . . adversantur legi in commodum privatorum . . . strictam interpretationem recipiunt; cetera omnia latam." Cf. Van Hove, *Commentarium Lovaniense*, V (*De Privilegiis*), pp. 161-162; Michiels, *Normae Generales Juris Canonici*, II, 441-442.

*"si"* or *"dummodo"* or by any other particle of like significance and juridic force, then there would be no question of its essential character.

Thus far consideration has been given to the text of the faculties *as it actually appears* in the indult to American ordinaries. To introduce a hypothetical question, it may here be stated that an apostolic indult could go so far as to demand, as an essential condition for the dispensation, the Catholic's express promise to strive to procure the non-Catholic's conversion, and yet in so doing would not contradict the present common law. A contradiction would indeed be present, if the common law expressly and explicitly forbade the demanding of such a promise as an essentially required condition for the validity of the dispensation. But even in this further hypothesis, though a factual contradiction would be inescapable, it would still be within the competence of the supreme authority of the Holy See, which is itself the juridic source of the common law, to run counter to that law by demanding in a particular indult the express promise of the Catholic as an essentially requisite condition for the valid granting of the dispensation. In reality the Code is silent on the matter of an express promise. It reiterates the former law solely on the point of the Catholic's obligation to seek the non-Catholic's conversion. An Apostolic indult, therefore, by introducing the essential necessity of an express promise to this effect, would not contradict the present common law juridically, but would simply go beyond it in its present demand.

The further question as to what may be prescribed by local ordinaries with regard to this obligation on the part of the Catholic must now be weighed. To what extent may local ordinaries go in particular law or in curial practice on the point of demanding a written promise that the Catholic will work prudently for the conversion of the non-Catholic spouse?

One thing is certain. Ordinaries must bring the knowledge of this obligation to the attention of the Catholic party. This is implied in canon 1062 and is explicitly mentioned in the clauses of the indult of the Quinquennial Faculties, though, as has been seen, it is not to be considered as an essential condition for the validity of their dispensation. While this is primarily a pastoral problem involving methods of instruction, etc., certain canonical inquiries may be made. May the ordinary exact an express promise from the Catholic to fulfill this obligation? May he demand it in writing? May he exact it *ad validitatem dispensationis?*

The authors who consider these questions are agreed that the ordinary can exact an express and even written promise of the Catholic to fulfill this obligation.[21] Certainly this view is tenable. Actually many of the bishops of the United States, either by diocesan law or simply in curial practice, do provide for a written promise of the Catholic party in this regard. In so doing they do not contradict the Code any more than would an Apostolic indult were it to insist upon such a written promise.

The question of the admissibility of demanding a written promise is hardly a matter for a merely hesitant admission, for it must be remembered that the local ordinary is within his competence to determine for his diocese the form in which the written *cautiones* normally required by the common law are to be given.[22] For if it be permitted him at all to add to the common law content of the *cautiones* by insisting on this promise of the Catholic, then it is certainly also his right to exact such additional guarantees in writing.

Whether the ordinary may so strongly insist upon this express promise of the Catholic that its refusal will render the dispensation invalid is another question. It appears that this is beyond the power of an ordinary.[23] The essential conditions for a valid

[21] "At ex tali silentio iuris communis non sequitur a parocho non esse inculcandam illam obligationem atque adeo non posse exigere *promissionem etiam scripto consignatam,* si iure particulari aut legitimo praescripto Ordinarii id cautum fuerit."—Wernz-Vidal, *Ius Matrimoniale,* pp. 191, 193-194, nota 31. Cf. also Chelodi, *Ius Matrimoniale,* p. 69, where he cites the Council of Salzburg which exacts a written promise of the Catholic.

[22] All due consideration is to be given, of course, to the fundamental requirements of canon 1061, § 2, of the Code, but equal attention must also be paid to the circumstances of time, place, and person in the diocese. It is these circumstances that will suggest the form best suited for acquiring the necessary moral certitude that the promises will be fulfilled.

[23] "Imo probati auctores non prohibent quin, hac de re, *veram promissionem* exigat, *dummodo* non eam requirat sub poena denegandae dispensationis."—Payen, *De Matrimonio,* I, 658. Cf. also *ibid.,* pp. 666-667, where

dispensation are recounted in canon 1061 of the Code. The Catholic's promise to strive for the non-Catholic partner's conversion is not included among these conditions. To place it once more among the essential conditions for a valid dispensation is a matter which rests within the province of the Holy See, and not within that of the local ordinary. It has been seen that an Apostolic indult may decree that this condition must be met before a valid dispensation can be granted, but before any such insistence be acknowledged, it must be clear beyond a doubt that the clauses of the indult expressly mention this condition as an essential requisite in the approved form of canon 39 or in some similar unmistakable language. The faculties which are presently granted to the local ordinaries of the United States do not demand such a condition *ad validitatem.* Were a local ordinary to insist arbitrarily upon demanding this promise from the Catholic as an essential condition, he would demand more than the Holy See demands in this regard, and would be restricting the exercise of the right of the parties to marry in accordance with the Church's willingness to dispense in the cases of mixed religion and disparity of worship. Such a procedure, *in effect,* would approximate the establishment of a new impediment which is expressly reserved to the Holy See.[24] Such a rigid requirement of the Catholic's promise would not be unlike a diocesan statute which insisted upon confession and communion as a prerequired condition for permitting the contracting parties to enter marriage. Such a statute would offend against the more lenient requirement of the common law[25] and, in the

---

Payen excludes from the concern of the pastor, after the mixed marriage has taken place (canon 1064), the matter of the Catholic's promise to strive for the spouse's conversion.

[24] Canon 1038, § 2: Eidem supremae auctoritati privative ius est alia impedimenta matrimonium impedientia vel dirimentia pro baptizatis constituendi per modum legis sive universalis sive particularis. Cf. also canon 1040. Diocesan custom of demanding such an essential condition would be interdicted by the express terms of canon 1041: Consuetudo novum impedimentum inducens aut impedimentis existentibus contraria reprobatur.

[25] Canon 1033: . . . [sponsos] vehementer adhortetur [parochus] ut ante matrimonii celebrationem sua peccata diligenter confiteantur, et sanctissimam Eucharistiam pie recipiant. Cf. Ayrinhac-Lydon, *Marriage Legislation,* p. 48; Chelodi, *Ius Matrimoniale,* p. 23; Gasparri, *De Matrimonio,* I, 118; Cappello, *De Matrimonio,* P. I, 233-234.

opinion of at least two authors, would be tantamount to introducing a new prohibitive impediment.[26] What is true with reference to canon 1033 in this regard is equally true with reference to canon 1062.

It may be argued, however, that the circumstances of a given case may induce a bishop to insist upon an express promise from the Catholic party that he strive for the conversion of the non-Catholic, in order to acquire for himself the *required moral certitude* that the *cautiones* are given sincerely and will be fulfilled in future. In such a contingency the essential requirement of the canon that the bishop have the requisite moral certitude may be fully achieved only with the presence of such an express promise. Although the validity of this reasoning in jurisprudence cannot be effectively questioned, yet the hypothetical circumstances of such a case seem, to say the least, to be extremely far-fetched.

Here it will not be amiss to summarize. The obligation to seek the conversion of the non-Catholic spouse is a profound obligation in charity which arises from the natural law and besides is expressly stressed in canon 1062 of the Code. An express promise of the fulfillment of this obligation, however, is no longer to be considered one of the *cautiones* of the common law, essential for the dispensation from the impediment of mixed religion or of disparity of worship. A particular indult or rescript of the Holy See may demand such a promise as a condition for a valid dispensation. One must look to the clauses of the indult to determine this question. Indults granting faculties to the ordinaries of the United States to dispense from these impediments actually do *not* include the demand of such an express promise, or even the notification of this obligation in charity on the part of the Catholic among the essential conditions for the valid use of these faculties. It seems quite conclusive that, were an ordinary to include the demand of such an express promise from the Catholic among the essential conditions for the valid granting of the dispensation, he would be overreaching his power by demanding more than that which the Holy See alone can demand, inasmuch as the Holy See has exclusive authority and competence

[26] De Smet, *De Sponsalibus et Matrimonio*, p. 161; Payen, *De Matrimonio*, I, 387-388.

in determining the limits within which the celebration of Christian marriage is either prohibited or foredoomed to nullity.

### II PROMISES FROM THE NON-CATHOLIC PARTY ALONE

Before the Council of Trent one of the conditions upon which the Church permitted marriage between a Catholic and a non-Catholic was the obtaining of a promise of conversion from the non-Catholic party or his actual renunciation of heresy and the insisting upon his profession of faith. This condition gave way under the breakdown of Christian civil authority and the juridic recognition of other churches which resulted from the "Reformation." In the period of time between the Council of Trent and the Code of Canon Law, the non-Catholic wishing to marry a Catholic had to promise, among other things, that he would in no way interfere with the free exercise of the Catholic's religion. Generally that promise had to be attended with an oath and given in the presence of several witnesses. No longer was conversion or the profession of faith demanded.

With some mitigation regarding the form and manner in which it is to be exacted, the promise by the non-Catholic to obviate all danger of perversion from the Catholic spouse is now received into the Code, as an essential part of the *cautiones*.[27] There is no question of the essential condition which this promise entails for a valid dispensation. Its inclusion as an essential condition in canon 1061 after the particle *nisi,* as well as its express mention in the Apostolic indult of the Holy Office after the particle *dummodo,* places the essential requirement of this promise beyond all question.[28]

The wording of the canon is sufficiently general to be applicable to a host of particular details. "It implies the removal of every obstacle to the observance of all the obligations of the marital

[27] Canon 1061, § 1, 2°: Ecclesia super impedimento mixtae religionis non dispensat *nisi* cautionem praestiterit coniux acatholicus de amovendo a coniuge catholico perversionis periculo. . . . Cf. also canon 1071.

[28] "dummodo . . . ipse R.P.D. Ordinarius moraliter certus sit easdem [cautiones] impletum iri, scilicet: ex parte nupturientis acatholici de amovendo a parte catholica perversionis periculo . . ."—Beste, *Introductio in Codicem,* Appendix (Allegatum I), p. 974.

state which the parties wish to enter; a removal of any inducement to immoral practices which in a certain sense would be equivalent to a contumely of the Creator. Every hindrance must be removed from the Catholic's fulfillment of such duties as the attendance at Mass on Sundays and Holy Days of obligation; the reception of the sacraments; the observance of the laws of fast and abstinence; the Catholic's reasonable support of the Church."[29]

The negative connotation of this promise (*de amovendo*) must not be unduly emphasized. While the ante-nuptial agreements in many curiae are so edited as to be open to a strictly negative interpretation of this promise by the non-Catholic,[30] situations will arise, in the multiform occurrences of every-day life, wherein positive action by the non-Catholic is virtually demanded of him lest he interfere with the Catholic's religious practices. The non-Catholic may be requested to call a priest for his dying Catholic spouse; the non-Catholic bread-winner may be asked by the Catholic for money to make a reasonable offering to the Church. Thus positive acts may, at times, come within the scope of the promise of the non-Catholic if and when his/her refraining from such an act would interfere with the Catholic's practice of her/his religion.

It has been seen that the phrase *perversionis periculo* would be unduly and unreasonably restricted were it made to apply only to matters which involve a denial or loss of faith. Faith and morals are so intimately related that an interference with one frequently involves an interference with the other. The removal of the "danger of perversion", therefore, entails not only the refraining from words or acts which would ensnare a Catholic and try his faith, but also whatever would interfere with the reasonable and appointed practices of Catholic morals and Catholic liturgical worship. One can readily see how reasonable is the regulation in many dioceses which prescribes a certain number of instruc-

---

[29] Schenk, *Mixed Religion and Disparity of Cult,* p. 236. Cf. also Ayrinhac-Lydon, *Marriage Legislation,* p. 106; Ter Haar, *Mixed Marriages and Their Remedies,* pp. 17-18; 82.

[30] E.g. "The party of the first part [non-Catholic] further promises that he/she shall *in no way interfere* with the party of the second part in the free exercise of her/his religion," or, "I promise on my word of honor that I *will not* in any way *hinder* or obstruct the said [Catholic party] in the exercise of his/her religion . . ."

tions to be given to the parties contemplating a mixed marriage. The zealous pastor and assistant will make use of these instructions to review the essential doctrines of the Catholic Faith and the moral obligations of a Catholic life. How can a non-Catholic be expected to cooperate with the Catholic in the fulfillment of these obligations unless he knows their nature, importance, and extent?

### III PROMISES FROM BOTH SPOUSES CONJOINTLY

It has always been the conscious concern of the Church that the faith of the offspring of a mixed marriage be not placed in jeopardy. The experience and observation of the pastors of souls pay tribute to that concern in bearing first-hand evidence of the great leakage from the Church as a result of mixed marriages. One missionary has said that nine out of ten mixed marriages result in loss of faith in the first or second generations.

The Church's law always has reflected that conscious concern. It has made every effort through *opportune* CAUTIONES to safeguard the faith and morals of the Catholic party who ventures upon such a marriage and of the children who are born of that marriage.

Prior to the Code the non-Catholic party was asked to promise solemnly that all the children of either sex born of their proposed marriage would be baptized and educated in the Catholic religion alone. Usually this promise had to be accompanied with an oath.[31] It was only occasionally that the Catholic party was asked to make the same promise regarding the offspring. While the burden of this obligation toward the children of a mixed marriage generally

---

[31] Cf. e.g., Greg. XVI, litt. ap. "*Quas vestro,*" 30 apr. 1841—*Fontes,* n. 497; Greg. XVI, litt. ap. "*Non sine gravi,*" 23 maii, 1846—*Fontes,* n. 503; Faculties granted to bishops in France by Pius IX in 1858—*NRT,* XV (1883), 529-530; instr. S.C.S.Off., (ad Archiep. Scopien.), 15 nov. 1882—*Fontes,* n. 1074, wherein Catholics who pretended to be Mohammedans were expected to make a public profession of their faith, and under oath to give *cautiones* safeguarding the Catholic education of their children, before they were permitted to marry another Catholic; S.C.S.Off., instr. (ad omnes Ep. Ritus Orient.), 12 dec. 1888—*Fontes,* n. 1112.

lay upon the Catholic party, it was perhaps assumed that the intention of the Catholic parent would naturally be to seek the Catholic baptism and education of the children.

### *A. "Uterque Coniux"*

The present Code demands explicitly of both the non-Catholic and the Catholic parties to the marriage a strict *cautio* with regard to the Catholic baptism and training of the offspring. This is clear law according to canon 1061, § 1, 2°,[32] and forms one of the essential conditions as expressed in the Holy Office's rescript of faculties to American ordinaries for dispensing in case of mixed marriages, whether the impediment be one of mixed religion or of disparity of worship.[33] Hence it is an essential condition for a valid dispensation in mixed religion and in disparity of worship since the advent of the Code that the Catholic as well as the non-Catholic party give this promise. It is the parties themselves that must make this promise. It will not suffice that the parents of the parties give the *cautiones* in their stead.[34]

The absence of the signature of the Catholic party on the *cautio*, however, will not immediately constitute full proof that the Catholic party did not furnish the guarantee required by law. In many cases it is probable, or at least possible, that such a guarantee was exacted orally of the Catholic party by the priest. Such may well be brought to light through an investigation and interrogation of the priest, of the non-Catholic party, and even of the Catholic party himself. Doheny, in expressing this very opinion, states that such a case "cannot be summarily declared invalid nor can the case be hastily decided under the provisions of canon 1990."[35]

---

[32] "Ecclesia . . . non dispensat nisi cautionem praestiterit *uterque coniux* de universa prole catholice tantum baptizanda et educanda."

[33] "dummodo prius regulariter . . . cautum omnino sit conditionibus ab Ecclesia requiritur, . . . scilicet . . . *ab utroque contrahente* de universa prole utriusque sexus in catholicae religionis sanctitate omnino baptizanda et educanda."—Beste, *Introductio in Codicem,* Appendix (Allegatum I), p. 974.

[34] Cf. Schenk, *Mixed Religion and Disparity of Cult,* p. 237.

[35] *Canonical Procedure in Matrimonial Cases,* p. 449.

The recent response of the Holy Office bears out the opinion that the absence of the Catholic's signature is not sufficient of itself for regarding the granted dispensation as invalid.[86] The response goes so far as to admit even the implicit *cautiones* of the parties as a sufficient fulfillment of the condition for a valid dispensation and explains that implicit *cautiones* consist in such acts from which it may be concluded in the external forum that the obligation of fulfilling the *cautiones* is sufficiently known by the parties and firmly accepted for execution. The response furthermore indicates that if the conditions of canon 1990 are certainly fulfilled, then the summary process may be employed for the judgment concerning the invalidity of the disparate marriage. It is pointed out by Roelker that if a dispensation has been granted, at once the use of canon 1990 for establishing a judgment concerning the valid or invalid status of such a disparate marriage is precluded.[87] It appears equally conclusive, however, that if the dispensation is proved to have been invalid, it is equivalent to no dispensation at all, and the use of the summary procedure of canon 1990 can be admitted.[88]

The reply of the Holy Office applies a *post factum* norm for judging about the validity of a marriage celebrated between a Catholic and one certainly not baptized, and is not to be construed as an instruction on the manner in which the *cautiones* may be obtained with a view to receiving the necessary dispensation.

### B. *"De Universa Prole"*

The language of canon 1061, § 1, 2° leaves no doubt that all the children of both sexes are comprised in the *cautio* regarding

---

[86] *AAS,* XXXIII (1941), 294; cf. *supra,* pp. 55-56.

[87] "Decrees and Decisiones,"—*The Jurist,* II (1942), 59-60.

[88] Payen (*De Matrimonio,* III, 575) considers this very case of a dispensation granted for disparity of worship when the *cautiones* were not obtained from the parties and clearly states that such an invalid dispensation is equivalent to no dispensation. Cf. also Mahoney, "Roman Documents,"—*Clergy Review,* XXI (1941), 302. Mahoney is of the opinion that one "could rarely be certain that the dispensation was invalidly given, owing to the sufficiency of an 'implied' guarantee. Accordingly, the conditions for the summary process of canons 1990-1992 will rarely be verified."

Catholic baptism and education. Against such a law no custom or civil law statute can in any way effectively invoke the agency of legal prescription so as to protect and make enforceable any pacts or agreements in line with which the boys may be reared in the religion of their father, and the girls in the religion of their mother.

There is some question, however, as to the extent of meaning to be connected with the phrase *"universa prole."* Neither in canon 1061, §1, nor in canon 1065, § 2, does this phrase receive any definite qualification. Consequently it has been a matter of discussion among canonists as to whether this phrase is to be understood to include: 1. only the children yet to be born of the proposed marriage; 2. also the children born of the couple in concubinage or in a putative marriage; 3. solely the children of the Catholic party from a former marriage; 4. also the children of the non-Catholic from a former marriage; 5. the children of a former mixed marriage of either of the two parties; 6. the adopted children of either of the two parties.

1-2. The first and obvious sense of the words *"de universa prole"* embraces the children *to be born* of the proposed mixed marriage. These are so necessarily comprised in the *cautio*, that, if the subsequent dispensation is to stand as valid, then assurance must be had through moral certitude that all without exception will be baptized and reared as Catholics. While all the authors were agreed upon this matter,[39] their opinions varied on the question as to whether children already born of a couple now seeking to be married *in facie Ecclesiae* were also to be included in the strict *cautio*. This matter of divergent opinion arose as a result of a very general response given by the Holy Office in 1891 to some highly specific queries on the extent of the *cautiones*.[40] As a consequence, a number of canonists held that children already born of a couple should be included in the *cautio* in the same manner as the children to be born in future.[41] Even Gasparri was of

[39] Cf. e.g., Gasparri, *De Matrimonio*, I, 266; Payen, *De Matrimonio*, I, 654; Ayrinhac-Lydon, *Marriage Legislation*, p. 106.

[40] S.C.S.Off. (Leopolien.), 18 mart. 1891—*Fontes*, n. 1132.

[41] O'Neil, "Extent of Guarantees in Mixed Marriages,"—*IER*, 5th Series, XXIII (1924), 416-417; Konings-Putzer, *Commentarium in Facultates Apostolicas*, pp. 336-337; Vlaming, *Praelectiones Iuris Matrimonii*, I, 190-

this opinion, although he recommended that only such means of conversion be employed with regard to children no longer without the complete use of their reason as were compatible with their own freedom of action in adopting the Catholic faith.[42] Vromant seems to have been alone in opposing this opinion, for he included in the strict *cautio* only children *to be born* in future and explicitly excluded all others.[43]

A recent response of the Holy Office now places this matter beyond further debate. Because of its definitiveness the entire response received by cablegram by the National Catholic Welfare Conference News Service, is here reproduced:

> Citta del Vaticano
> Feb. 5, 1942.
>
> TO HOLY OFFICE WAS SUBMITTED DOUBT IF CAUTION REQUIRED BY CANON LAW ON CATHOLIC EDUCATION OF SONS BORN FROM MIXED MARRIAGE REFERS ONLY TO SONS TO BE BORN OR ALSO TO SONS ALREADY BORN PREVIOUSLY TO MIXED MARRIAGE IF THEY EXIST. HOLY OFFICE REPLIED WITH DECREE APPROVED BY POPE SAYING CAUTION REFERS ONLY TO SONS TO BE BORN AFTER MIXED MARRIAGE BUT EXPLAINS THAT INTENTION IS THAT COUPLE TO MARRY WITH MIXED MARRIAGE MUST BE SERIOUSLY INFORMED ON THEIR GRAVE OBLIGATION BY DIVINE RIGHT, OF EDUCATING IN CATHOLIC RELIGION ALSO SONS BORN PREVIOUSLY MIXED MARRIAGE IF THEY EXIST.
>
> PUCCI.[44]

---

191; Anonymous writer, "The Promises in Mixed Marriages 'De Prole Jam Nata'"—*ER,* LXXIV (1926), 630-632. Payen (*De Matrimonio,* I, 654, 823) extends the strict *cautio* to embrace children already born of the couple now proposing marriage as well as children born of either party in a former mixed marriage wherein the *cautiones* were not observed. Cf. also Schenk, *Mixed Religion and Disparity of Cult,* pp. 243-244.

[42] *De Matrimonio,* I, 266.

[43] "Collatis documentis S. Sedis, nobis videtur probabile, cautionem per se non respicere nisi prolem nascituram, non vero prolem iam natam."—*De Matrimonio,* p. 134.

[44] *AAS,* XXXIV (1942), 22. Cf. *The Jurist,* II (1942), 185-186.

No longer will there be reason to doubt whether children already born to a couple who now seek to be married are to be included in the *cautio.* The authoritative response restricts the application of the words *"universa prole"* to children *to be born* after the mixed marriage. The inclusion in the *cautio* of children already born to a couple would assuredly be demanding more than the Holy See in this matter. The only avenue open for further content in the pre-nuptial guarantees will be found in exceptional cases by way of the essential requirement of the presence of the canonical moral certitude. Hence if a bishop truly felt that the only way in which he could have moral certitude of the fulfillment of the *cautiones* with regard to children to be born of a particular couple was to include in the *cautiones* children already born to them, clearly the *cautiones* would have to be extended to embrace even these. How often a practical case of that kind will arise, will remain to be seen.

The intention of the Holy Office that the couple about to enter a mixed marriage be seriously informed of their grave obligation in the face of the divine law to educate in the Catholic religion also other children born previously to the mixed marriage would include primarily children already born of this very couple. No express promise in this matter is required of the parties. Neither can the inculcation of this obligation be considered an essential condition for a valid dispensation. The manner of fulfilling this serious obligation will be a pastoral problem which may vary with the individual case. Certainly, if the children are already adults, this obligation will not assume the serious character which it obtains in the event that the children are still infants or at least under parental control. Children who have reached the use of reason and are old enough to make their own judgment in a matter of this kind will not be treated in the same manner as infants entirely dependent in religious affairs upon the judgment of the parents.

3. The distinctions just mentioned are applicable as well to the children of the Catholic party alone if they were born of an earlier union and are not yet baptized, though they will be under the care of the Catholic parent in his or her proposed marriage with a non-Catholic party. The Catholic parent must be seriously

warned of the incumbent grave obligation to rear in the Catholic religion all the unbaptized children which were born previously to the contemplated marriage with the non-Catholic party. And this warning must be made relative also to those previously born children which may already have received baptism, for in both cases the duty is one which derives from the divine law itself concerning which the Church can exercise no other authority than that of calling for its fulfillment. But the lack of imparting such information and of administering such a warning does not invalidate the dispensation for the contemplated marriage between the Catholic and the non-Catholic. If the declaration which must be made to the Catholic party concerning the obligation to use prudent measures for the conversion of the non-Catholic party does not constitute an essential condition for a subsequent valid dispensation, then with equal if not with greater reason, the inculcation of the obligation to provide a Catholic training for the previously born children of the Catholic party is not to be considered as essential for a valid dispensation. The question of the lawfulness of granting a dispensation when such a warning has not been given is a matter separate and distinct from that which concerns the validity of the dispensation. The sole assurance that the dispensation can be granted validly does not at all imply that it can also be granted lawfully. Cases could easily arise in which an ordinary would have to abstain from granting a desired dispensation lest scandal ensue, or lest his action of dispensing link him with the Catholic party in the latter's foreknown repudiation of the obligation to rear in the Catholic faith those children which were born previously to the marriage for which the dispensation is being granted.

4-5. The obligation of the divine law regarding the Catholic baptism and education of children grows less pronounced and less pressing when one considers the children born of the non-Catholic party alone in a former marriage. Indeed if the former marriage was one between two non-Catholics there seems to be no obligation whatsoever entailed by the present nupturients except that which is prompted by charity and good common sense. The obligation seems more pointed however, touching children who were born to the non-Catholic party in a former mixed marriage. For if *cautiones* were not observed in a former mixed marriage, there may be solid basis for doubt of future fulfillment of *cautiones* now being procured.

6. The authors who treat this problem do not touch the question of a child who is adopted by the parties of a mixed marriage. This question will seldom arise at the time the parties furnish the *cautiones* for couples rarely enter marriage with the premeditated purpose of adopting a child. Even if such were the case, the clear text of the recent response of the Holy Office cannot be interpreted in such a way as to include children to be adopted. In matters of validity in law only those conditions are necessary which are expressly or equivalently required. If it is known at the time of the marriage that children will be adopted, certainly such children need not be given more consideration in the obligation of their Catholic baptism and education than would be given with regard to children already born of the couple before their proposed mixed marriage. Certainly children adopted after the mixed marriage who were not within the prospective intention of the parties at the time of their marriage can hardly be subject to *cautiones* relative to a dispensation for the said marriage. At most, such children will come within the scope of the obligation of the divine law in so far as it binds parents to care for the spiritual birth and welfare of their adopted children as they would of their very own.

### C. *"Catholice tantum Baptizanda et Educanda"*

Exclusive Catholic baptism and education of the children as prescribed in canon 1061 precludes any double ceremony of baptism, one in the Catholic religion and the other in a non-Catholic religion. The present phrase precludes, moreover, simultaneous or consecutive education in any religion other than the Catholic faith, and outlaws any contrary pacts the parties may secretly have made regarding the baptism and education of their children. Indeed, such pacts are entered upon not only illicitly, but of their very nature they cannot exercise any morally binding force.[45]

[45] Gasparri, *De Matrimonio*, I, 266. Such pacts, however, do not of themselves affect the validity of the disparate marriage, for as long as the dispensing ordinary has derived a prudent moral certitude from the furnished *cautiones*, and this moral certitude is present when he dispenses, his dispensation *must* be regarded fully valid in its desired effect.

Moreover, if the marriage is contracted with such an agreement, be it done explicitly or only implicitly, the Catholic incurs an excommunication by force of canon 2319, § 1, 2°. Again the fulfillment of such a pact by offering one's children to a non-Catholic minister for baptism or by sending them to a school whose purpose it is to impart training and instruction in a non-Catholic religion, occasions for the Catholic the same censure of excommunication as enacted in canon 2319, § 1, 3° and 4°. In addition such a Catholic becomes suspect of heresy in view of the law contained in canon 2319, § 2.

The obligations assumed by the parties to a mixed marriage imply that they will have their newly born children baptized as soon as possible in the Catholic Church,[46] that they will aid in the preparation of the children for their first confession and communion, and see to their catechetical instruction, normally in a Catholic school,[47] and that they will cooperate with the pastor in having the children confirmed in due time.[48] It is only in circumstances wherein attendance at a Catholic school is impossible that the use of any other means for their Catholic education may be tolerated.[49]

### D. *Law of Canon 1063*

> Canon 1063, § 1: Etsi ab Ecclesia obtenta sit dispensatio super impedimento mixtae religionis, coniuges nequeunt, vel ante vel post matrimonium coram Ecclesia initum, adire quoque, sive per se sive per procuratorem, ministrum acatholicum uti sacris addictum, ad matrimonialem consensum praestandum vel renovandum.

The content of this law, which forbids the contractants of mixed marriages (canon 1071) to appear before a non-Catholic minister in his capacity and status of a minister of religion, either personally or by proxy, for the purpose of giving or renewing matrimonial consent, is but a specific application of the general principle

[46] Canon 770. Cf. Cappello, *De Matrimonio,* P. II, 228.
[47] Canons 860; 906; 1113; 1335; 1372, § 2-1374.
[48] Canon 787.
[49] Canon 1374.

which bars every Catholic from partaking in non-Catholic rites and ceremonies. Such participation in the rites of heretics is forbidden to the Catholic by the divine law itself, since it involves at least an implicit profession of heresy or schism.[50] The same prohibition finds express mention in the Code of Canon Law[51] and in the case of marriage is fortified with a penal sanction through the infliction of a *latae sententiae* excommunication which for its absolution is reserved to the ordinary.[52] In addition this law carries with it its own sanction in paragraph two of canon 1063[53] which forbids the pastor to assist at a marriage wherein he knows this law will be violated or even has already been violated. Such interdicted assistance will assuredly impress upon the contractants the seriousness of the ecclesiastical law which forbids participation by Catholics in non-Catholic rites.

Serious as is this prohibition, it is not made a part of the content of the *cautiones* by the common law, and an express promise not to offend against this law is not required. The indult of faculties granted to ordinaries in the United States for dispensing in the cases of mixed marriages make explicit mention of this prohibition, but it is placed outside and beyond the control of the *dummodo* clause which introduces the conditions which must be verified for the valid use of the faculties. There is no question either of the use of an ablative absolute. There is simply the injunction that the contracting parties be warned to observe the requirement of canon 1063, § 1.[54]

An Apostolic indult, however, may include this prohibition among the conditions which are designated as essential for a valid dis-

[50] S.C.S.Off. (ad Ep. Osnabrugen.), 17 feb. 1864—*Fontes,* n. 976; S.C.S.Off., instr. (ad omnes Ep. Ritus Orient.), 12 dec. 1888—*Fontes,* n. 1112; Benedict XIV, *De Synodo Dioecesana,* Lib. VI, cap. 7, n. 2; Cappello, *De Matrimonio,* P. I, 403-404; Ayrinhac-Lydon, *Marriage Legislation,* p. 112.

[51] Canon 1258, § 1: Haud licitum est fidelibus quovis modo active assistere seu partem habere in sacris acatholicorum.

[52] Canon 2319, § 1, 1°.

[53] "Si parochus certe noverit sponsos hanc legem violaturos esse vel iam violasse, eorum matrimonio ne assistat, nisi ex gravissimis causis, remoto scandalo et consulto prius Ordinario."

[54] Cf. Beste, *Introductio in Codicem,* Appendix (Allegatum I), p. 974, for the text in this faculty.

pensation, just as it may exact for the validity of the dispensation an express promise on the part of the Catholic to strive for the non-Catholic's conversion.[55] Hence, one must study the terms of the indult.

While the authors observe that a *cautio* regarding the prohibition to go before a non-Catholic minister is not demanded in the Code, they are in agreement that an ordinary may exact such a promise if he sees fit to do so.[56] Indeed, some ordinaries have seen fit to include within the ante-nuptial agreements for the Catholic party alone, or for both parties conjointly a promise not to offend against this prescription. Since, however, the common law does not exact such a promise as an essential condition for the dispensation, it is quite certain that neither can an ordinary. By doing so he would be exacting more of the parties than does the Holy See. The ordinary, on the other hand, is charged with obtaining for himself a moral certitude that the regular canonical *cautiones* will be fulfilled in the future. It may well be that an ordinary, in a given case, may rest that moral certitude upon a sincere promise that the parties, or the Catholic party alone will not break the law of the Church in this important matter. It may

[55] Wernz-Vidal (*Ius Matrimoniale*, pp. 198-199, nota 40) indicates that ever since the instruction of the Holy Office, Feb. 17, 1864, the Holy Office customarily appends this condition as essential to the grant of a valid dispensation. Gasparri (*De Matrimonio*, II, 437-444) does not corroborate this statement in the formularies which he reproduces, not even in the case of intermarriage between Catholic and Mohammedan. Ojetti (*Commentarium in Codicem Iuris Canonici*, I, 218-219) quotes the clause of the Sacred Penitentiary which includes this prohibition among the essential conditions, but he himself raises a doubt as to its essential character. Van Hove (*Commentarium Lovaniense*, IV [*De Rescriptis*], pp. 125-126) as well as Chelodi (*Ius Matrimoniale*, pp. 57; 70) limit the essential character of this condition to the actual intention of the parties to the marriage. Thus if the parties have the intention of presenting themselves before a non-Catholic minister to pronounce their matrimonial consent, and that intention was present at the time the dispensation was granted, Van Hove and Chelodi would consider the dispensation invalid, even if the parties did not carry out their sinister intention.

[56] Schenk, *Mixed Religion and Disparity of Cult*, p. 258, note 6; De Smet, *De Sponsalibus et Matrimonio*, pp. 444; 732; Wernz-Vidal, *Ius Matrimoniale*, p. 193, nota 31; Vermeersch-Creusen, *Epitome Iuris Canonici*, II, 233.

stand as a test of the strength and sincerity of the *cautiones* furnished by the parties. In such circumstances, although the indult does not exact this promise as an essential condition, undoubtedly the ordinary must do so. This is not to be considered a regular norm, but only the exceptional case. The obtaining of such a promise in such a case is in effect reducible and tantamount to the use of an essentially requisite means for gaining the moral certitude which is needed by the one who dispenses. While such a promise, therefore, is not necessary of itself for the validity of the dispensation, it may in exceptional circumstances become an indispensable condition without which moral certitude could not be achieved.

### *E. Corollary*

The principles heretofore considered also apply to other promises which ordinaries are wont to include in the prenuptial guarantees.

1. Some pre-nuptial agreements are so drawn as to include the phrase "in a Catholic school wherever possible" in connection with the promise of the parties that they will educate their children in the Catholic religion alone. This condition is not exacted by the Holy See, nor is it found mentioned in the canon on the *cautiones.* The common law, however, in canon 1373 and 1374 explicitly requires religious instruction for youth and forbids Catholic children to go to non-Catholic or neutral schools. The ordinary alone may judge under what circumstances the attendance at other schools may be tolerated. Some ordinaries have considered this matter so serious that they have declared it a reserved case for parents to refuse the sending of their children to the Catholic schools. Faculties to absolve such parents in confession have been withdrawn from the priests in some dioceses and the absolution is reserved to the ordinary.[57]

The duty of attendance at Catholic schools is a doubly serious matter in the case of children which are born of mixed marriages. Particularly when the non-Catholic party is the mother of the

---

[57] This discipline obtains, for example in the Archdiocese of Milwaukee.

family is there danger of neglect in the religious training of the very young children. The cradle of a man's Catholicism must normally be sought at his mother's knee.

Ordinaries are within their rights, therefore, in adding to the ante-nuptial agreements a clause which pertains to the attendance at a Catholic school. Should they further consider that only through this medium they can assure themselves with moral certitude that the children will be given a Catholic education, then such a clause can be considered as introducing *an essential condition for a valid dispensation.* Parties who do not hesitate to make use of the ordinary and accepted means for some specific purpose will usually be ready and willing to make the promise that they will procure the proper religious education of their children by sending them to an available Catholic school for in most instances the Catholic school is the recognized ordinary means for gaining a well-grounded training in the Catholic faith. Conversely, parties who are unwilling to send their children to a Catholic school often, if not usually, are disinclined to use any of the regular or ordinary means by which they can effectively provide for the Catholic Education of their children.

2. In some ante-nuptial agreements there appears the wording of a promise to be given by both parties to the effect that they shall "lead a married life in conformity with the teachings of the Church regarding birth control, realizing fully the attitude of the Catholic Church in this regard."

Such a condition is nowhere demanded in the common law or in the Quinquennial Faculties. A marriage would be rendered invalid, however, on the grounds of an intention *contra bonum prolis,* if the parties to the marriage were not to give their consent in that substantial element in the matrimonial contract which is called the *bonum prolis.*[58]

The difficulty with such cases in their definitive settlement and solution is to be able to prove satisfactorily in the external forum the nature of the intention and condition under which the marriage was contracted.

[58] Canon 1092, 2°. Cf. Bouscaren, *Canon Law Digest,* I, 532-533, under canon 1092, for cases declared null by the Rota on grounds of an intention *contra bonum prolis* in the exchange of the matrimonial consent.

The distinction must be clearly drawn between the right to the marital act and the exercise of that right. An agreement, tacit or expressed, or even an intention of only one of the parties to abuse the marital right, even though perpetually, does not invalidate the marriage, as long as the right itself is mutually interchanged. Indeed the intention to abuse the right argues the presence of the right which lends itself to being violated.[59] At most such intention to abuse the right perpetually can set up a *presumption* that the right itself was intended to be excluded and denied.[60]

In view of the conditions in this country an ordinary may feel in duty bound to exact in this matter a promise from the nupturients. Even though few cases would arise wherein the very validity of the marriage might be questioned on this score, there is always involved the consideration of grave sin when marriage is entered with an intention to abuse its sacred rights. In consequence an ordinary may feel it necessary to employ such effective means as will avert this moral danger. It is extremely doubtful, however, whether such a promise can, in view of general circumstances, be exacted by the ordinary as a condition which is essential for the validity of the dispensation.

3. Many dioceses of the United States prescribe by diocesan law or statute that several instructions be given to the parties who contract a mixed marriage. The wisdom of such a regulation is apparent. The Catholic is given an opportunity to review the doctrines and practice of his faith. The non-Catholic party is informed of the religious obligations of the Catholic spouse and of his own moral obligations in view of the promises he is about to make. The moral code of Catholic married life, the high ideals of Christian family life, the mutual obligations of the spouses toward each other, the parental obligations towards the children—all these factors can be given due consideration and

---

[59] Cf. McCarthy, "Marriage under Birth Control Conditions,"—*IER*, 5th Series, LVII (1941), 71-76; 348-356 for a popular treatment of this subject.

[60] It is in this sense one must read the opinions of Noldin-Schmitt, *Summa Theologiae Moralis*, III, 635 and Cappello, *De Matrimonio*, P. II, 80-81.

discussion. Through the medium of such a course of instruction the canonical investigation required by canon 1020 can be more adequately made, and the proper imparting of the requisite knowledge as prescribed by canons 1018 and 1033 can be more fully provided. In addition, these instructions may furnish a splendid opportunity to lay the foundation for the conversion of the non-Catholic party, while the Catholic (privately) can be informed of the obligation to strive for that conversion and be advised of the prudent as well as practical and effective means to attain that end.

Normally, however, it seems that a bishop would go beyond his powers if he were to make the granting of a dispensation in cases of mixed religion and disparity of worship invariably dependent upon the completion of a set number of instructions. Adequate instructions, of course, should be given in accordance with the common law, but the law does not demand them for the validity of the dispensation. Bishops are within their right to prescribe not only the subject-matter of such instructions, but they may also indicate by way of law at which time prior to the marriage, under which circumstances of place, and in which number these instructions are to be imparted. It even seems permissible, in a given case, for the bishop to forbid a party to marry for a time until such instructions are given, if in his prudence he deems this procedure to constitute a necessary measure of pastoral discipline.[61] But to make it a general rule that no dispensation will be granted until after such instructions are given seems to offend against the prescription of canon 1038, § 2.[62]

---

[61] Canon 1039, § 1.

[62] Cf. Vermeersch-Creusen (*Epitome Iuris Canonici*, II, 234) who mentions the existence of this condition in some American dioceses, but makes no comment on its juridic force; cf. also Noldin-Schmitt, *Summa Theologiae Moralis*, III, 567; De Smet, *De Sponsalibus et Matrimonio*, p. 445, nota 4.

# CHAPTER EIGHT

## Pastoral Problems on Moral Certitude and the *Cautiones*

Some practical problems will confront the pastor and assistant who are personally responsible for the observance of the law of the Church in their dealings with persons who propose to enter a mixed marriage. It is impossible, of course, to imagine or anticipate all such problems, but the more commonly occurring pastoral and canonical questions will be given some attention in this chapter. The busy pastor is not devoid of interest in canonical opinions and arguments, but he is eminently more concerned about practical conclusions. Since the latter, however, have no independent character of their own, they must rest upon the pertinent and reasonable bases of the former.

With no pretense at exhausting the range of the subjects, consideration will be given to the following canonical and pastoral questions: a) The obtaining of moral certitude regarding the sincerity of the parties and concerning the fulfillment of the *cautiones* in the future; b) Practical consideration of the case in which the *cautiones* are given insincerely; c) The obligation of the pastor according to canon 1064; d) The question of the *cautiones* in the case of convalidation; e) The *cautiones* and the *sanatio in radice;* f) The requirement of the *cautiones* when one or the other of the contracting parties is in danger of death.

### I THE OBTAINING OF MORAL CERTITUDE

Simply because "certitude" is a subjective element, which relates to the mind knowing, and consequently is to be distinguished from "certainty", which, by way of contrast, points rather to the objective truth (the thing known), it is not to be gathered that certitude is something intuitive or psychic or simply a kind of prescience. Certitude has a foundation in reality, an objective basis upon which to rest, for no man can have certitude in the mind without the presence of some objective evidence in the thing. The kind of evidence determines the kind of certitude. Evidence founded upon moral standards and human conventions will necessarily result in moral certitude.

Moral certitude that the ante-nuptial promises will be fulfilled is an essential requirement for a valid dispensation from either the impediment of mixed religion or that of disparity of worship.[1] The source of this moral certitude in a given case will normally be the pastor's practical judgment, which is inferred on the basis of all the known circumstances of person, time, and place in conjunction with his knowledge of human nature which reveals to him in general how people are likely to act in a given situation, and in particular what reaction the contracting parties do reflect on the occasion of their petition for the dispensation. The bishop who dispenses can in turn derive his moral certitude from the testimony and recommendation of the pastor who has dealt with the case.[2]

The canonists are substantially agreed upon the description of the various elements that must be taken into account in the obtaining of this certitude. Indeed, whatever discrepancy of opinion may occur seems to be rooted rather in a difference of accidental degree than in one of essential nature or substantial kind. Thus one author may be more specific than another in mentioning some item or quality that contributes to the ultimate picture of the many-sided situation from which must be inferred the moral certitude of the sincerity of the promises and the further assurance that these promises will be fulfilled. Substantially the authors[3] are agreed that the serious promise which is given by the parties will form the starting point for such certitude, though this promise alone, aside from other circumstantial considerations, does not suffice to beget the ultimate assurance that they will be put into effect.[4] Hence, one must consider

---

[1] Cf. canons 1061, § 1, 3° and 1071.

[2] De Smet, *De Sponsalibus et Matrimonio,* p. 732, note 5.

[3] Gasparri, *De Matrimonio,* I, 265; Payen, *De Matrimonio,* I, 655; Ter Haar, *Mixed Marriages and Their Remedies,* p. 90.

[4] The refusal to give the required promises necessitates the refusal of the dispensation; hesitancy in giving them may weaken the basis of certitude, but, on the other hand, all other things being weighed, such hesitancy

especially the character of both the Catholic and the non-Catholic parties, the attitude which probably will be taken by the families of the respective parties to these promises, the local circumstances under which the promises are made, the stand of the civil law relative to such promises, the locality where the parties intend to live after their marriage, the earlier fulfillment or non-fulfillment of similar promises when one or the other of the parties lived in a mixed marriage, etc.[5] If either party was married before in a mixed marriage and such promises were not kept, it will be rather difficult, apart from strong present indications to the contrary, to arrive at moral certitude that the promises will be fulfilled in the mixed marriage now contemplated.

The form in which the *cautiones* are to be furnished, either as described by the common law or as outlined by the specific direction of the ordinary, who is presumed to know the best practical solution of this problem for his territory, is simply a matter which is designed to aid in the acquiring of the necessary moral certitude.[6] An ordinary may insist upon an accompanying oath of the parties if he sees fit to do so.

In the last analysis, each mixed marriage case must be given its separate and individual consideration to the exclusion of any *a priori* presumptions militating either for or against the sincerity of the promissors or the assurance of fulfillment regarding the *cautiones.* Ter Haar, however, while he admits the individual considerations in each case to be paramount, argues for the presence of an *a priori* presumption in favor of the fulfillment of the promises from the general upright character and reliable honor

---

may actually strengthen the basis of certitude. It may indicate an initial lack of knowledge regarding the full meaning of the promises, or it may reflect a settled attitude of solid caution in giving one's abiding word of honor. Hasty, almost flippant, signing of the *cautiones* can in many instances arouse more suspicion regarding the possible or even probable unreliability and subsequent worthlessness of the promises than a show of hesitancy in furnishing the *cautiones.*

[5] Cf. Ter Haar, *Mixed Marriages and Their Remedies,* pp. 91-93; Bangen, *De Sponsalibus et Matrimonio,* IV, 16-17; Vlaming, *Praelectiones Iuris Matrimonii,* I, 191-192.

[6] Cf. Konings-Putzer, *Commentarium in Facultates Apostolicas,* p. 337; Chelodi, *Ius Matrimoniale,* p. 69.

of the promissors in a certain district.[7] Thus, if in a locality most of the promises in this regard are fulfilled, he argues that such an existing factor will raise a presumption for the fulfillment of the promises in the case presently under consideration. Significantly Vermeersch-Creusen deny the presence of any presumption for ultimate failure in the fulfillment of the promises on the simple grounds that many in a given region have failed to carry them out.[8] If a favorable presumption can be admitted in the former hypothesis, then must it not also be acknowledged that an unfavorable one is admissible in the latter supposition? In reality it is rather to be accepted that neither presumption can find outright application, and that each case will stand or fall upon its own proper merits or demerits.[9]

## II PROMISES GIVEN INSINCERELY

While the pastor and the ordinary are charged with obtaining moral certitude regarding the sincerity of the *cautiones* and the assurance of their fulfillment in the future, it is nevertheless true that both may be deceived. The parties may have feigned the promises with a view to obtaining the requisite dispensation for their contemplated marriage.

If such insincerity be brought to light before the time when the dispensation is to be granted, then the dispensation must be refused, for the required moral certitude in such a case can certainly not be said to exist.

Should the knowledge of this insincerity arise on the part of the pastor or ordinary after the granting of the dispensation but before the celebration of the marriage, what is to be done? Since the pastor and bishop had moral certitude at the time the dispen-

---

[7] *Mixed Marriages and Their Remedies*, p. 90; Donovan, *The Pastoral Obligation in Pre-Nuptial Investigation*, pp. 247-249.

[8] *Epitome Iuris Canonici*, II, 232.

[9] The reader may profitably consult a recent answer to this entire problem of how to obtain moral certitude in the case of a Catholic soldier who presents himself and his non-Catholic bride to be married before a parish priest who knows neither of the parties. Cf. McCarthy, "Moral Certainty Regarding the Fulfillment of the 'Cautiones' in a Mixed Marriage,"—*IER*, 5th Series, LIX (1942), 74-78.

sation was granted, it is to be considered a valid dispensation, and the ecclesiastical law no longer prohibits the marriage from the sole viewpoint of the required valid dispensation. It is apparent, however, that the requirements of the natural divine law, which likewise constitutes a prohibitive impediment in the case of a mixed marriage, have not been satisfied. It would be rash, therefore, and gravely illicit on the part of Church authorities to approve the celebration of the marriage in the face of the evident offense against the natural law which such a celebration would necessarily entail.[10] The practical solution, it seems, resolves itself into one course of action. The bishop will see fit to prohibit the marriage until such time that he can assure himself that the intention of the parties has changed and is in conformity with the demand of the natural law.[11] To support his judgment in the case he may order further instructions to be given to the parties and may make inquiries into the reasons for such duplicity on their part. If he have some well-founded reason for suspicion, he will particularly investigate whether the Catholic party was equally guilty with the non-Catholic party in feigning the required promise. Even when the Catholic party has cleared himself of his past duplicity, the ordinary may thereupon demand that new promises be given under oath and in the presence of new witnesses. Under no conditions may the ordinary permit a pastor to witness a mixed or disparate marriage under the circumstances here considered as long as the direct occasion of scandal is not obviated. Even if all scandal be successfully averted, there must nevertheless be present a most urgent and serious cause before the Church allows herself to be drawn even as a passive partner into an act that offends against the known dictates of the natural divine law in so important a matter.[12]

---

[10] Canon 1064, 2°.

[11] Canon 1039, § 1.

[12] The fact that a valid dispensation has been granted in favor of the parties does not of necessity place the bishop on the defensive. He may recall his granted dispensation or declare it null and void for potential use, since he dispenses by virtue of faculties given *"ad universitatem causarum."* Cf. Reilly, *The General Norms of Dispensation,* The Catholic University of America Canon Law Studies, n. 119 (Washington, D. C.: The Catholic University of America Press, 1939), pp. 128-129.

When the insincerity of the promise is detected only after the marriage has taken place, the Catholic's possible complicity in an explicit or implicit pact to rear the future children outside of the Catholic faith may call for searching scrutiny, for the Catholic surely is liable to the censure of excommunication enacted by law in canon 2319, § 1, 2°. This situation presents the exact setting in which the question will arise as to the validity of a dispensation granted in the face of insincere *cautiones.* In the case of the prohibitive impediment of mixed religion no adverse consequence will result as to the status of the marriage; in the case of disparity of worship, if the dispensation is invalid, the marriage will be invalid. Since the emphasis of the law for a valid dispensation is placed upon the presence of moral certitude on the part of the one dispensing rather than on the objective veracity of the promises, the dispensation cannot be said to be invalid. Insincere *cautiones* alone, therefore, cannot be advanced to impugn the validity of the marriage. This view will surely receive the support of those canonists who defend the position that insincere *cautiones* do not invalidate the dispensation.[13]

On what canonical grounds would the question of such a marriage be brought into court for a judgment concerning its juridic status? There is no certain canonical text which declares that insincere guarantees invalidate the dispensation. Hence such insincerity does not give rise to a suit for the declaration of nullity.[14] Nor will a judicial rescissory action on the part of the ordinary in accordance with the norms of canons 103, § 2, and 1684-1686 avail in the case, for once the marriage is validly contracted, no one can place an act which by way of rescission has any retroactive effect upon the previous valid status of a mar-

[13] Doheny (*Canonical Procedure in Matrimonial Cases,* p. 450) holds this view and cites in his support *S.R.R. Nullitas Matrimonii,* 11 aug. 1926, *coram R.P.D. Ubaldo Mannucci,* dec. XLI—*S.R.R. Decisiones,* XVIII (1926), 325-331. He remarks, however, that the marriage may be found to be null for want of true matrimonial consent inasmuch as the consent may have been conditioned upon the other party's intention to fulfill the guarantees. Cf. also Ter Haar, *Mixed Marriages and Their Remedies,* p. 95, n. 4.

[14] Canon 1679; Park, "Insincere Ante-Nuptial Guarantees,"—*ER,* XCI (1934), 455-456.

riage. Such a rescissory action could at most obtain with regard to the dispensation but not with regard to the marriage, for the ordinary's sole act in consequence of the fraud of the parties was his granting of the dispensation. Now, the granted dispensation was but a passing act. As soon as the utilization of the dispensation achieved its desired effect, the marriage obtained a status which placed it within the favor of the law that continues to honor that marriage as valid as long as the proof of its invalidity has not evoked a final judicial sentence of nullity. The argument, namely, that in the face of existing facts the ordinary could not rightfully have granted the dispensation, and in consequence of this would not have granted it, is of no practical value. For the declaration of a judicial fact one must depend, not on interpretative human acts but on the actually performed human acts. If it stands approved that the ordinary, though unwittingly betrayed, nevertheless granted a valid dispensation, then it is equally clear that the subsequent marriage is valid inasfar as it depends for its status upon a validly granted dispensation.

Certainly the much discussed question whether insincere *cautiones* render valid or invalid not only the dispensation from the impediment of disparity of worship, but also the marriage itself for which this dispensation is prerequired as an essential condition can at most—in the absence of an authentic interpretation of the Holy See—result in a *dubium iuris*. Practically, therefore, such a marriage cannot be declared invalid by a diocesan tribunal on the exclusive grounds of the invalidity of the previous dispensation.[15] If there be desired any greater certitude in this question than that which is already possessed, then the question will have to be submitted to the Code Commission for an interpretation. If the settlement of a particular case is pending, then the case may be remitted to the Holy Office.[16]

### III PASTORAL DUTIES IN MIXED MARRIAGES

The obtaining of the *cautiones* from the parties as well as the achieving of certitude regarding their fulfillment for the future

---

[15] Canon 15.

[16] Schenk, *Mixed Religion and Disparity of Cult,* p. 254.

does not end the concern of the Church in the matter of mixed marriages. The Code of Canon Law imposes upon local ordinaries and upon the pastors of souls additional pastoral duties which derive not only from their pastoral office but also from the very claims of Christian charity.[17]

The first of these duties of the ordinaries and pastors is that of deterring the faithful, as much as they can, from the contraction of mixed marriages.[18] Ways and means to accomplish this purpose will tax the ingenuity of the zealous pastor, but the tried and experienced method of frequent instructions, administered both publicly and privately, on the dangers, both to faith and to morals, which are inherent in such unions, will necessarily hold an important place in the campaign against mixed marriages. Such instructions and exhortations are contemplated in the explicit direction of the III Council of Baltimore (1884),[19] are strongly prescribed by diocesan synods,[20] and are highly recommended by canonists and by such persons as are profoundly versed in the practical sciences of pastoral and moral theology.[21] Perhaps equally important, and perhaps even more fruitful for the desired effect, is a well-developed C.Y.O. program of religious, social, and

---

[17] Canon 1064. Cf. Cappello, *De Matrimonio,* P. I, 407; Wernz-Vidal, *Ius Matrimoniale,* p. 195.

[18] Canon 1064, 1°: Ordinarii aliique animarum pastores fideles a mixtis nuptiis, quantum possunt, absterreant.

[19] N. 133.

[20] E.g., *Synodus Dioecesana Fargensis Prima* (Milwaukee: Bruce, 1941), pp. 70-71, statutum 362; *Synodus Dioecesana Bellevillensis Quinta* (Belleville: Buechler, 1940), pp. 54-55, statutum 146; *Statuta Dioecesis Ogdensburgensis (XIII)* (Ogdensburg, 1928), pp. 26-27, statutum 108.

[21] Cf. Wernz-Vidal, *Ius Matrimoniale,* p. 195; Blat, *De Rebus,* P. I, 563; Payen, *De Matrimonio,* I, 662; Chelodi, *Ius Matrimoniale,* p. 73. De Smet (*De Sponsalibus et Matrimonio,* p. 445, note 2) among other things notes that the refusal of the dispensation for mixed marriages has been a powerful deterrent particularly in Holland; Ter Haar (*Mixed Marriages and Their Remedies,* pp. 98-103) highly recommends such instructions as a means to deter Catholics from entering mixed marriages, and in his thorough treatment of this subject mentions other practical employable means, especially a just severity on the part of confessors with those who contemplate a mixed marriage, pp. 126-140, and a prudent severity in granting the dispensation, pp. 140-175.

cultural activities in the parish for the Catholic youth of both sexes. Such a program will reveal the Church's official solicitude and concern in a less patently manifest vein, but the very condition of the veiled presence of the Church's challenge to youth may invite a more sympathetic docility and correspondingly a greater compliance with her purpose to endear to them the interests of their holy faith. Youth activities of this character will provide natural and easy opportunities for mutual acquaintanceship. They furnish the occasion for the young people within the parish to seek one another's companionship and company, and thus prepare the way for Catholic courtship and marriage.

The second duty of ordinaries and pastors is to see to it that mixed marriages, if they cannot be averted, will be celebrated in accordance with the laws of God and of the Church.[22] Hence a just and grave cause for the marriage must be recognized as present, the required *cautiones* must be duly given, and the pastor and the ordinary must have moral certitude that these promises will be fulfilled. Undoubtedly one of the most practical steps taken to fulfill this law of the Code is the statutory prescription which, current in so many dioceses throughout the United States, requires the giving of a series of instructions to the persons who contemplate a mixed marriage.[23]

Canon 1064, 4°, which prescribes the observance of the due form for the celebration of the marriage seems to be but an amplification and a more specific application of canon 1064, 2°.[24]

Another very real duty incumbent upon pastors and ordinaries is to watch over the faithful fulfillment of the promises made before a mixed marriage, whether such a marriage was contracted in their territory or outside of it.[25] This duty as specified in the

[22] Canon 1064: 2°: Ordinarii aliique animarum pastores, si eas impedire non valeant, omni studio curent ne contra Dei et Ecclesiae leges contrahantur.

[23] Cf. *supra,* pp. 142-143; *Synodus Dioecesana Fargensis Prima,* p. 71, statutum 363; *Synodus Dioecesana Bellevillensis Quinta,* pp. 55-56, statutum 147, § 4.

[24] Canon 1064, 4°: Ordinarii aliique animarum pastores assistentes matrimonio servent praescriptum can. 1102; cf. also canon 1095, § 1, 3°.

[25] Canon 1064, 3°: Ordinarii aliique animarum pastores mixtis nuptiis celebratis sive in proprio sive in alieno territorio, sedulo invigilent ut coniuges promissiones factas fideliter impleant.

Code could easily be deduced from the more general pronouncements of the canons which define a parish[26] and a pastor[27] both of which make mention of the "care of souls" as the charge inherent in the pastoral office.[28]

The practical method of fulfilling this duty is a pastoral problem which causes much concern even to pastors of long pastoral experience. Obviously the facts must be known: it must be known who are the parties who have entered mixed or disparate marriages; whether or not they are living up to their promises; why they have failed to carry out their promises; whether the non-Catholic party alone or the Catholic party alone, or both parties are responsible for the non-execution of the promises. Many pastors meet this primary problem through an accurate, complete, and up-to-the-minute census of their parishes. To this end they visit the parties from time to time to encourage them in the fulfillment of their obligations. When the family moves to another parish, then the former pastor writes a letter to the new pastor and explains the spiritual background and present status of the new parishioners.[29]

While the instructions privately given to the parties, the visits to their homes, etc., may be effective in encouraging the parties to carry out their promises, at times more severe measures may have to be employed. If the non-Catholic alone is responsible for the repudiation of the *cautiones,* then a consultation with the Catholic party may suffice to impart the needed advice in the matter of striving to change the wilful or perhaps even embittered viewpoint of the non-Catholic spouse. Should this fail, then it may be advisable to confer with the non-Catholic party directly. He can

---

[26] Canon 216, § 1.

[27] Canon 451, § 1.

[28] Cf. S.C. de Prop. Fide, instr. (ad Archiep. Baltimoren.), 25 iun. 1884, ad 1: "Post celebratas mixtas nuptias, parochi gravi conscientiae onere se gravari sciant invigilandi ut promissae a coniugibus conditiones observentur, et effectum sortiantur."—*Fontes,* n. 4904; *Coll. S.C.P.F.,* n. 1621. On the office of the bishop, cf. canons 334 and 335.

[29] Ter Haar, *Mixed Marriages and Their Remedies,* pp. 176-180; Payen, *De Matrimonio,* I, 667-668; *Synodus Dioecesana Fargensis Prima,* p. 18, stat. 87; p. 19, stat. 94; p. 72, stat. 367.

be shown the document which records the promises that were signed. It can also be indicated that full freedom and all lack of coercion accompanied the signing of these promises. As a last resort, though in rare circumstances and only when the canonical conditions are truly present, the Catholic may have to be advised to seek, upon consultation with the ordinary, canonical separation from bed and board according to canon 1131, § 1. The Catholic must be made to understand, however, that the matrimonial bond remains. Such action must, of course, be undertaken only rarely and even then most carefully. Perhaps the sole threat of such an action will be sufficient to move the non-Catholic to conform to the intention he expressed in the *cautiones*. The ecclesiastical grant of a separation for the Catholic must also be weighed in the possible consequence of a suit of divorce entered by the non-Catholic on the charge of desertion, as well as the possibility of a suit for alienation of affections.

Should the Catholic alone be at fault with regard to the fulfillment of the promises, then an earnest instruction regarding the duties of a Catholic parent with respect to the Catholic education of the children may suffice. Should stronger measures be deemed necessary, then the Catholic should be advised of the meaning and seriousness of the application of canon 2319. Further, until such a Catholic has complied with the promises and has taken definite steps to provide in the future for the Catholic education of the children, or at least has seriously promised to do so as soon as possible, the reception of the sacraments must be denied as to a public sinner.[80]

[80] S.C.S.Off., litt. 23 aug. 1877: Dubium: "Utrum in contractis matrimoniis (cum haereticis) pastores animarum partem poenitentem, dummodo seclusum sit scandalum, tuta conscientia ad receptionem sacramentorum admittere valeant." R.: "Quoad matrimonia valida, ad sacramenta percipienda posse admitti sine praevia renovatione consensus, sed ab iisdem percipiendis arcendos, donec vera dederint resipiscentiae signa, et promiserint se curaturos totis viribus tam conversionem partis haereticae, quam educationem in religione catholica prolis universae natae et forsan nasciturae et tandem donec obtinuerint absolutionem a censuris incursis una cum poenitentiis salutaribus, casu quo contraxerint coram ministro haeretico."—*Fontes*, n. 1052; Ter Haar, *Mixed Marriages and Their Remedies*, pp. 179-180.

Recourse to civil law to uphold the contractual character of the pre-nuptial guarantees has found little support among ordinaries and pastors of our country. As White has pointed out, however, test cases of this kind, particularly if the contract is drawn in the language of civil law injunctions, may prove surprisingly effective in favor of the Catholic party in spite of the common law tradition of England.[81] Favorable decisions by the civil courts in this regard, in addition to setting a precedent in the States, would implicitly indicate the contractual form in which the *cautiones* would thereafter have to be made if a dispensation from the impediment of mixed religion and of disparity of worship is to be granted with valid effect.[82]

### IV THE *cautiones* IN THE CASE OF CONVALIDATION

Two cases are to be given consideration here. They come to the attention of the pastor, either after a valid marriage or simply an attempt at marriage has taken place. Only the latter of these constitutes the case of a true convalidation.

First, there is the case which involves the prohibitive impediment of mixed religion, wherein the priest either through personal inadvertence, or as a consequence of the erroneous consciences of the parties, or in view of some undetected error in the documents relating to the status of the parties, has assisted at the marriage without obtaining the required *cautiones* and the needed dispensation. The marriage was contracted validly, of course, but not licitly, and hence there arises no question of convalidation or of a *sanatio in radice*. In such circumstances what must the priest undertake to do?

If the Catholic party is at fault because he was knowingly and consciously silent regarding the need of a dispensation upon properly furnished *cautiones*, then every effort must be made to reconcile him with the Church. The failure of the Catholic to

[81] *Canonical Ante-Nuptial Promises and the Civil Law*, pp. 66-73, especially p. 73; Chelodi, *Ius Matrimoniale*, p. 73.

[82] S.C.S.Off., decr. 14 ian. 1932—*AAS*, XXIV (1932), 25; Ter Haar, *Mixed Marriages and Their Remedies*, pp. 185-196; Ayrinhac-Lydon, *Marriage Legislation*, pp. 109-111; 388-389.

respond will classify him as a public sinner, especially if the children are baptized and educated in heresy. Thus the Catholic most assuredly becomes liable to the censure of excommunication which is reserved for its absolution to the ordinary by virtue of canon 2319, § 1, 3° and 4°. He is denied the reception of the sacraments[33] until he has been legitimately absolved[34] and he is furthermore denied the participation in "legitimate ecclesiastical acts" as enumerated in canon 2256, 2° and the use of the sacramentals until he has received a dispensation from the ordinary.[35] If he perseveres in this contumacious attitude without any sign of repentance before death, he is to be denied ecclesiastical burial by force of canon 1240, § 1, 6°, provided, of course, the delict is notorious. And if the incurred excommunication has also been publicly declared by ecclesiastical authority, then this condition at death likewise constitutes a reason for the denial of Christian burial according to the law of canon 1240, § 1, 2°.[36] A further canonical basis for the punishment of the Catholic party who in this case is the *minister of a Sacrament,* may be inferred from canon 2364. This canon provides for punishment in accordance with the gravity of the offense relative to those who administer the sacraments to persons forbidden to receive them. The nature and necessity of cooperation, as delineated in canon 2209, may involve the priest in the pertinent punishment of suspension from the further administration of the sacraments, as is indicated in canon 2364, if he has presumed to assist at a mixed marriage without receiving the required *cautiones* and the necessary dispensation.[37]

If the Catholic desires in a duly penitent spirit to become reconciled with the Church, then the following considerations obtain: 1) Renewal of consent is not needed inasmuch as the marriage was validly contracted. 2) There is likewise no need of a dispensation from the impediment of mixed religion even

---

[33] Canon 2260, § 1.

[34] Canon 2248, § 1.

[35] Canons 2263; 2375.

[36] Payen, *De Matrimonio,* I, 668; Cappello, *De Matrimonio,* P. I, 407-408; De Smet, *De Sponsalibus et Matrimonio,* p. 451, nota 2.

[37] Cf. Coronata, IV (*De Delictis et Poenis*), p. 509.

though the marriage was unlawfully contracted. 3) A thorough instruction must be given to the parties regarding the meaning and purpose of the *cautiones.* 4) The usual *cautiones* should then be received from both parties in the marriage, but if the non-Catholic refuses to give them, they should then be obtained from the Catholic party alone and every effort is to be made to provide for their fulfillment. 5) If the Catholic has incurred excommunication according to canon 2319, the faculties to absolve therefrom must be sought from the ordinary. To make use of the sacramentals and to participate in "legitimate ecclesiastical acts" the Catholic needs a dispensation from the ordinary according to canon 2375. But ignorance of any kind, except affected ignorance and the presence of even a slight duress or fear will suffice to excuse the offender from incurring the vindicative penalty enacted in canon 2375.[38] 6) The Catholic should be admitted to sacramental penance. 7) There may be a necessity of obviating the scandal which may be occasioned by the Catholic's reception of the sacraments in view of his past failure to provide a Catholic education for the children. 8) The pastor and ordinary have the duty to watch over the fulfillment of the *cautiones,* perhaps with even more reason in the case under consideration than in the ordinary cases of mixed marriage wherein the *cautiones* were furnished prior to the marriage.[39]

Secondly, there is the case which involves a possible dual aspect, but which under either supposition calls for the same manner of solution. The marriage may have been one which was forbidden by the prohibitive impediment of mixed religion, but which in the absence of any furnished *cautiones* and granted dispensation was contracted invalidly because of the non-observance of the required canonical form; or the marriage may have been one which was interdicted by the diriment impediment of disparity of worship, and which was contracted invalidly because of the absence of the *cautiones* and in view of the invalidity of the dispensation. In either supposition the way is open for one of three

[38] Canon 2229, § 1, and § 2.

[39] Payen, *De Matrimonio,* I, 669-670. Cf. also Cappello, *De Matrimonio,* P. I, 408-409; De Smet, *De Sponsalibus et Matrimonio,* pp. 449-451; Chelodi, *Ius Matrimoniale,* p. 72.

possible courses of action: the separation of the parties, the simple convalidation of their invalid union,[40] or the application of the extraordinary remedy of the *sanatio in radice*.[41]

Under certain sinister or even adverse circumstances insistence upon the separation of the parties may be the only justified as well as expedient course of action that may be followed. Such a course would be necessitated when the parties are devoid of all firmness of good will and lack every indication of a docile disposition so that it can be morally foreseen that desertion or divorce would follow upon their rectified marriage. The same course of action would be necessary if the convalidated marriage were to place the Catholic party in an imminent danger of perversion in his faith. And the same course of action would have to be invoked when both parties refuse to furnish the required *cautiones*.

But the circumstances under which such a separation has to be urged occur with relative infrequency in comparison with the situation in which a proper convalidation of the marriage can be undertaken. If both parties are so well disposed that they show good faith in furnishing the *cautiones,* and besides are willing to renew their matrimonial consent in the due canonical form, then the needed dispensation should be obtained and thereupon the simple convalidation of the marriage can readily follow. If the Catholic party has incurred the censure of excommunication[42] through his previously attempted marriage, then a prior absolution from this censure must be imparted in view of his proper repentance, and the absolution of his sins in the Sacrament of penance should likewise be urged in preparation for the convalidation of the marriage. It does not matter whether the previously attempted marriage was invalid in view of the undispensed impedi-

---

[40] Canons 1133-1137.

[41] Canons 1138-1141.

[42] Quinquennial Faculties require absolution from the excommunication of canon 2319, § 1, 1° *if the parties are living in concubinage* and desire to return to the Church. Hence a double ceremony, one before the Protestant minister, the other before the Church is not necessary to incur this censure. The same reasoning is evident in the faculty to grant a *sanatio in radice*—cf. Bouscaren, *The Canon Law Digest,* Supplement, 1941, pp. 27; 29, under canon 66.

ment of disparity of worship or in view of the unobserved canonical form; in either event the renewal of the matrimonial consent must be undertaken in the canonical form as established by the law.[43]

### V THE *cautiones* AND THE *sanatio in radice*

A situation can arise in which the non-Catholic party refuses to renew his earlier matrimonial consent in the due canonical form or declines to have a part in the furnishing of the *cautiones*. A last resort in the use of the *sanatio in radice* may be employed by the bishop in order to give the Catholic party, now penitent and well-disposed, the opportunity to live in a true marriage and to receive the sacraments.[44] It is assumed that a separation cannot be expediently effected for various grave reasons, particularly if children have been born of the union, or if the parties are well advanced in age and have no separate means of support. In the present consideration the Church finds herself face to face with two evils. If she refuses to dispense from her own law regarding the required canonical form for the expression of matrimonial consent or regarding the stipulated manner for the furnishing of the *cautiones* by the non-Catholic party, then there is imminent danger of the loss of the soul of the Catholic party who now

---

[43] Canon 1135: Si impedimentum sit publicum, consensus ab utraque parte renovandus est forma iure praescripta. Canon 1137: Matrimonium nullum ob defectum formae, ut validum fiat, contrahi denuo debet legitima forma. The impediment of disparity of worship is readily recognized to be a public impediment according to the definition supplied by the Code in canon 1037, inasmuch as proof for its existence can be established in the external forum. Cf. Payen, *De Matrimonio*, I, 671; De Smet, *De Sponsalibus et Matrimonio*, p. 451; Ayrinhac-Lydon, *Marriage Legislation*, p. 117; Petrovits, *The New Church Law on Matrimony*, pp. 172-173; Wernz-Vidal, *Ius Matrimoniale*, p. 196; Schenk, *Mixed Religion and Disparity of Cult*, p. 174; Chelodi, *Ius Matrimoniale*, p. 72.

[44] The authors are in agreement on the required presence of the already-mentioned conditions as well as of the continued perseverance of the non-Catholic's matrimonial consent for the licit and valid use of the *sanatio in radice*. Cf. Chelodi, *Ius Matrimoniale*, p. 73; Wernz-Vidal, *Ius Matrimoniale*, p. 196; Payen, *De Matrimonio*, I, 653; 671; De Smet, *De Sponsalibus et Matrimonio*, pp. 451; 763; Ter Haar, *Mixed Marriages and Their Remedies*, p. 80.

desires reconciliation. If as a result of the non-Catholic's refusal to furnish the *cautiones* in due written form, she dispenses from the use of this form, or even foregoes his positive verbal assurance to respect the demands inherent in the legally required *cautiones,* then she sacrifices her normally greater security against the possible danger of perversion by tolerating a merely negative assurance, namely, that the non-Catholic is not opposed to the Catholic baptism and education of each and every one of the children, and that he has not prior to the attempted marriage, entered upon a pact with the Catholic party to procure the education of the children in a non-Catholic belief. In permitting the application of a *sanatio in radice* in such a stubborn case the Church's intervention simply bespeaks her active toleration of the lesser evil. She turns her attention in the meantime to the immediate positive need of the Catholic party. She trusts that the grace of God will furnish the necessary safeguard against the emergence of spiritual harm as a result of her indulgent action.[43] No mixed marriage is permitted without the furnished *cautiones,* and hence no dispensation is granted when they are not furnished. The case under consideration presupposes an earlier attempt at marriage. It presents additional stubborn elements and hence calls for a rectification in the most practical way that can be utilized in harmony with the divine law. There is question here of salvaging as much as possible in the spiritual lives of all concerned. This is not to say, however, that the Church will in any case whatsoever apply a *sanatio* contrary to the dictates of the natural divine law. In addition to sincere penance for the sin of his attempted marriage and the subsequent concubinage, the Catholic must be solemnly warned of his obligation regarding the Catholic baptism and education of all the children already born or yet to be born of their marital union. On the other hand, the refusal of the non-Catholic to furnish the *cautiones* may be a matter of merely negative import. Should he go further, however, and positively oppose the baptism and Catholic education of the children already born, or indicate such contrary intention with regard to children who may be born in the future, no *sanatio* may

[43] Schenk, *Mixed Religion and Disparity of Cult,* p. 178.

be given.[46] Nor may the *sanatio* be applied in the case wherein a mutual agreement was entered into before the attempted marriage, either privately or publicly, to educate the children in a non-Catholic religion. This restriction, however, obtains only if one or both of the parties still adhere to the agreement to give the children a non-Catholic education. If the parties have receded from such an agreement, then a *sanatio* may be granted.

A third curtailment of the use of the *sanatio* would have place if both parties are in ignorance of the invalidity of their marriage and another diriment impediment, in which the ordinary has no power to dispense or to grant a *sanatio,* were present in the case.

These three restrictions of the use of the *sanatio* in upholding the known dictates of the natural divine law are express modifications introduced in the recent Quinquennial Faculties which are granted to ordinaries in the United States by the Holy Office.[47]

Regarding the application of the *sanatio* it is to be noted that "it is the mind of the Holy Office that the bishop exercise this faculty personally, that is, that he do not subdelegate it to anyone."[48] The vicar general, of course, may exercise this same faculty to sanate invalid marriages because the faculty is not given *ex industria personae.*[49]

---

[46] De Smet (*De Sponsalibus et Matrimonio,* pp. 451, 445) points out that even the *sanatio in radice* cannot be granted if danger of perversion be present; Payen (*De Matrimonio,* I, 671, 653) includes in the consideration for the use of the *sanatio* the absence of the danger of perversion, or, at least, a sufficient remoteness of that danger that there is still compatible with it the moral certitude that the non-Catholic will not oppose the Catholic education of the children.

[47] Cf. Beste, *Introductio in Codicem,* Appendix (Allegatum I), 975; for the English, cf. Bouscaren, *The Canon Law Digest,* Supplement, 1941, p. 28 under canon 66. Neither Ter Haar (*Mixed Marriages and Their Remedies,* pp. 196-197) nor Ayrinhac-Lydon (*Marriage Legislation,* p. 149) mention the third exception which appears in the faculties relative to the use of the *sanatio.*

[48] Bouscaren, *The Canon Law Digest,* Supplement, 1941, p. 29, under canon 66. It may here be noted that an earlier grant of this faculty permitted the bishop to subdelegate the power of granting a *sanatio* only to pastors and for individual cases (*The Canon Law Digest,* I, 64, under canon 66). Such a faculty to subdelegate no longer exists.

[49] Cf. Canon 368, § 2; Harrigan, *The Radical Sanation of Invalid Marriages,* The Catholic University of America Canon Law Studies, n. 116 (Washington, D. C.: The Catholic University of America, 1938), p. 155.

Should the bishop consider that good reasons are present for a *sanatio* even in such cases which are beyond his power to administer, he may have recourse for faculties to the Holy See or to the Apostolic Delegate.

### VI THE *cautiones* OF PARTIES IN DANGER OF DEATH

The extraordinary remedy of the *sanatio in radice* is the only dispensation which can be given for the impediment of mixed religion and of disparity of worship without the *cautiones* on the part of non-Catholics. There is no reason why this remedy may not also be used when one of the parties is in danger of death, should circumstances permit. It may be that the non-Catholic party refuses to make the promises, but does not positively oppose the Catholic education of the children already born or yet perhaps to be born. Upon duly warning the Catholic party of his obligation toward the children and with a moral certitude that the danger of perversion either is not present or has been rendered remote, the ordinary may grant the *sanatio*.

Time may not permit recourse to the ordinary. What is the priest to do? In all dispensations from the impediments of mixed religion and disparity of worship, apart from the *sanatio,* the obtaining of the promises is an essential condition for a valid dispensation. This is the clear law of canon 1061, § 1, 2°. Even in such unusual circumstances wherein one of the parties is in danger of death, on which occasion the ordinary in virtue of the native powers of his office enjoys the right to dispense in accordance with canon 1043, the *cautiones* are clearly postulated (*praestitis consuetis cautionibus*). The same condition is present when, by virtue of canon 1044, the pastor as well as the priest of whom mention is made in canon 1098, 2°, and the confessor in the internal forum dispenses if he cannot reach the ordinary.[50]

[50] Koudelka ("Assistants and Matrimonial Dispensation Urgente Mortis Periculo,"—*The Salesianum,* XXX (April, 1935), 22-30) is of the opinion that the same faculty under the same conditions is very probably enjoyed by assistants who have a general delegation to assist at marriages in the parish. Cf. also Ayrinhac-Lydon (*Marriage Legislation,* pp. 71-72) who appeal to canon 209 to supply such an assistant with the necessary faculties in the given circumstances. Delegation of the power contained in canon 1043 and 1044 can be given the assistant by the ordinary or the pastor and thus the practical problem will be solved.

There has been a dispute among canonists whether the obtaining of the *cautiones* in such extreme circumstances as these must be considered an essential condition for the dispensation, so that without them the dispensation would be invalid. The discussion centered upon a response of the Holy Office under date of June 21, 1912,[51] wherein the dispensation for the impediment of disparity of worship, if it was granted when the *cautiones* either had been refused or had not been sought at all, was indicated to be null and void. The question is now definitely settled by a recent decree of the same Holy Office[52] in favor of the strict opinion which required the *cautiones* for the validity of the dispensation even when one of the parties was in danger of death.[53] Consequently, to make valid use of the faculty to dispense, which is granted in canon 1044 when the ordinary cannot be approached, the pastor, the priest designated in canon 1098, 2°, and also the assistant with due and proper delegation, must secure the *cautiones*.

The procedure, then, will be that the priest absolves in the internal sacramental forum, at the same time requesting the penitent to repeat the details of the case in the external forum. The faculty may then be used to dispense in the external forum after the promises are given, and a record of the granted dispensation

---

[51] *Fontes*, n. 1293, or *AAS*, IV (1912), 442-443; Schenk (*Mixed Religion and Disparity of Cult*, pp. 216-234) gives a thorough treatment of the controversy. He examines the arguments of the canonists on both sides of the question and ranges himself with those who uphold the strict opinion that the *cautiones* are necessary even in the extreme circumstances of danger of death for one of the parties.

[52] 14 ian. 1932—*AAS*, XXIV (1932), 25. It is irrelevant whether or not the decree applies to the United States as far as the present question is concerned; cf. Ter Haar, *Mixed Marriages and Their Remedies*, p. 189. This decree mentions expressly both *disparity of worship* and *mixed religion* as well as the circumstances of *danger of death*, and hence it is not open to dispute, as was the former response. Cf. Payen, *De Matrimonio*, I, 652-653.

[53] The use of the ablative absolute, "*praestitis consuetis cautionibus*", at the end of canon 1043 serves as a striking example of the expression of an essential condition for it necessarily involves that condition which elsewhere in the common law (canon 1061, § 1, 2°) is unmistakably designated as essential for a valid dispensation in the cases of mixed religion and of disparity of worship. Cf. *supra*, pp. 120-121.

will thereupon be made in accordance with the rule enacted in canon 1046. It is, of course, not necessary in the unusual circumstances of the case that the *cautiones* be given in writing, even though the Code and the diocesan statutes may so prescribe. The written form of the *cautiones* is a matter which even in normal circumstances is required only for licit use of the faculties, and the very wording of canon 1061, § 2—*"regulariter in scriptus"* —seems to contemplate just such a situation wherein an exception may be allowed. It is advisable, however, when the *cautiones* are not obtained in writing, to have a witness for the *cautiones* and the granted dispensation if one can be had, though the official entry of the granting of the dispensation in the matrimonial book and in the diocesan archives with a notation that the *cautiones* were given will suffice to render proof in the external forum that the marriage was contracted free of all hindrance on the part of that particular impediment.

As in the case of the *sanatio,* so in the use of the extraordinary faculties granted by canons 1043-1044, the Church may have to stand face to face with two evils. On the one hand, the natural divine law does not permit the celebration of a marriage in connection with which a danger of perversion threatens or is patently present. The securing of the *cautiones* is the normal method of obviating this danger. On the other hand, the Catholic party may be well disposed and sincerely penitent, but is now placed in danger of death. There is this difference, however, between the *sanatio* and the use of the faculty granted in canon 1044; the *sanatio* can be applied even apart from the acceptance of any *cautiones* from the non-Catholic party, but the faculty of canon 1044 does not become operative until the *cautiones* have been furnished. If *explicit cautiones* cannot be obtained in these urgent circumstances, the *implicit* or *equivalent cautiones* will suffice for the validity of the subsequently granted dispensation.

Though the recent response of the Holy Office[54] set up a *post factum* norm for judging about the validity of the dispensation when it declared that, with relation to the impediment of disparity of worship, a marriage was to be considered valid if *implicit cautiones* were furnished when the dispensation was granted, the

---

[54] Cf. *supra,* pp. 55-56.

emergency of the presently contemplated situation will surely admit as valid the use of *implicit cautiones* in order to satisfy the demand of canon 1061, § 2. After all, the moral certitude regarding the obviation of the danger of perversion is all that the natural divine law demands. *Implicit cautiones* will suffice not only to furnish that moral certitude, but also to satisfy at the same time the essential positive canonical requirement that the *cautiones* be obtained even in this unusual case. Just what will constitute *implicit cautiones* must be left to the prudent judgment of the one who dispenses. If the Catholic party has always enjoyed freedom to practice his religion, and the children already born are baptized and are receiving a Catholic education, it seems reasonable to conclude that implicit *cautiones* exist in the case. The likely future attitude of the non-Catholic to the Catholic education of the children in the event of the death of the Catholic party must surely be taken into account in every case.

It may be that even *implicit cautiones* in given circumstances cannot be obtained. Thus it may happen that the non-Catholic party positively opposes the Catholic education of the children, and that in consequence of this, though he try as he may, the priest who attends the dying Catholic can receive no assurance that the natural divine law requirements are satisfied. In such a case both the use of the *sanatio* as well as the use of the extraordinary faculty granted in canon 1044 would be of no avail. The priest may impart sacramental absolution from censure and sin to the Catholic party upon receiving his promise to do all in his power to procure a Catholic education for the children if he recovers. But it likewise appears necessary to exact a promise of the Catholic to renounce the illicit union, or if it appears that this is impossible, to continue to cohabit in the fashion of brother and sister, should the circumstances of age or health indicate that this can feasibly be done without serious danger or harm to the spiritual life.

In summary, therefore, four possibilities may present themselves to the priest or ordinary who attends a dying Catholic whose marriage of mixed religion or disparity of worship took place before a non-Catholic minister or a civil judge. 1) A refusal to furnish the *cautiones* on the part of the non-Catholic may not mean a positive antipathy to the substance of the promises, but only a negative, unconcerned attitude thereto. In such a case, all other required conditions being present (n. V.), the *sanatio in radice* may be applied if time will permit a recourse to the ordinary. 2) Upon ascertaining the presence of the conditions expressed in canons 1043-1044, the ordinary or priest will obtain the *cautiones,* assure himself of his jurisdiction, absolve in the internal forum, and then dispense in the external forum. 3) All other conditions of canons 1043-1044 being present, it seems justifiable that the ordinary or priest can dispense, as above indicated, upon assuring himself of the presence of *implicit cautiones* when positive promises cannot be had. 4) Total failure in all these attempts to rectify the marriage may leave but one course open to the priest, namely, to administer sacramental absolution upon the Catholic's promise to abandon the illicit union, or to take definite steps only in such a way to continue in it as to place himself and his children beyond the danger of perversion or of jeopardy for the faith.

## CONCLUSIONS

1) The impediments of mixed religion and of disparity of worship with their respective juridic effects upon matrimony were mutually distinguished by the time of Gratian, but the full basis of this distinction as inherent in the respective baptism or non-baptism of the non-Catholic party came to be recognized only in the scholastics' interpretation of the papal decretals during the twelfth and thirteenth centuries.

2) Prior to the "Reformation," when all of Europe was Catholic and when no juridic recognition was given to any other religion, the only condition upon which the marriage of a Catholic with a non-Catholic was permitted consisted in the latter's conversion, or promise of conversion, to the Catholic faith.

3) The first *cautiones* after the "Reformation" consisted in long, involved politico-religious agreements between the Holy See and the heretic in the mixed marriages of the royalty.

4) *Cautiones,* although of ecclesiastical origin, are the normal means of certifying the presence of the *cautelae* or *conditiones* demanded by the natural divine law before a mixed marriage may be tolerated.

5) While the question of the validity of a dispensation from mixed marriages in the face of *insincere* CAUTIONES remains unsettled and awaits an authoritative solution by the Holy See, it seems far more consistent with the known jurisprudence of the Sacred Roman Rota, as well as with the philosophical and canonical concept of *moral certitude,* to acknowledge such dispensation as valid.

6) The content of the *cautiones* in mixed marriages is limited, as far as the essential conditions for a valid dispensation are concerned, to the demands made by canon 1061, § 1, 2°; if any further content accedes to the *cautiones* through the action of minor Church authorities, it must be considered to be incidental in character.

7) The recent response of the Holy Office limits the extent of the words *"de universa prole"* in canon 1061, § 1, 2°, to the

future children of the contemplated marriage, but simultaneously stresses the necessity of informing the couple of their obligation to educate in the Catholic religion also those children, if any exist, of whom they are the parents in common.

8) *Cautiones* are required for the validity of all dispensations for mixed marriages except in the relatively infrequent case of the *sanatio in radice;* the unusual circumstance of danger of death offers no exception to the general rule, though implicit *cautiones* in such case will satisfy.

# BIBLIOGRAPHY

## Sources

*Acta Apostolicae Sedis, Commentarium Officiale,* Romae, 1909-

*Acta et Decreta Concilii Plenarii Baltimorensis Tertii, A.D. MDCCCLXXXIV,* Baltimorae: John Murphy, 1886.

*Acta et Decreta Sacrorum Conciliorum Recentiorum, Collectio Lacensis,* 7 vols., Friburgi Brisgoviae: Herder, 1870-1890.

*Acta Gregorii Papae XVI, scilicet Constitutiones, Bullae, Litterae Apostolicae,* cura ac studio Antonii M. Bernasconi, 4 vols., Romae: Typographia Polyglotta, 1901-1904.

*Acta Sanctae Sedis,* 41 vols., Romae, 1865-1908.

*Ante-Nicene Fathers,* 14 vols., American Reprint of the Edinburg ed., New York: Scribner & Sons, 1903.

*Codex Iuris Canonici Pii X Pontificis Maximi iussu digestus Benedicti XV auctoritate promulgatus,* Romae: Typis Polyglottis Vaticanis, 1917.

*Codicis Iuris Canonici Fontes cura Emi. Petri Card. Gasparri Editi,* 9 vols., Romae [postea Civitate Vaticana]: Typis Polyglottis Vaticanis, 1923-1939. (Vols. VII, VIII, et IX ed. cura et studio Emi. Iustiniani Card. Serédi.

*Collectanea S. Congregationis Propaganda Fide,* Romae: Ex Typographia Polyglotta, 1893.

*Collectanea S. Congregationis de Propaganda Fide,* 2 vols., Romae: ex Typographia Polyglotta Vaticana, 1907.

*Concilii Plenarii Baltimorensis II, in Ecclesia Metropolitana Baltimorensi, a die VII. ad diem XXI Octobris,* A.D. MDCCCLXVI, *Habiti, et a Sede Apostolica Recogniti, Acta et Decreta,* ed. altera mendis expurgata, Baltimorae: John Murphy, 1894.

*Corpus Iuris Canonici,* ed. Lipsiensis 2 post Aemilii Ludovici Richteri curas . . . instruxit Aemilius Friedberg, 2 vols., Lipsiae: Tauchnitz, 1879-1881; ed. anastatice repetita, 1928.

*Corpus Iuris Civilis,* (Krueger-Mommsen-Schoell-Kroll), 3 vols., Berolini: Apud Weidmannos, 1928-1929:
    Vol. I (*Institutiones et Digesta*), ed. stereotype quinta decima, 1929;
    Vol. II (*Codex Iustinianus*), ed. stereotypa decima, 1929;
    Vol. III (*Novellae*), ed. stereotypa quinta, 1928.

*Corpus Scriptorum Ecclesiasticorum Latinorum,* Vindobonae, 1866-

*Decretum Gratiani Emendatum et Notationibus Illustratum una cum Glossis,* Venetiis, 1605.

Jaffé, Philippus, *Bibliotheca Rerum Germanicarum,* 6 vols., Berolini: Apud Weidmannos, 1864-1873.

Mansi, J. D., *Sacrorum Conciliorum Nova et Amplissima Collectio,* 53 vols. in 59, Paris-Leipzig-Arnhem, 1901-1927.

*Monumento Germaniae Historica, Epistolae,* Tom. III Berolini: Apud Weidmannos, 1892.

*Monumenta Germaniae Historica, Legum Sectio III (Concilia Aevi Merovingici),* Tom. I, recensuit Fridericus Maassen, Hannoverae, 1893.

Rushworth, John, *Historical Collections . . . Beginning the Sixteenth year of King James, anno 1618 and ending Fifth year of King Charles, anno 1629,* 8 vols., London: 1682.

*S. Romanae Rotae Decisiones seu Sententiae* . . . quae *prodierunt anno* 1909-1932, 24 vols., Romae: Typis Vaticanis, 1912-1940.

Schannat-Hartzheim, *Concilia Germaniae,* 11 vols., Coloniae Augustae Agrippinensium, 1759-1790.

*Synodus Dioecesana Bellevillensis Quinta,* Belleville: Buechler, 1940.

*Synodus Dioecesana Fargensis Prima,* Milwaukee: Bruce, 1941.

*Statuta Dioecesis Ogdensburgensis* quae in *Synodo Ogdensburgensi XIII . . . Lata ac Promulgata,* Ogdensburg, 1928.

*Thesaurus Resolutionum Sacrae Congregationis Concilii,* 167 vols., Romae, 1718-1908.

## Authors

Aichner, Simon, *Compendium Iuris Ecclesiastici,* 11. ed., Brixinae, 1911.

Albertus Magnus, *Opera Omnia,* 38 vols., cura ac labore Steph. Caes. Aug. Borgnet, Parisiis, 1890-1899; Vol. XXIX, *Commentarium IV Sententiarum,* Dist. I-XXII; Vol. XXX, Dist. XXIII-L, 1894.

Albitius, Francesco, *De Inconstantia in Iure Admittenda vel Non,* Amstelaedami, 1683, *Tractatus de Inconstantia in Fide*—Private typewritten copy of this tract alone was used.

Arregui, Antonius, *Summarium Theologiae Moralis,* 12. ed., Bilbao: El Mensajero del Corazón de Jesús, 1934.

Ayrinhac-Lydon, *Marriage Legislation in the New Code of Canon Law,* New Revised Ed., New York: Benziger Bros., 1935.

[Bachofen], Charles Augustine, *Rights and Duties of Ordinaries According to the Code and Apostolic Faculties,* St. Louis: Herder, 1924.

Ballerini, A.,-Palmieri, P., *Opus Theologicum Morale,* 7 vols., Prati: Giachetti, 1889-1893.

Bangen, Ioannes H., *Instructio Practica de Sponsalibus et Matrimonio,* IV Partes in 1 vol., Monasterii, 1858-1860.

Bellarmine, Robert, *Opera Omnia,* 12 vols., Parisiis: ex editione Veneta, iterum edidit Justinus Fevre, 1870-1874; Tom. V, *De Sacramento Matrimonii,* 1873.

Benedictus XIV, *De Synodo Dioecesana,* 2 vols., Romae, 1767.

Bernard of Pavia, *Summa Decretalium,* ed. E. A. T. Laspeyres, Ratisbonae, 1861.

Beste, Udalricus, *Introductio in Codicem, Collegeville:* St. John's Abbey Press, 1938.

Bittle, Celestine, *Reality and The Mind,* 3. ed., Milwaukee: Bruce, 1940.

Blat, Albertus, *Commentarium Textus Codicis Iuris Canonici,* 5 vols. in 6, 1921-1927, Vol. III, P. I. (*De Rebus*), 2. ed., Romae: Typographia Pontificia in Instituto Pii IX, 1924.

Bouscaren, T. Lincoln, *The Canon Law Digest,* 2 vols. and Supplement—1941, Milwaukee: Bruce, 1934-1941.

Calmet, Augustinus, *Commentarius Literalis in Omnes Libros Veteris et Novi Testamenti,* 8 vols., ed. Latina, A. J. D. Mansi, Venetiis, 1754-1756.

*Cambridge Medieval History,* 8 vols., New York: Macmillan, 1911-1936.

Cappello, Felix M., *Tractatus Canonico-Moralis De Censuris iuxta Codicem Iuris Canonici,* 3. ed., Augustae Taurinorum et Romae: Marietti, 1933.

———, *Tractatus Canonico-Moralis de Sacramentis,* 3 vols. in 6, Taurini: Marietti, 1932-1939; Vol. III, Partes I et II, *De Matrimonio,* 4. ed., 1939.

Carrière, Joseph, *Praelectiones Theologicae—De Matrimonio,* 2 vols., Parisiis, 1837.

Cathrein, Victor, *Cursus Philosophicus,* Pars VI, *Philosophia Moralis,* 15. ed., Friburgi Brisgoviae: Herder, 1929.

Chelodi, Ioannes, *Ius Matrimoniale iuxta Codicem Iuris Canonici,* 4. ed., Tridenti: Libreria Moderna Editrice A. Ardesi, 1937.

———, *Ius Poenale et Ordo Procedendi in Iudiciis Criminalibus iuxta Codicem Iuris Canonici,* 4. ed., Tridenti: Libreria Moderna Editrice A. Ardesi, 1935.

Cicognani, Amleto, *Canon Law,* Authorized English version by J. O'Hara and F. Brennan, 2. ed., Philadelphia: Dolphin Press, 1935.

Coffey, P., *The Science of Logic,* 2 vols., New York: Peter Smith, 1938. (First published 1912, reprinted 1938 by special arrangement with Longmans, Green & Co., London.)

Cornely, Rudolphus, *Commentarius Scripturae Sacrae,—Cursus Scripturae Sacrae,* II, *Prior Epistola ad Corinthios,* III, *Epistolae ad Corinthios Altera et ad Galatas,* Parisiis, 1890-1892.

Coronata, Matheus Conte a, *Institutiones Iuris Canonici,* 5 vols., Taurini (Italia): Marietti, Vol. III, *De Processibus,* 1933; Vol. IV, *De Delictis et Poenis,* 1935.

Dale, Alfred W., *The Synod of Elvira and Christian Life in the Fourth Century,* London, 1882.

De Smet, Aloysius, *Tractatus Theologico-Canonicus De Sponsalibus et Matrimonio,* 4. ed., Brugis: Beyaert, 1927.

Doheny, William J., *Canonical Procedure in Matrimonial Cases,* Milwaukee: Bruce, 1938.

Donat, J., *Summa Philosophiae Christianae,* 8 vols., Innsbruck: Verlag Felizian Rauch, 1933-1936, Vol. II (*Critica*), 7. ed., 1933.

Donovan, James J., *The Pastor's Obligation in Pre-Nuptial Investigation,* The Catholic University of America Canon Law Studies, n. 115, Washington, D. C.: The Catholic University of America, 1938.

Esmein, A., *Le Mariage en Droit Canonique,* 2. ed., 2 vols., Paris: Libraire de Recueil Sirey, 1929-1935.

Estius, Guilielmus, *In Quatuor Libros Sententiarum Commentaria,* 2 vols., Parisiis, 1696.

Feije [Feye], Henricus J., *De Impedimentis et Dispensationibus Matrimonialibus,* 3. ed., Lovanii, 1885.

———, *Dissertatio Canonica de Matrimoniis Mixtis,* Lovanii, 1847.

Ferreres, Ioannes, *Compendium Theologiae Moralis,* 14. ed., 2 vols., Barcinone: Eugenius Subirana, 1928.

Forcellini, Aegidius, *Lexicon Totius Latinitatis,* 4 vols., consilio et cura Jacobi Facciolati, Patavii: Bettinelli, 1805.

Gasparri, Petrus, *Tractatus Canonicus de Matrimonio,* ed. nova, 2 vols., Romae: Typis Polyglottis Vaticanis, 1932.

Génicot, E.-Salsmans, J., *Institutiones Theologiae Moralis,* 10. ed., 2 vols., Bruxellis: Alb. Dewit, 1922.

Gredt, Iosephus, *Elementa Philosophiae,* 3. ed., 2 vols., Friburgi Brisgoviae: Herder, 1921-1922.

Guilielmus Durantis, *Speculum Iuris,* 3 vols., Venetiis, 1577.

Harrigan, Robert, *The Radical Sanation of Invalid Marriages,* The Catholic University of America Canon Law Studies, n. 116, Washington, D. C.: The Catholic University of America, 1938.

Hickey, J. S., *Summula Philosophiae Scholasticae,* 3 vols., Dublini: Browne et Nolan, 1905-1908, Vol. I (*Logica et Ontologia*), 2. ed., 1908.

Joannes a S. Thoma, *Cursus Philosophicus Thomisticus,* ed. nova, 3 Toms., Parisiis, 1883.

Joannes Duns Scotus, *Opera Omnia,* 26 vols., Parisiis, 1891-1895, Vol. XIX (*Quaestiones in Quartum Librum Sententiarum*), 1894.

Joyce, George, *Christian Marriage,* Heythrop Theological Series: I, London: Sheed & Ward, 1933.

Kelly-Geniesse, *Efficax Antidotum ad Matrimonii Mixta Praecavenda,* Romae: Pustet, 1923.

Knecht, August, *Handbuch des katholischen Eherechts,* Freiburg im Breisgau: Herder, 1928.

Konings, A.-Putzer, J. L., *Commentarium in Facultates Apostolicas,* 3. ed., Ilchestriae: Typis Congregationis Sanctissimi Redemptoris, 1893.

Kuttner, Stephan, *Repertorium der Kanonistik, 1140-1234.* Studi e Testi, 71, Città del Vaticano: Biblioteca Apostolica Vaticana, 1937.

Lega, M.-Bartoccetti, V., *Commentarius in Iudicia Ecclesiastica,* 3 vols., Romae: Anonima Libraria Cattolica Italiana, 1938-1942.

Lehmkuhl, Augustinus, *Theologia Moralis,* 4. ed., 2 vols., Friburgi Brisgoviae: Herder, 1887.

Leitner, Martin, *Lehrbuch des katholischen Eherechts,* 3. ed., Paderborn, 1920.

Michiels, Gommarus, *Normae Generales Juris Canonici,* 2 vols., Lublin, Polonia: Universitas Catholica, 1929.

Migne, P. J., *Patrologiae Cursus Completus, Series Latina,* 221 vols., Parisiis, 1844-1864.

Morrison, Bakewell, *Marriage,* Milwaukee: Bruce, 1934.

Nau, Louis J., *Manual of the Marriage Laws of Canon Law,* New York: Pustet, 1933.

Noldin, H.-Schmitt, A., *Summa Theologiae Moralis iuxta Codicem Iuris Canonici,* 21. et 22. ed., 3 vols., Oeniponte: Typis et Sumptibus Fel. Rauch, 1932-1934.

Noval, P., *Commentarium Codicis Iuris Canonici,* Lib. IV, *De Processibus,* 2 vols., Augustae Taurinorum et Romae: Marietti, 1920-1932.

Ojetti, B., *Commentarium in Codicem Iuris Canonici,* 4 vols., Romae: Apud Aedes Universitatis Gregorianae, 1927-1931.

O'Mara, William, *Canonical Causes for Matrimonial Dispensations,* The Catholic University of America Canon Law Studies, n. 96, Washington, D. C.: The Catholic University of America, 1935.

O'Neil, W. H., *Papal Rescripts of Favor,* The Catholic University of America Canon Law Studies, n. 57, Washington, D. C.: The Catholic University of America, 1930.

Panormitanus, Abbas (Nicholaus de Tudeschis), *Commentaria in Quinque Libros Decretalium,* 5 vols. in 7, Venetiis, 1588.

Pastor, Ludwig Freiherr von, *The History of the Popes from the Close of the Middle Ages,* 32 vols., St. Louis: Herder, 1906-1940.

Payen, G., *De Matrimonio in Missionibus ac Potissimum in Sinis Tractatus Practicus et Casus,* 2. ed., 3 vols., Zi-ka-wei: Typographia T'OU-SÈ-WÈ, 1935-1936.

Perrone, Ioannes, *De Matrimonio Christiano,* 3 vols., Romae: Typis S. Congregationis De Propaganda Fide, 1858.

Petrovits, Joseph, *The New Church Law on Matrimony,* Philadelphia: McVey, 1921.

Petrus Lombardus, *Petri Lombardi Libri IV Sententiarum,* studio et cura PP. Collegii S. Bonaventurae in lucem editi, 2. ed., 2 vols., Ad Claras Aquas, 1916.

Raymundus de Peñafort, *Summa,* Veronae: apud Augustinum Carattonium, 1744.

Reiffenstuel, Anacletus, *Ius Canonicum Universum,* 5 vols. in 7, Parisiis, 1864-1882.

Reilly, Edward, *The General Norms of Dispensations,* The Catholic University of America Canon Law Studies, n. 119, Washington, D. C.: The Catholic University of America Press, 1939.

Rice, Patrick, *Proof of Death in Pre-Nuptial Investigation,* The Catholic University of America Canon Law Studies, n. 123, Washington, D. C.: The Catholic University of America Press, 1940.

Roberti, F., *De Processibus,* 2 vols. in 1, Romae: Officina Tipografica Ausonia, 1926.

Roskovány, Augustinus, *De Matrimoniis Mixtis inter Catholicos et Protestantes,* 8 vols., Pestini et Nitriae, 1842-1887.

Sabetti-Barrett, *Compendium Theologiae Moralis,* 27. ed., Neo-Eboraci: Pustet, 1919.

Sanchez, Thomas, *De Sancto Matrimonii Sacramento Disputationum Libri Tres,* Lugduni, 1669.

Schenk, Francis J., *The Matrimonial Impediments of Mixed Religion and Disparity of Cult,* The Catholic University of America Canon Law Studies, n. 51, Washington, D. C.: The Catholic University of America, 1929.

Schmalzgrueber, Franciscus, *Ius Ecclesiasticum Universum,* 5 vols. in 12, Romae, 1843-1845.

Slater, Thomas, *A Manual of Moral Theology,* 3. ed., 2 vols., New York: Benziger Bros., 1909.

Sturzo, Don Luigi, *Church and State,* New York: Longmans, Green & Co., 1939.

Suarez, Franciscus, *Opera Omnia,* ed. nova, 26 vols., Parisiis, 1856-1866, Vols. V et VI, *Tractatus de Legibus.*

Tanquerey, Ad., *Synopsis Theologiae Moralis et Pastoralis,* 3. ed., 3 vols., New York: Benziger Bros., 1907.

Ter Haar, Francis, *Mixed Marriages and Their Remedies,* translation by Aloysius Walter, New York: Pustet, 1933.

*Thesaurus Linguae Latinae,* Lipsiae, 1900-; Vol. III, 1906-1912.

Thomas Aquinas, *In Omnes D. Pauli Apostoli Epistolas Doctissima Commentaria,* restituit F. Remigius Florentinus, Venetiis, 1562.

———, *Summa Theologica,* 6 vols., Taurini (Italia): Marietti, 1937.

Van Hove, A., *Commentarium Lovaniense in Codicem Iuris Canonici,* Vol. I, Tom. I (*Prolegomena*), Mechliniae: H. Dessain, 1928; Tom. IV (*De Rescriptis*), Mechliniae: H. Dessain, 1936; Tom. V (*De Privilegiis*), Mechliniae: H. Dessain, 1939.

Vermeersch, Arthurus, *Theologia Moralis,* 2. ed., 3 vols., Romae: Università Gregoriana, 1926-1927.

Vermeersch, A.-Creusen, J., *Epitome Iuris Canonici,* 3 vols., Vol. I, 6. ed., 1937, Vols. II et III, 5. ed., 1934-1936, Bruxellis: H. Dessain.

Vlaming, Th. M., *Praelectiones Iuris Matrimonii,* 3. ed., 2 vols., Bussum in Hollandia, 1919-1921.

Vromant, G., *Ius Missionariorum,* 8 Toms., Tom. V. (*De Matrimonio*), Louvain: Museum Lessianum, 1931.

Wernz, Franciscus X., *Ius Decretalium,* 6 vols., Romae et Prati, 1898-1905, Vol. IV (*Ius Matrimoniale*), 1904.

Wernz, Franciscus, et Vidal, Petrus, *Ius Canonicum,* 7 vols. in 8, Romae: Apud Aedes Universitatis Gregorianae, 1923-1938, Vol. V (*Ius Matrimoniale*), 2. ed., 1928.

White, Robert J., *Canonical Ante-Nuptial Promises and the Civil Law,* The Catholic University of America Canon Law Studies, n. 91, Washington, D. C.: The Catholic University of America, 1934.

Winslow, Francis J., *Vicars and Prefects Apostolic,* Maryknoll, New York: Catholic Foreign Mission Society of America, Inc., 1924.

Woywod, S., *A Practical Commentary on the Code of Canon Law,* 2 vols., New York: Jos. F. Wagner, 1925.

ARTICLES

Aich, Hrn., "Ueber die gemischten Ehen mit besonderer Rücksicht auf die Verhältnisse in Würtemberg."—*AKKR,* XIV (1865), 322-344.

Bernardini, Philip, "The Decree of the Holy Office respecting Ante-Nuptial Agreements in Mixed Marriages."—*ER,* LXXXVIII (1933), 185-190.

Czibulka, "Ungarische Staatskirchengesetze vom Jahre 1868."—*AKKR,* XXIV (1870), 104-107.

Foley, Leo P., "Insincere Ante-Nuptial Guarantees."—*ER,* XCII (1935), 72-73.

———, "Second Marriage Ceremony before a Minister."—*ER,* XC (1934), 173-175.

———, "Sincerity of the Promises Before Mixed Marriages."—*HPR,* XXXIII[2] (1933), 743-743.

Harrington, J. C., "The Importance of the *Cautiones* in Disparity of Worship."—*ER,* LXV (1921), 257-262.

Koudelka, Charles, "Assistants and Matrimonial Dispensation *Urgente Mortis Periculo.*"—*The Salesianum,* XXX (April, 1935), 22-30.

Mahoney, E. J., "Roman Documents."—*Clergy Review,* XXI (1941), 300-302.

McCarthy, J., "Marriage Under Birth Control Conditions."—*IER,* 5th Series, LVII (1941). 71-76; 348-356.

———, "Moral Certainty Regarding the Fulfilment of the 'Cautiones' in a Mixed Marriage."—*IER,* 5th Series, LIX (1942), 74-78.

O'Donnell, M. J., "Mixed Marriage Guarantees."—*IER,* 5th Series, XVIII (1921), 411-418.

Oesterle, G., "Circa Declarationem Authenticam Can. 1102 De Passiva Assistentia."—*JP,* X (1930), 292-314.

———, "De Cautionibus Matrimonialibus."—*JP,* XIV (1934), 270-276; XV (1935), 64-81; 191-195.

———, "Quaestio de Cautionibus in Missionibus."—*CpRM,* XIX (1938), 101-109.

O'Neil, P., "Disparity of Worship and Fictitious Guarantees."—*IER,* 5th Series, XLI (1933), 630-635.

———, "Extent of the Guarantees in Mixed Marriages."—*IER,* 5th Series, XXIII (1924), 416-417.

Park, Charles, "Insincere Ante-Nuptial Guarantees."—*ER,* XCI (1934), 446-459.

Planchard, J., "Dispense de Disparité de Cult et de Religion Mixte."—*NRT,* XV (1883), 392-441; 500-531; 573-601.

Roelker, Edward, "Decrees and Decisions."—*The Jurist,* II (1942), 59-60.

Schaaf, Valentine T., "In How Far Does the Recent Decree Regarding The *Cautiones* Apply to the United States?"—*ER,* LXXXVI (1932), 408-411.

Toso, A., "De Cautionibus Matrimonialibus."—*JP*, XIII (1933), 207-214.
Vermeersch, Arthurus, "Annotationes."—*Periodica, Pars Altera (Monumenta)*, XXIII (1934), 145-147.
Woywod, S., "Insincere Promises and Validity of Dispensation from Impediment of Disparity of Cult."—*HPR*, XXXIV (1933-1934), 518-520.
———, "Dispensation From Disparity of Cult and Secret Agreement of the Parties to Raise Children Non-Catholic."—*HPR*, XXXI (1930-1931), 630-631.
Anonymous, "Questions de science ecclésiastique."—*L'Ami du Clergé*, XLIII (1926), 383-384.
———, "The Promises in Mixed Marriages 'De Prole Jam Nata.'"—*ER*, LXXIV (1926), 630-632.

## Periodicals

*Analecta Ecclesiastica*, Romae, 1893-1911.
*Apollinaris*, Romae, 1928-
*Archiv für katholisches Kirchenrecht*, Innsbruck, 1857-1861; Mainz, 1862-
*Clergy Review, The*, London, 1931-
*Commentarium pro Religiosis*, Romae, 1920-1934; *Commentarium pro Religiosis et Missionariis*, Romae, 1935-
*Ecclesiastical Review, The* (originally *The American Ecclesiastical Review*), Philadelphia, 1889-
*Homiletic and Pastoral Review, The*, New York, 1900-
*Irish Ecclesiastical Record*, Dublin, 1864-; 5th Series, 1913-
*Jurist, The*, Washington, 1941-
*Jus Pontificium*, Romae, 1921-
*L'Ami du Clergé*, Paris-Bruxelles, 1879-1883; Bruxelles-Genève, 1883-1887; Paris, 1887-1888; Langres, 1889-
*Le Canoniste Contemporain*, Paris, 1878-1922.
*Nouvelle Revue Théologique*, Paris, 1869-
*Periodica de Re Canonica et Morali utili Praesertim Religiosis et Missionariis*, Bruges, 1905-
*Salesianum, The*, St. Francis, Wis., 1905-

## ABBREVIATIONS

*AAS—Acta Apostolicae Sedis.*
*AKKR—Archiv für katholisches Kirchenrecht.*
*ASS—Acta Sanctae Sedis.*
*Coll. S.C.P.F.—Collectanea S. Congregationis de Propaganda Fide*, ed. 1907.
*CpRM—Commentarium pro Religiosis et Missionariis.*
*CSEL—Corpus Scriptorum Ecclesiasticorum Latinorum.*
*ER—The Ecclesiastical Review.*

*Fontes—Codicis Iuris Canonici Fontes cura . . . Gasparri editi.*
*HPR—Homiletic and Pastoral Review.*
*IER—Irish Ecclesiastical Record.*
*JP—Jus Pontificium.*
*MPL—Migne, Patrologia Latina.*
*NRT—Nouvelle Revue Théologique.*

## BIOGRAPHICAL NOTE

David John Boyle was born in Waupun, Wisconsin, June 13, 1912. He attended St. Thomas Aquinas parish school in Milwaukee, Wisconsin, and St. Francis Seminary High School, St. Francis, Wisconsin, graduating in June 1930. He enrolled in the College Department of St. Francis Seminary and received the A.B. degree in June 1934, and the A.M. degree in January 1938, after completing his theological course in the same Seminary. He was ordained to the Sacred Priesthood on May 26, 1938. After a year as curate in St. Mary's Cathedral, Fargo, North Dakota, he enrolled in the School of Canon Law of the Catholic University of America in September 1939. In June 1940 he received the degree of J.C.B., and in June, 1941, the degree of J.C.L.

## INDEX

## CANON LAW STUDIES

1. Freriks, Rev. Celestine A., C.PP.S., J.C.D., Religious Congregations in Their External Relations, 121 pp., 1916.
2. Galliher, Rev. Daniel M., O.P., J.C.D., Canonical Elections, 117 pp., 1917.
3. Borowski, Rev. Aurelius L., O.F.M., J.C.D., De Confraternitatibus Ecclesiasticis, 136 pp., 1918.
4. Castillo, Rev. Cayo, J.C.D., Disertacion Historico-Canonica sobre la Potestad del Cabildo en Sede Vacante o Impedida del Vicario Capitular, 99 pp., 1919 (1918).
5. Kubelbeck, Rev. William J., S.T.B., J.C.D., The Sacred Penitentiaria and Its Relations to Faculties of Ordinaries and Priests, 129 pp., 1918.
6. Petrovits, Rev. Joseph, J.C., S.T.D., J.C.D., The New Church Law On Matrimony, X-461 pp., 1919.
7. Hickey, Rev. John J., S.T.B., J.C.D., Irregularities and Simple Impediments in the New Code of Canon Law, 100 pp., 1920.
8. Klekotka, Rev. Peter J., S.T.B., J.C.D., Diocesan Consultors, 179 pp., 1920.
9. Wanenmacher, Rev. Francis, J.C.D., The Evidence in Ecclesiastical Procedure Affecting the Marriage Bond, 1920 (Printed 1935).
10. Golden, Rev. Henry Francis, J.C.D., Parochial Benefices in the New Code, IV-119 pp., 1921 (Printed 1925).
11. Koudelka, Rev. Charles J., J.C.D., Pastors, Their Rights and Duties According to the New Code of Canon Law, 211 pp., 1921.
12. Melo, Rev. Antonius, O.F.M., J.C.D., De Exemptione Regularium, X-188 pp., 1921.
13. Schaaf, Rev. Valentine Theodore, O.F.M., S.T.B., J.C.D., The Cloister, X-180 pp., 1921.
14. Burke, Rev. Thomas Joseph, S.T.D., J.C.D., Competence in Ecclesiastical Tribunals, IV-117 pp., 1922.
15. Leech, Rev. George Leo, J.C.D., A Comparative Study of the Constitution, "Apostolicae Sedis" and the "Codex Juris Canonici," 179 pp., 1922.
16. Motry, Rev. Hubert Louis, S.T.D., J.C.D., Diocesan Faculties According to the Code of Canon Law, II-167 pp., 1922.
17. Murphy, Rev. George Lawrence, J.C.D., Delinquencies and Penalties in the Administration and Reception of the Sacraments, IV-121 pp., 1923.
18. O'Reilly, Rev. John Anthony, S.T.B., J.C.D., Ecclesiastical Sepulture in the New Code of Canon Law, II-129 pp., 1923.
19. Michalicka, Rev. Wenceslas Cyrill, O.S.B., J.C.D., Judicial Procedure in Dismissal of Clerical Exempt Religious, 107 pp., 1923.

20. Dargin, Rev. Edward Vincent, S.T.B., J.C.D., Reserved Cases According to the Code of Canon Law, IV-103 pp., 1924.
21. Godfrey, Rev. John A., S.T.B., J.C.D., The Right of Patronage According to the Code of Canon Law, 153 pp., 1924.
22. Hagedorn, Rev. Francis Edward, J.C.D., General Legislation on Indulgences, II-154 pp., 1924.
23. King, Rev. James Ignatius, J.C.D., The Administration of the Sacraments to Dying Non-Catholics, V-141 pp., 1924.
24. Winslow, Rev. Francis Joseph, A.F.M., J.C.D., Vicars and Prefects Apostolic, IV-149 pp., 1924.
25. Correa, Rev. Jose Servelion, S.T.L., J.C.D., La Potestad Legislativa de la Iglesia Catolica, IV-127 pp., 1925.
26. Dugan, Rev. Henry Francis, A.M., J.C.D., The Judiciary Department of the Diocesan Curia, 87 pp., 1925.
27. Keller, Rev. Charles Frederick, S.T.B., J.C.D., Mass Stipends, 167 pp., 1925.
28. Paschang, Rev. John Linus, J.C.D., The Sacramentals According to the Code of Canon Law, 129 pp., 1925.
29. Pointek, Rev. Cyrillus, O.F.M., S.T.B., J.C.D., De Indulto Exclaustrationis necnon Saecularizationis, XIII-289 pp., 1925.
30. Kearney, Rev. Richard Joseph, S.T.B., J.C.D., Sponsors at Baptism According to the Code of Canon Law, IV-127 pp., 1925.
31. Bartlett, Rev. Chester Joseph, A.M., LL.B., J.C.D., The Tenure of Parochial Property in the United States of America, V-108 pp., 1926.
32. Kilker, Rev. Adrian Jerome, J.C.D., Extreme Unction, V-425 pp., 1926.
33. McCormick, Rev. Robert Emmett, J.C.D., Confessors of Religious, VIII-266 pp., 1926.
34. Miller, Rev. Newton Thomas, J.C.D., Founded Masses According to the Code of Canon Law, VII-93 pp., 1926.
35. Roelker, Rev. Edward G., S.T.D., J.C.D., Principles of Privilege According to the Code of Canon Law, XI-166 pp., 1926.
36. Bakalarcyzk, Rev. Richardus, M.I.C., J.U.D., De Novitiatus, VIII-208 pp., 1927.
37. Pizzuti, Rev. Lawrence, O.F.M., J.U.L., De Parochis Religiosis, 1927. (Not printed.)
38. Bliley, Rev. Nicholas Martin, O.S.B., J.C.D., Altars According to the Code of Canon Law, XIX-132 pp., 1927.
39. Brown, Mr. Brendan Francis, A.B., LL.M., J.U.D., The Canonical Juristic Personality with Special Reference to Its Status in the United States of America, V-212 pp., 1927.
40. Cavanaugh, Rev. William Thomas, C.P., J.U.D., The Reservation of the Blessed Sacrament, VIII-101 pp., 1927.
41. Doheny, Rev. William J., C.S.C., A.B., J.U.D., Church Property: Modes of Acquisition, X-118 pp., 1927.
42. Feldhaus, Rev. Aloysius H., C.PP.S., J.C.D., Oratories, IX-141 pp., 1927.

43. Kelly, Rev. James Patrick, A.B., J.C.D., The Jurisdiction of the Simple Confessor, X-208 pp., 1927.
44. Neuberger, Rev. Nicholas J., J.C.D., Canon 6 or the Relation of the Codex Juris Canonici to the Preceding Legislation, V-95 pp., 1927.
45. O'Keefe, Rev. Gerald Michael, J.C.D., Matrimonial Dispensations, Powers of Bishops, Priests and Confessors, VIII-232 pp., 1927.
46. Quigley, Rev. Joseph, A.M., A.B., J.C.B., Condemned Societies, 139 pp., 1927.
47. Zaplotnik, Rev. Johannes Leo, J.C.D., De Vicariis Foraneis, X-142 pp., 1927.
48. Duskie, Rev. John Aloysius, A.B., J.C.D., The Canonical Status of the Orientals in the United States, VIII-196 pp., 1928.
49. Hyland, Rev. Francis Edward, J.C.D., Excommunication, Its Nature, Historical Development and Effects, VIII-181 pp., 1928.
50. Reinmann, Rev. Gerald Joseph, O.M.C., J.C.D., The Third Order Secular of Saint Francis, 201 pp., 1928.
51. Schenk, Rev. Francis J., J.C.D., The Matrimonial Impediments of Mixed Religion and Disparity of Cult, XVI-318 pp., 1929.
52. Coady, Rev. John Joseph, S.T.D., J.U.D., A.M., The Appointment of Pastors, VIII-150 pp., 1929.
53. Kay, Rev. Thomas Henry, J.C.D., Competence in Matrimonial Procedure, VIII-164 pp., 1929.
54. Turner, Rev. Sidney Joseph, C.P., J.U.D., The Vow of Poverty, XLIX-217 pp., 1929.
55. Kearney, Rev. Raymond A., A.B., S.T.D., J.C.D., The Principles of Delegation, VII-149 pp., 1929.
56. Conran, Rev. Edward James, A.B., J.C.D., The Interdict, V-163 pp., 1930.
57. O'Neil, Rev. William H., J.C.D., Papal Rescripts of Favor, VII-218 pp., 1930.
58. Bastnagel, Rev. Clement Vincent, J.U.D., The Appointment of Parochial Adjutants and Assistants, XV-257 pp., 1930.
59. Ferry, Rev. William A., A.B., J.C.D., Stole Fees, V-135 pp., 1930.
60. Costello, Rev. John Michael, A.B., J.C.D., Domicile and Quasi-domicile, VII-201 pp., 1930.
61. Kremer, Rev. Michael Nicholas, A.B., S.T.B., J.C.D., Church Support in the United States, VI-1930.
62. Angulo, Rev. Luis, C.M., J.C.D., Legislation de la Iglesia sobre la intencion en la application de la Santa Misa, VII-104 pp., 1931.
63. Frey, Rev. Wolfgang Norbert, O.S.B., A.B., J.C.D., The Act of Religious Profession, VIII-174 pp., 1931.
64. Roberts, Rev. James Brendan, A.B., J.C.D., The Banns of Marriage, XIV-140 pp., 1931.
65. Ryder, Rev. Raymond Aloysius, A.B., J.C.D., Simony, IX-151 pp., 1931.

66. Campagna, Rev. Angelo, Ph.D., J.U.D., Il Vicario Generale del Vescovo, VII-205 pp., 1931.
67. Cox, Rev. Joseph Godfrey, A.B., J.C.D., The Administration of Seminaries, VI-124 pp., 1931.
68. Gregory, Rev. Donald J., J.U.D., The Pauline Privilege, XV-165 pp., 1931.
69. Donohue, Rev. John F., J.C.D., The Impediment of Crime, VII-110 pp., 1931.
70. Dooley, Rev. Eugene A., O.M.I., J.C.D., Church Law on Sacred Relics, IX-143 pp., 1931.
71. Orth, Rev. Raymond Clement, O.M.C., J.C.D., The Approbation of Religious Institutes, 171 pp., 1931.
72. Pernicone, Rev. Joseph M., A.B., J.C.D., The Ecclesiastical Prohibition of Books, XII-267 pp., 1932.
73. Clinton, Rev. Connell, A.B., J.C.D., The Paschal Precept, IX-108 pp., 1932.
74. Donnelly, Rev. Francis B., A.M., S.T.L., J.C.D., The Diocesan Synod, VIII-125 pp., 1932.
75. Torrente, Rev. Camilo, C.M.F., J.C.D., Las Processiones Sagradas, V-145 pp., 1932.
76. Murphy, Rev. Edwin J., C.PP.S., J.C.D., Suspension Ex Informata Conscientia, XI-122 pp., 1932.
77. Mackenzie, Rev. Eric F., A.M., S.T.L., J.C.D., The Delict of Heresy in Its Commission, Penalization, Absolution, VII-124 pp., 1932.
78. Lyons, Rev. Avitus E., S.T.B., J.C.D., The Collegiate Tribunal of First Instance, XI-147 pp., 1932.
79. Connolly, Rev. Thomas A., J.C.D., Appeals, XI-195 pp., 1932.
80. Sangmeister, Rev. Joseph V., A.B., J.C.D., Force and Fear as Precluding Matrimonial Consent, V-211 pp., 1932.
81. Jaeger, Rev. Leo A., A.B., J.C.D., The Administration of Vacant and Quasi-vacant Episcopal Sees in the United States, IX-229 pp., 1932.
82. Rimlinger, Rev. Herbert T., J.C.D., Error Invalidating Matrimonial Consent, VII-79 pp., 1932.
83. Barrett, Rev. John, D.M., S.S., J.C.D., A Comparative Study of the Third Plenary Council of Baltimore and the Code, IX-221 pp., 1932.
84. Carberry, Rev. John J., Ph.D., S.T.D., J.C.D., The Juridical Form of Marriage, X-177 pp., 1934.
85. Dolan, Rev. John L., A.B., J.C.D., The Defensor Vinculi, XII-157 pp., 1934.
86. Hannan, Rev. Jerome D., A.M., S.T.D., LL.B., J.C.D., The Canon Law of Wills, IX-517 pp., 1934.
87. Lemieux, Rev. Delisle A., A.M., J.C.D., The Sentence in Ecclesiastical Procedure, IX-131 pp., 1934.
88. O'Rourke, Rev. James J., A.B., J.C.D., Parish Registers, VII-109 pp., 1934.

89. Timlin, Rev. Bartholomew, O.F.M., A.M., J.C.D., Conditional Matrimonial Consent, X-381 pp., 1934.
90. Wahl, Rev. Francis X., A.B., J.C.D., The Matrimonial Impediments of Consanguinity and Affinity, VI-125 pp., 1934.
91. White, Rev. Robert J., A.B., LL.B., S.T.B., J.C.D., Canonical Ante-Nuptial Promises and the Civil Law, VI-152 pp., 1934.
92. Herrera, Rev. Antonio Parra, O.C.D., J.C.D., Legislation Ecclesiastica sobra el Ayuno y la Abstinencia, XI-191 pp., 1935.
93. Kennedy, Rev. Edwin J., J.C.D., The Special Matrimonial Process in Cases of Evident Nullity, X-165 pp., 1935.
94. Manning, Rev. John J., A.B., J.C.D., Presumption of Law in Matrimonial Procedure, XI-111 pp., 1935.
95. Moeder, Rev. John M., J.C.D., The Proper Bishop for Ordination and Dismissorial Letters, VII-135 pp., 1935.
96. O'Mara, Rev. William A., A.B., J.C.D., Canonical Causes for Matrimonial Dispensations, IX-155 pp., 1935.
97. Reilly, Rev. Peter, J.C.D., Residence of Pastors, IX-81 pp., 1935.
98. Smith, Rev. Mariner T., O.P., S.T.L., J.C.D., The Penal Law for Religious, VII-169 pp., 1935.
99. Whalen, Rev. Donald W., A.M., J.C.D., The Value of Testimonial Evidence in Matrimonial Procedure, XIII-297 pp., 1935.
100. Cleary, Rev. Joseph F., J.C.D., Canonical Limitations on the Alienation of Church Property, VIII-141 pp., 1936.
101. Glynn, Rev. John C., J.C.D., The Promoter of Justice, XX-337 pp., 1936.
102. Brennan, Rev. James H., S.S., A.M., S.T.B., J.C.D., The Simple Convalidation of Marriage, VI-135 pp., 1937.
103. Brunini, Rev. Joseph Bernard, J.C.D., The Clerical Obligations of Canons 139 and 142, X-121 pp., 1937.
104. Connor, Rev. Maurice, A.B., J.C.D., The Administrative Removal of Pastors, VIII-159 pp., 1937.
105. Guilfoyle, Rev. Merlin Joseph, J.C.D., Custom, XI-144 pp., 1937.
106. Hughes, Rev. James Austin, A.B., A.M., J.C.D., Witnesses in Criminal Trials of Clerics, IX-140 pp., 1937.
107. Jansen, Rev. Raymond J., A.B., S.T.L., J.C.D., Canonical Provisions for Catechetical Instruction, VII-153 pp., 1937.
108. Kealy, Rev. John James, A.B., J.C.D., The Introductory Libellus in Church Court Procedure, XI-121 pp., 1937.
109. McManus, Rev. James Edward, C.SS.R., J.C.D., The Administration of Temporal Goods in Religious Institutes, XVI-196 pp., 1937.
110. Moriarity, Rev. Eugene James, J.C.D., Oaths in Ecclesiastical Courts, X-115 pp., 1937.
111. Rainer, Rev. Eligius George, C.SS.R., J.C.D., Suspension of Clerics, XVII-249 pp., 1937.
112. Reilly, Rev. Thomas F., C.SS.R., J.C.D., Visitation of Religious, VI-195 pp., 1938.

113. Moriarty, Rev. Francis E., C.SS.R., J.C.D., The Extraordinary Absolution from Censures, XV-334 pp., 1938.
114. Connolly, Rev. Nicholas P., J.C.D., The Canonical Erection of Parishes, X-132 pp., 1938.
115. Donovan, Rev. James Joseph, J.C.D., The Pastor's Obligation in Prenuptial Investigation, XII-322 pp., 1938.
116. Harrigan, Rev. Robert J., M.A., S.T.B., J.C.D., The Radical Sanation of Invalid Marriages, VIII-208 pp., 1938.
117. Boffa, Rev. Conrad Humbert, J.C.D., Canonical Provisions for Catholic Schools, X-211 pp., 1939.
118. Parsons, Rev. Anscar John, O.M., Cap., J.C.D., Canonical Elections, XII-236 pp., 1939.
119. Reilly, Rev. Edward Michael, A.B., J.C.D., The General Norms of Dispensation, X-156 pp., 1939.
120. Ryan, Rev. Gerald Aloysius, A.B., J.C.D., Principles of Episcopal Jurisdiction, XII-172 pp., 1939.
121. Burton, Rev. Francis James, C.S.C., A.B., J.C.D., A Commentary on Canon 1125, X-222 pp., 1940.
122. Miaskiewicz, Rev. Francis Sigismund, J.C.D., Supplied Jurisdiction According to Canon 209, XII-340 pp., 1940.
123. Rice, Rev. Patrick William, A.B., J.C.D., Proof of Death in Prenuptial Investigation, VIII-156 pp., 1940.
124. Anglin, Rev. Thomas Francis, M.S., J.C.D., The Eucharistic Fast, VIII-183 pp., 1941.
125. Coleman, Rev. John Jerome, J.C.L., The Minister of Confirmation, VI-153 pp., 1941.
126. Downs, Rev. John Emmanuel, A.B., J.C.D., The Concept of Clerical Immunity, XI-163 pp., 1941.
127. Esswein, Rev. Anthony Albert, J.C.D., Extrajudicial Penal Powers of Ecclesiastical Superiors, X-144 pp., 1941.
128. Farrell, Rev. Benjamin Francis, M.A., S.T.L., J.C.D., The Rights and Duties of the Local Ordinary Regarding Congregations of Women Religious of Pontifical Approval, V-195 pp., 1941.
129. Feeney, Rev. Thomas John, A.B., S.T.L., J.C.D., Restitutio in Integrum, VI-169 pp., 1941.
130. Findlay, Rev. Stephen William, O.S.B., A.B., J.C.D., Canonical Norms Governing the Deposition and Degradation of Clerics, XVII-279 pp., 1941.
131. Goodwine, Rev. John, A.B., S.T.L., J.C.L., The Right of the Church to Acquire Property, VIII-119 pp., 1941.
132. Heston, Rev. Edward Louis, C.S.C., Ph.D., S.T.D., J.C.D., The Alienation of Church Property in the United States, XII-222 pp., 1941.
133. Hogan, Rev. James John, S.T.L., J.C.D., Judicial Advocates and Procurators, VIII-200 pp., 1941.

134. Kealy, Rev. Thomas M., A.B., Litt. B., J.C.D., Dowry of Women Religious, IX-152 pp., 1941.
135. Keene, Rev. Michael James, O.S.B., J.C.D., Religious Ordinaries and Canon 198, 1941.
136. Kerin, Rev. Charles A., S.S., M.A., S.T.B., J.C.D., The Privation of Christian Burial, XVI-279 pp., 1941.
137. Louis, Rev. William Francis, M.A., J.C.D., Diocesan Archives, X-109 pp., 1941.
138. McDevitt, Rev. Gilbert Joseph, A.B., J.C.D., Legitimacy and Legitimation, X-247 pp., 1941.
139. McDonough, Rev. Thomas Joseph, A.B., J.C.D., Apostolic Administrators, X-217 pp., 1941.
140. Meier, Rev. Carl Anthony, A.B., J.C.D., Penal Administrative Procedure Against Negligent Pastors, XI-240 pp., 1941.
141. Schmidt, Rev. John Rogg, A.B., J.C.D., The Principles of Authentic Interpretation in Canon 17 of the Code of Canon Law, XII-331 pp., 1941.
142. Slafkosky, Rev. Andrew Leonard, A.B., J.C.D., The Canonical Episcopal Visitation of the Diocese, X-197 pp., 1941.
143. Swoboda, Rev. Innocent Robert, O.F.M., J.C.D., Ignorance in Relation to the Imputability of Delicts, IX-271 pp., 1941.
144. Dubé, Rev. Arthur Joseph, A.B., J.C.D., The General Principles for the Reckoning of Time in Canon Law, VIII-299 pp., 1941.
145. McBride, Rev. James T., A.B., J.C.D., Incardination and Excardination of Seculars, XX-585 pp., 1941.
146. Król, Rev. John J., J.C.L., The Defendant in Contentious Trials.
147. Comyns, Rev. Joseph J., C.SS.R., J.C.L., The Papal and Episcopal Administration of Church Property.
148. Barry, Rev. Garrett Francis, O.M.I., J.C.L., Violation of the Cloister.
149. Bolduc, Rev. Gatien, C.S.V., A.B., S.T.L., J.C.L., Les études dans les religions cléricales.
150. Boyle, Rev. David John, M.A., J.C.L., The Juridic Effects of Moral Certitude on Pre-Nuptial Guarantees.
151. Canavan, Rev. Walter Joseph, M.A., Litt.D., J.C.L., Profession of Faith.
152. Desrochers, Rev. Bruno, A.B., Ph.L., S.T.B., J.C.L., Le Premier Concile Plénier de Québec et le Code de Droit Canonique.
153. Dillon, Rev. Robert Edward, A.B., J.C.L., Common Law Marriage.
154. Dodwell, Rev. Edward John, Ph.D., S.T.B., J.C.L., The Time and Place for the Celebration of Marriage.
155. Donnellan, Rev. Thomas Andrew, A.B., J.C.L., The Obligation of the Missa pro Populo.
156. Eltz, Rev. Louis Anthony, A.B., J.C.L., Co-operation in Crime.
157. Gass, Rev. Sylvester Francis, M.A., J.C.L., Ecclesiastical Pensions.
158. Guiniven, Rev. John Joseph, C.SS.R., J.C.L., The Precept of Hearing Mass on Sundays and Holy Days of Obligation.

159. Gulczynski, Rev. John Theophilus, J.C.L., The Desecration and Violation of Churches.
160. Hammill, Rev. John Leo, M.A., J.C.L., The Obligations of the Traveler According to Canon 14.
161. Haydt, Rev. John Joseph, A.B., J.C.L., Reserved Benefices.
162. Huser, Rev. Roger John, O.F.M., A.B., J.C.L., The Crime of Abortion in Canon Law.
163. Kearney, Rev. Francis Patrick, A.B., S.T.L., J.C.L., The Principles of Canon 1127.
164. Linahen, Rev. Leo James, S.T.L., J.C.L., De Absolutione Complicis in Peccato Turpi.
165. McCloskey, Rev. Joseph Aloysius, A.B., J.C.L., The Subject of Ecclesiastical Law according to Canon 12.
166. O'Neill, Rev. Francis Joseph, C.SS.R., J.C.L., The Dismissal of Religious in Temporary Vows.
167. Prince, Rev. John Edward, A.B., S.T.B., J.C.L., The Diocesan Chancellor.
168. Riesner, Rev. Albert Joseph, C.SS.R., J.C.L., Apostates and Fugitives from Religious Institutes.
169. Stenger, Rev. Joseph Bernard, J.C.L., The Mortgaging of Church Property.
170. Waldron, Rev. Joseph Francis, A.B., J.C.L., The Minister of Baptism.
171. Willett, Rev. Robert Albert, J.C.L., The Probative Value of Documents in Ecclesiastical Trials.
172. Woeber, Rev. Edward Martin, M.A., J.C.L., The Interpellations.

www.ingramcontent.com/pod-product-compliance
Lightning Source LLC
LaVergne TN
LVHW050237080826
844660LV00012B/546

* 9 7 8 0 8 1 3 2 2 3 3 9 1 *